D0560622

What the critics say

These authors have a real penchant for provoking their readers. They love to shake old certainties and orthodoxies. And in this new book, they have excelled themselves by penning a magnificently iconoclastic dialogue. *Pierre Vidal-Naquet, Le Nouvel Observateur*

Readers will be grateful to these authors for having opened up, and so richly, the 'Jewish Question' today – placing centre stage once again the figure of the Jew in exile. *Sylvain Cypel, Le Monde*

This book positively invites debate. But on condition one first recognizes the deep knowledge and openminded spirit that inspires it. *L'Histoire*

These authors share a common passion for the history of Judaism, and an equal repugnance for the prejudices, taboos, even panic that characterize Judaism when it thinks it is under attack. Taking the form of a dialogue in the manner of certain old rabbinical texts, the authors upset the intellectual or spiritual quietude in which contemporary Jewry tends to indulge more than it would like to admit. *Jean-Luc Allouche, Libération*

What does it mean to be Jewish today? Is it to live in the cocoon of the Shoah and the fear of a resurgence of fascism? Is it to cover one's head, to support Sharon? Or is it to have a sense of belonging across boundaries? To answer these questions, the authors revisit such central and inevitable issues as the diaspora, zionism, anti-semitism, and the 'Jewish mother', as well as the tensions between ashkenazi and sephardic Jews, and deconstruct them with a delicate touch. *François Dufay, Le Point*

'… after Auschwitz the life of the Jews is more sacred than the death of the Jews, even for the sanctification of the Divine Name.'

Emile Fackenheim, Jewish philosopher and theologian

'After the death camps we are left with only one supreme value: existence.'

Amos Kenan, left-wing secular Israeli

Esther Benbassa & Jean-Christophe Attias

The Jews and Their Future

a conversation on Judaism and Jewish identities

translated by Patrick Camiller

Zed Books
LONDON · NEW YORK

JERICHO PUBLIC LIBRARY

The Jews and their future: a conversation on Judaism and Jewish identities
was first published by Zed Books Ltd, 7 Cynthia Street, London N1
9JF, UK and Room 400, 175 Fifth Avenue, New York, NY 10010,
USA in 2004.

www.zedbooks.co.uk

Copyright © éditions Jean-Claude Lattès, 2001
Translation copyright © Patrick Camiller, 2004

The rights of Esther Benbassa and Jean-Christophe Attias to be
identified as the authors of this work has been asserted by them
in accordance with the Copyright, Designs and Patents Act,
1988.

Cover designed by Andrew Corbett
Indexed by Ed Emery
Set in Bembo and Futura Bold by Ewan Smith, London
Printed and bound in Malta by Gutenberg Press Ltd

Distributed in the USA exclusively by Palgrave Macmillan, a division
of St Martin's Press, LLC, 175 Fifth Avenue, New York, NY 10010.

A catalogue record for this book is available from the British Library
Library of Congress cataloging-in-publication data: available

ISBN 1 84277 390 9 cased
ISBN 1 84277 391 7 limp

Contents

A note of thanks

We would like to thank Isabelle Laffont and the Jean-Claude Lattès publishing house for having conceived the idea of this book. We feel especially indebted to Jean-François Colosimo, with whom we spent many gratifying hours considering what it means to be a Jew. Insightful and stimulating, he was in fact the third partner in this dialogue. Born of friendship, let it be dedicated to our friendship.

We are deeply grateful to Robert Molteno and everyone at Zed Books, as well as to our translator Patrick Camiller; their joint efforts made it possible for the work to have a second life in the English-speaking world.

Preface to the English edition

When we were reading the proofs of the English translation of this book, American troops had just captured Baghdad and the anti-war demonstrations that had preceded the invasion were still continuing; the calm following the election of Jacques Chirac had been broken. It had not taken long for the Israeli–Palestinian and Iraqi–American conflicts to be rolled into one. Combined in many people's minds, they compensated for an ideological vacuum or disarray manifest since the death of the great ideologies of the twentieth century. It was thought that the Americans and Israelis had together loosed their fury on the Arabs, and so on. But, in reality, such views were a long way from a genuinely critical attitude to American policy or Israeli policy – not to mention a critique of Palestinian or Iraqi policies. Some of the peace marchers carried Israeli flags adorned with swastikas, while others held pro-Iraq banners. Their slogans reviled '*Busharon assassin*'. Jewish left-wing activists were beaten up in Paris. A simplistic anti-Americanism reduced the United States to the bellicose policy of the Bush government and, in some cases, was coupled with an anti-Semitism in line with current tastes.

At the same time, North African strata of French society, more and more strongly identified with the Palestinians and Iraqis, came out in open opposition to the Jews. This new worsening of the climate is especially apparent on school premises, which have become a barometer of growing communitarian polarization and ethnic-religious confrontations in France. At school, children no longer hesitate to call one another 'dirty Arab' or 'dirty Jew' or 'dirty nigger'. In a context where racism is no longer taboo, tolerance is no longer in line with current tastes. If France's Jews and Arabs persist in strongly identifying with the opposing sides in Middle Eastern conflicts, and if those conflicts themselves continue, then the worst is to be feared. Unfortunately, ideologies without much substance have a remarkable capacity to adapt and to enlist any means available to them.

It is worth recalling that mutual understanding among ethnic-religious groups in France and Europe is not a pious wish but a necessity. The school system, the public authorities and the structures representing the various communities are all required to play their part. Only genuine dialogue is capable of preventing tolerance from becoming merely a concept emptied of all meaning. It is not by encouraging communitarian withdrawal, whether in the Muslim world or the Jewish world, that advances will be made in this direction. The fight against racism must involve genuine and positive attempts to draw communities closer together, in ways that highlight what unites them without denying the reality of what separates them. There still seems to be a long road ahead.

E. B. and J.-C. A.,
Paris, April 2003

Introduction[†]

'Do the Jews have a future?' It was before 11 September that we tried to answer this question – a question as old as Judaism and one the Jews, as a dispersed minority, have always asked of themselves. Modernity has rendered it more urgent and insistent, both because the integration of Jews as citizens into non-Jewish societies has favoured their acculturation, and because it has become much more a matter of choice than of destiny whether an individual is or remains a Jew. The issue arises spontaneously from an awareness of the vicissitudes of Jewish life – not only in the West but also in the East, where the fall of communism has had a major impact on Jewish identities – and the only ones who will dare sidestep it are those few (fewer than one might think) who blindly believe in an immutable, eternally stable Jewish being. Even the most religious and traditional layers of the Jewish Diaspora cannot entirely escape the major existential anxiety, since for them too the identity questions shaking our ever restless modern societies pose a genuine challenge even in their everyday lives.

The fact remains, however, that the first French edition of our book appeared after 11 September, and that the question forming its title in French (*Les Juifs ont-ils un avenir?*) suddenly began to look provocative. Bombarded with pictures from the scene, the world seemed to participate directly in the Twin Towers collapse, identifying with the death and anguish of thousands of innocent people who had simply gone to work that day like the rest of us. A kind of secular apocalypse unfolded before the eyes of viewers glued to their television screens, and struck right to the depths of their beings. The agents of this tragedy were Muslim fundamentalists. This fact triggered a huge uproar in our secular, individualist Judeo-Christian societies, which had forgotten those distant times when, in the name of religion, it had still been possible to sacrifice one's life for a 'sacred' cause. What some saw as a 'sacred' cause thus seemed to the West (which had long since 'neutralized' religion) no more than a pretext for an odious massacre. The sudden and, in our eyes, perverse irruption of death and the sacred, coming from an occult faraway place, was liable to arouse strong feelings in us citizens of an

† Originally published as an Afterword to the French edition.

increasingly aseptic world – feelings of compassion for the victims as well as hatred and absolute rejection of those who planned and carried out the terrible deed.

In the space of a few minutes, the world was divided into the 'good' and the 'bad'. The cause of Good was clear and the Evil was precisely located; the dividing line between the two allowed nothing to cross. The 'civilized' West, now a victim, could even adorn itself with the immaculate dress of a politically correct morality. It was a question of 'them' and 'us'. Faced with the Manichaean rhetoric that this situation encouraged, and the warlike culture that it established as a norm, moderate discourses had little room in which to operate. The pressure was on to take sides, clearly and as a matter of urgency; abstention was enough for you to be instantly ranged on the side of the 'enemy'. A world divided into 'us' and 'them', however, is a space of closure and paranoia, in which others can never wish us anything but harm. Of course, the policies and speeches of Western leaders played their part in influencing people, as they set off on a 'crusade' against Muslim fundamentalism as the source of all evil.

This interlocking of politics and morality, this insidious injection of religion back into politics within the West, came at a time in 2001 when the second Intifadah was reaching new peaks of violence, after a summer of mourning overshadowed by deadly attacks. The way in which attention was focused on a Muslim world mortally threatening the enlightened West was certainly not likely to advance the cause of peace in the Middle East. On the contrary, everything was clear and gave meaning to the war. The Americans were conducting theirs in Afghanistan, and the Israelis theirs against the Palestinians.

Where was right? Who had reason on their side? But war thrives precisely when reason abdicates its responsibility. Palestinians were mercilessly attacking the Israeli population, while Israelis were entering the territories and committing various exactions. On both sides, civilians were paying with their blood for the interminable, seemingly insoluble conflict, and the world's major powers did not seem to be contemplating any active intervention to try to find a way out. The West, itself freshly bruised by its live encounter with death and blind violence, rediscovered another terrorism raging in specific forms but with the same violence in the Middle East. There too men and women were sacrificing their lives for a 'noble' and 'sacred' cause, killing other men and women in the process. As in New York. As in Washington.

The Middle Eastern conflict soon stretched outside the arena of combat. France directly felt the effects in sensitive city suburbs where Jewish and Muslim populations rubbed shoulders with each other on a daily basis, veritable barometers of the poor integration or simple nonintegration of sections of North African immigrants, especially among the second generation. In these suburbs that had become fortresses of insecurity, as a result of a stand back approach on the part of leaders seemingly incapable of coming up with more than fine words and sentiments, the new positioning of identities soon created explosive situations. The reality on the ground was not entirely new, though, as tensions had existed for ten to fifteen years in these difficult suburbs between the Jewish population and young North Africans or West Indians.[1] Outside events merely fanned the flames, until the anti-Jewish incidents of recent months signalled that things were getting out of control.

As they watched what was happening in the Palestinian territories, many young North Africans identified with their 'brothers' in the Middle East. The religious link, with its common Islamic reference, doubtless contributed to this, but so too did a vaguer yet strong and painful sense of being completely abandoned. The hostility of large sections of the French population towards the Arabs was evidently another factor strengthening the religious ties: there were 'we Muslims' and 'the rest'. 'The French' were placed in the opposite camp, but as they were the majority they could not be opposed head on. Everything therefore pointed to 'the Jews' as the target.

In this logic of ghettoization which began to appear in France, each group braced itself against the other. The first victims of the acts of incivility that were soon being recorded were Jews who stood out as Jews; most of these had also come from North Africa and were living side by side with Arabs. Blithely amalgamated with 'Israelis' in a way hardly likely to calm matters, these Jews had been more successful in making a way for themselves in France and could also easily be bracketed together with 'the French'. One young man put it like this in an interview: 'The Jews haven't got any poor people like us. Even the ones who live in our part of town can get a job more easily. And they've got people representing them everywhere, in the government and especially the media. There are ten times more of us and we don't exist. That really screws you up inside.'[2]

In this context, although these young North Africans do not

regularly practise their religion, the identification with the Palestinians operated to the full, if only because the latter had been promoting the holiness of their cause and the land at issue in their struggle (land, of course, which is holy for everybody, Jews, Muslims and Christians). This is not to say that every young Arab in France or Belgium went around 'beating up Jews'. But 'desperate', uncontrollable elements in the sub-urbs did find in the Palestinian struggle an ideal that could lift them out of their confusion and their lack of anything to do with their lives.

By committing acts of incivility towards Jews, by attacking their places of worship and their schools, some could therefore feel that they were taking part in the 'just struggle' of the Palestinians and becoming heroes in their turn – heroes at a lesser cost, but heroes all the same. Media reporting of their actions also seemed to give them extra meaning or 'value'. If they had not been given such a high and noisy profile, they would surely have made less impact on others who were likely to commit similar actions. But now the forgotten ones in the council blocks burst on to centre stage, their delinquency suddenly lifting them out of anonymity.

Contrary to the views of Pierre-André Taguieff, whose work *La Nouvelle Judéophobie* caused a sensation but is far from providing all the keys to the present crisis,[3] it is not rigorous indoctrination nor fully conscious militancy that moves these young people. If we are to believe a study conducted in 2000–01 for the Higher Research Institute on Internal Security (IHESI), Islam has certainly become a major reference for young members of the North African immigration in France. But the authors of the study consider that this tells us nothing about the actual place of religion in their everyday lives, and that the religious reference plays more the role of a 'social marker'.[4] It would thus not seem to be ideological Islam which lies behind the anti-Jewish actions of young people from this milieu. Neither at the ministry of the interior nor at the ministry of justice have there been any reports of 'organized gangs' or of a 'structured ideology in respect of Judeophobia'.[5] Nor does any call for a jihad for Palestine seem to have been heard, even if more or less concerted attempts to whip up violence cannot be ruled out. In any event, immigrant associations and Muslim religious authorities regularly condemn such deviant behaviour and call on their flock to use democratic means to express their opposition or support for the causes in which they have become active.

Denunciations of a new global anti-Semitic scourge have sometimes led people to lose sight of the complexity of local situations,
unduly creating anxieties and adding to uncertainty. There can be no
doubt that France is going through a serious identity crisis and that
its republicanism is in trouble. Yet French political leaders on both
the Right and the Left have vigorously condemned the signs of an
anti-Jewish drift; they have taken the necessary measures to strengthen
the security of Jewish places; and the media have neither kept quiet
nor shown any indulgence about the wave of attacks on the Jewish
community.

We must also distinguish between manifestations of 'Judeophobia'
in the French suburbs and the anti-Semitism which has been plaguing
the Arab-Muslim world for a number of decades, especially since the
creation and successive victories of the State of Israel, and which is
regularly ratcheted up a further notch when there is an exacerbation
of the Middle East conflict. New editions of the *Protocols of the Elders
of Zion* come thick and fast, as do translations of Hitler's *Mein Kampf*
and the outpourings of Holocaust revisionism. Anti-Semitic or
anti-Israeli propaganda is nothing new in the Arabic schoolbooks of
Palestine and the Middle East. But there is some way from this to any
idea that the juvenile instigators of anti-Jewish violence in Europe are
in the grip of the same tendency.

Obviously nothing can justify the acts of aggression. Indeed, they
point to a noxious atmosphere that is far from healthy, either, for
the Arabs of Europe. There have recently been reports in France of
a virulent 'rise of racism against North Africans',[6] and we should
remember that Muslims remain the chief victims of 'them and us'
xenophobia in the surrounding society.[7] The ethnicization of relations
between populations with different origins serves to worsen the
tensions, and one does not have to be excessively pessimistic to fear
that the republican consensus might break down at any moment. On
11 September the rejectionist attitudes in each 'camp' crystallized.
North African victims of racism had an opportunity to turn it
round against the Jews, and racist discourse lost its inhibitions in an
atmosphere favourable to closure. Jews too have suffered as a result of
this. For, as Nonna Mayer has suggested, although anti-Semitism has
been generally on the retreat, 'the explosive situation in the Middle
East and the widespread disapproval of Israel's policy in the territories
have adversely affected the image of all Jews and removed the barrier

to any expression of anti-Semitism'.[8] This trend hardly suggested that relations of trust were about to be restored between the different communities present in France. Nor was the theme of insecurity, taken up by politicians at the height of the presidential election campaign in 2002, likely to make dialogue between them any easier.

Also in 2002, the French Union of Jewish Students and the SOS Racisme organization listed 405 cases of assault against Jews between 1 September 2000 and 31 January 2002, ranging from minor acts of incivility to the burning of synagogues.[9] Not all were of extreme gravity, but they occurred at a time when things were on the boil and many Jews in France and Europe feared the worst for Israel. Identification with Israel is traditionally one of the pillars of Jewish identity in the Diaspora. But the shock waves coming from war in the Middle East, the revival of old bones of contention with the Arabs (more than half of French Jews being of North African origin), the often close family ties with Israel: all these factors served to heighten the fear already kindled by hypermnesia of the genocide in the last few decades.

To cultivate the memory of the Holocaust is one thing. To base Jewish identity on it is another thing, which involves many dangers. The institutions of the Jewish community represent at most a third of the Jews of France, and some officials of those institutions who waged a campaign against our book later admitted to us that they had devoted too much of their activity to remembrance of the genocide. The reason why they had done this was that they were otherwise unable, through a significant cultural project, to foster the Jewish identity of major sections of a largely secularized community with different persuasions. Week after week, month after month, whole pages of the Jewish press have for years focused on the 'duty to remember' and systematically listed anti-Semitic incidents throughout the world. If we add to this the abundant literature on the subject in French, the commemorations, the debates about property confiscated from Jews during the war, and the space given to all these issues in the general media and the cinema, then we can easily understand the hypersensitivity of Jews in France and elsewhere in Europe. The Holocaust is certainly part of the contemporary history of the Jews, and it is legitimate to want to preserve and deepen people's awareness of it. The huge trauma continues to weigh on the lives of survivors and their descendants. But excessive activation of the memory paved the way for Jews to retreat into themselves in a moment of crisis.

A similar retreat occurs from time to time in Israel, when a situation seen as critical leads some of its citizens to embrace a simplistic dichotomy that plays into the hands of extremist politicians by presenting Israel as exposed to universal hostility. Here again it is a question of 'them and us', where 'they' all wish to inflict harm on 'us'. The Israeli historian Zeev Sternhell has recently written: 'Israel's settler nationalism, like all extremist nationalisms, needs an enemy. The presence of such an enemy amounts to a methodological necessity. The formula "the whole world is against us" serves a function of this kind. It is a myth involving an element of conscious fraud, but it can ease people's consciences and allow them to bury their heads in the sand when reality becomes too difficult to bear.'[10]

If 9/11 gave a free hand to Sharon's anti-Palestinian policy, it also fuelled fear among Jews. Palestinian terrorism was killing dozens of innocent people in Israel, and Bin Laden's accomplices had endangered the whole of the democratic West. The threat seemed to be worldwide and might well hit France and other European countries. Were the Jews, persecuted since time immemorial, in danger of reliving the nightmare of the war years? Against a background of remembrance of the genocide, the anti-Jewish actions in France soon came to be interpreted without a proper sense of judgement. There could be no doubt, of course, that they had taken place and were distressing or actually painful for their direct victims. Calls for vigilance and a fight against the new drift were perfectly in order. But when people started relating these incidents to the major tragedy of the twentieth century, it gave them a scale and significance that could not but fuel the anxieties of Jews in sensitive suburbs and of the Jewish population in general.

The first anti-Jewish actions took place right at the beginning of the second Intifadah in autumn 2000, but the atmosphere grew continually worse after 11 September 2001. Did Bin Laden serve as a model for some young North Africans? Did the wave of Islamophobia after the Twin Towers collapse not encourage the Jewish leadership to use the displays of aggression against Jews as a political instrument to restore Israel's image after months in which it had been constantly dented? We should also consider that Israeli leaders were able to delude themselves that the flare-up of 'anti-Semitism' would encourage large numbers of French Jews to emigrate to Israel. France, it is true, houses the largest Jewish population in Europe. And, at a time when emigration to Israel has been drying up, two reserves seemed possible to exploit: Argentina (which is faced with the worst economic crisis in its history) and France (where a majority of the Jewish community is of Sephardi origin and has important family connections in Israel). In both cases, however, the hope that a new round of emigration would occur in these times of crisis would be mostly disappointed.

The Israeli authorities certainly spared no effort to achieve it. On 6 January 2002 deputy foreign minister Michael Melchior, then in February Ariel Sharon himself, and finally on 22 April (following the first round of the French presidential elections) deputy prime minister and interior minister Eli Yishai all expressed a view of France as the most anti-Semitic country in the West and called upon its Jews to depart. Mr Sharon felt it necessary to explain that French Jews 'might find themselves in danger' because of 'the presence of six million Arabs' in the country.[11] Everything possible was turned to account. Whereas the first two of the above statements banked on the Arab Muslim threat, the third cited the rise of Le Pen. By 10 April the Israeli government was arguing that the emigration of French Jews had become an 'immediate necessity', and on 22 April it urged them to start 'packing their bags'.[12] Emergency funds were released to assist in the process.

The negative repercussions of Israel's interference in the internal affairs of the French Jewish group, together with protests by the French government and Jacques Chirac, soon led the leaders of the Jewish community to try to limit the damage. The president of the CRIF, who had played a major role in creating a climate of tension around the issue of anti-Semitism in France, now called for Sharon's statements to be placed in a proper perspective. And he added: 'The context in which Ariel Sharon said what he did is very different from the context in France. I can understand that the Israeli government needs a flow of immigrants, but I do not think that this is the concern of France.'[13] Even the Israeli ambassador felt obliged to take a step in the same direction, thereby bringing out into the open, despite himself, the contradiction between his government's way of seeing things and his own. Thus, he declared on RTL that it was 'a big exaggeration' to say that the Jewish community was 'threatened with violence'.[14] It was becoming clear how much the whole operation had turned into a fiasco; attempts were made to limit the damage.

The fear was real enough, of course, and had to be taken into account. But perhaps it would have been more advisable to seek ways of stemming the evil that had aroused it, than to add fuel to the fire through exaggerated reactions in the media. Instead of engaging in vigorous dialogue with responsible figures in the various immigrant communities, the Jewish leadership chose to adopt a victim's position – victim of the North Africans, victim of the Arabs. In this vision, the same Arabs who wanted to destroy Israel were setting fire to Jewish synagogues and schools in France. Anti-Semitism in France and Europe was headline news in the Israeli papers; the danger for Jews was supposed to be the same everywhere. It was not long before the 'psychosis' was spreading to all quarters, including in the United States on the basis of a totally imaginary threat.

The place of the Holocaust in American Jewish culture has been well described by Peter Novick in a book the appearance of which in translation in autumn 2001 triggered a polemic, albeit limited in scope, in France.[15] The Jewish media mostly preferred to greet it with stony silence, or to point out that the United States was, in any case, not France. Things which might be true in the United States, never directly affected by the genocide, could surely not be applied to a Europe that would be forever marked by the tragedy. Things which, on the other side of the Atlantic, might belong more to the realm of the imagination were in France a real and painful memory. Things which at best might be overlooked in Novick's case would not be forgiven in ours. And yet, the distance was perhaps not as great as it was claimed to be. Can it really be said, for example, that identification with the genocide is less a matter of 'imagination' for the second or third generation of French Jews of North African origin than it is for many young Ashkenazi North Americans?

In France, the Jewish Consistory compared the 'anti-Semitic violence' to the early stages of a new Kristallnacht,[16] referring to that terrible night of 9–10 November 1938 when the authorities of the Third Reich organized pogroms in Germany during which hundreds of synagogues were wrecked, Jews murdered, Jewish shops plundered, cemeteries desecrated, and thousands arrested. What did the France of Jacques Chirac and Lionel Jospin, both known opponents of anti-Semitism, have in common with Hitler's Germany? Nevertheless, after the first incidents of autumn 2000, the term Kristallnacht was given quite an airing, when the brilliant intellectual Alain Finkielkraut unhesitatingly took it up and organic intellectuals of the Jewish community fell in behind him. The term was subsequently used in a wild manner to serve the interests of a dramatic new alarmism.

Curiously, faced with the imminent apocalypse that some liked to foretell, people's reactions were actually quite restrained. The rate of emigration to Israel remained very low – understandably, in view of the security situation there. Of course, emigration from the Diaspora to Israel has always been the basic goal of Zionism, but, since the leaders of the French Jewish community were able to produce so few results on this level, it has to be asked whether their agitation on the issue did not increase the danger to those whom they claimed to be protecting. By making anti-Semitism rather than a threat to the Republic the key problem for Jews, did it not express a disturbing lack of common sense and political judgement? After all, 'the French' could at any moment turn around and lump together the rowdy 'Arabs' and 'Jews'.

France was then entering a critical election period, soon to be dominated by the obsession with security, and the rightward leanings of the Jewish community organizations were expressing themselves ever more clearly in a strict alignment with the Israeli policies of the day. This explains why, from the last few months of 2001, these organizations flirted so readily with the French Right, themselves playing in their own way the card of 'security'. The Jewish leadership suspected that the Left would not be capable of stemming anti-Semitism in France – a phenomenon which it seemed ultimately unsure how to interpret, and which, around the middle of March, it preferred to start calling by the name of 'anti-Jewish acts' or, most fashionably, 'Judeophobia'.[17] In some circles, indeed, it had become customary to tar the Left and the Far Left with the same brush (if one can still speak of a Far Left in France), and to suspect of 'Judeophobia' anyone too keen on supporting the Palestinians and criticizing Israel.

Of course, the fear and reality of insecurity affected not only the Jewish community but a large part of the French population as a whole. And the various political parties, which wrongly continue to believe that there is a 'Jewish vote' in France,[18] tried to win support in the election by promising greater security to the Jews as well as to others. Le Pen did not miss the opportunity to ride this wave, and that was Lionel Jospin's undoing. On the morning after the first round of the presidential elections, the CRIF president opined that the Front National breakthrough was in the end quite a positive development, since it would convince the Muslims of France to quieten down. The next day, he stuck to this position at an emergency meeting of Jewish leaders to discuss ways of combating anti-Semitism in Western Europe.[19] We had to wait until 26 April, when the whole of France was beginning to mobilize against the Far Right, to learn from *Le Monde* that the same individual deplored the failure to reproduce his remarks 'accurately' and was now arguing that 'the Front National current of thought is dangerous for France and all French people'.

Such incoherence on the part of the French Jewish leadership, which had been noticeable since the beginning of the second Intifadah and had become a recurrent feature since 11 September, indicated an unusual and worrying degree of political amateurism. Divisions within the leadership burst into the open on the great day of demonstrations on 7 April 2002, in Paris and other large French cities, a day of struggle against anti-Semitism and solidarity with the Israeli population which, contrary to the wishes of some of its organizers and many participants, quickly turned into an expression of support for Ariel Sharon. Although it ended in some violent incidents, this initiative once more sowed confusion by amalgamating the struggle against anti-Semitism with unconditional support for Israel. How, after that, could the most excitable and least informed elements be asked to distinguish between Jews here and Israelis there? It would have been perfectly possible to reject the amalgamation, without in any way detracting from the principle of support for Israel.

It must be said that quite a large part of the Jewish establishment had a very narrow conception of 'support for Israel', as well as of the 'neutrality' that it felt entitled to demand of journalists covering events in the Middle East. In fact, the raising of doubts to implicate the media was a constant feature of those turbulent months. It is true that the flood of news and commentary in the aftermath of 11 September, as well as the resumption of violence in Palestine, did not pass without causing a few blunders; it is also true that the acts of anti-Jewish violence were not subjected to any censure in the radio, television or press. But the accusations against the media were actually deployed in a different connection. What was suggested was that, by systematically attacking Israel, they had somehow provoked or at least encouraged the surge of 'Judeophobia' in France and elsewhere in Europe. Each word spoken or written, each picture screened, was carefully weighed and judged. But was it really proof of the moderation demanded of others to prosecute this or that journalist on the slightest pretext: Pierre Assouline, for instance, for not having sufficiently censored the verbal excesses of Raymonda Hawa Tawil on France Culture; or, more recently, Daniel Mermet for having broadcast on France Inter violently anti-Israeli messages from various listeners, in the context of a series of reports on the Middle East conflict? No doubt some journalists were inclined to take liberties with the objectivity that they were expected to show. But did that mean they should have remained quiet about the exactions committed by the Israeli army?

While the number of civilian victims of the conflict kept increasing, in both Israel and Palestine, organic intellectuals of the French Jewish community thought it more urgent to deploy their rhetorical talents in denouncing the pernicious effects of the world conference on racial discrimination, xenophobia and intolerance, held in Durban from 31 August to 7 September 2001. It is true that several NGOs made clearly anti-Semitic statements there, and the press itself denounced these as a shameful lapse. Were the scandalous excesses in Durban reason enough to abstain for ever from the slightest criticism of Israeli policy towards the Palestinians? Did any questioning of Israel's actions contain the seeds of its blackballing from the international community?

There was a war on. Neither side was innocent. And one could expect that Israel and everyone really attached to it would accept the consequences of the normalization that Zionism had advocated and largely achieved. Politically independent, with a sovereign state and an army, the Jewish people of Israel could be judged like any other people with comparable status for the power they exercised and their tendency under certain circumstances to abuse it. They could not continue for ever claiming the privilege of absolute innocence. They could finally agree to enter the age of relativity – of relative innocence and relative guilt.

But Durban and the acts of anti-Jewish violence in Europe had set going the machine that pumped out denunciations of anti-Semitism and anti-Zionism. A surprising number of new books going more or less in the same direction appeared in the first quarter of 2002, the green light having been given in the last quarter of 2001.[20] Some saw in the new twists no more than the final disguise of an eternal hatred: the Jewish people had always been surrounded by enemies, and now they or their successors were bent on the destruction of Israel. Jewish websites took the same themes one step further. And, in Israel itself, the media served up long accounts of the anti-Semitism spreading across Europe – a region hostile to Jews from time immemorial, a region that had brought them nothing but persecution and tragedy.

Fear turned to 'paranoia'. It was impossible to say or write enough, or to do so well enough, about the new 'Judeophobia'. Violence against other groups, the anti-Arab racism of the French population: none of that counted. Everyone had it in for the Jews. Therefore, retreat into the community appeared to many a lesser evil, or even a solution. Begun long before, the retreat now took a clearer turn in favour of a new 'us against them' attitude, which on the whole seemed likely to strengthen the links of French Jews with the 'organized' community and to enhance the power and authority of its leaders and institutions. After all, anti-Semitism could always help to save the Jewishness of the Jews. In these times of identity crisis and exogamous marriage, a little hostility from the outside world might have a few beneficial effects.

There can be no question here of denying the reality of the acts of anti-Jewish violence, or of exonerating those responsible for them; all we have been trying to do is understand their impact and analyse the uses made of them. The case of France deserves to be dwelt on a little. Why did the state of panic arise? How are we to explain the particular sensitivity of the French Jewish community?

The majority of Jews in France originally came from North Africa. As the various countries in the region gained independence in the 1950s and 1960s, the Jews took the path of exile; those from Egypt did the same, especially after the Suez War. Virtually all the Algerian Jews headed for France, where they had the status of repatriated citizens and were therefore able to integrate more easily. Most of the Moroccan and Tunisian Jews, on the other hand, went to Israel, with a minority preferring to settle in Canada or France. Their integration in France proved more complicated, if only because they did not all have French nationality; the history of their exile has been forgotten, much as French people have preferred to forget the Algerian War. The bitterness resulting from this oblivion has, for these exiles, been compounded by the memory of a lingering bone of contention with the Arabs, although the country they left behind has meanwhile paradoxically taken on the colours of a lost paradise. Upon their arrival in France, it was obviously difficult for these North African Jews to gain attention for their sufferings in exile, when the Ashkenazi Jewish community that received them had been decimated by the war.

It must be said that the hour of hypermnesia had not yet sounded: it was only in the 1980s that the 'return of memory' began to occur in connection with the Vichy period and the Holocaust.[21] In this recall, however, the Sephardis of North Africa and Egypt had scarcely any place. Their own memory was overshadowed by the incomparably stronger one which then surfaced in France and elsewhere in the West, and which eventually became ubiquitous. Until very late, there was no talk in North African Jewish families about the genocide. And, although Sephardis began to dominate Jewish religious and community life in France, their own experience generally remained in obscurity – with the exception of some younger people who, having grown up in France, turned towards that experience nostalgically, in a literature that started to appear in the late 1970s. Their spectacular integration made them, in the eyes of others, fortunate Jews upon whom the sun had shone, so that they were as if excluded from the Holocaust remembrance that was gradually becoming one of the key components of Jewish identity in Europe and the United States. Slowly, the new generations descended from North African immigrants began their own identification with the genocide, as it seemed to be the only way of achieving a genuine Jewish identity.

It was no accident that, during a programme on LCI television in November 2001, Raphaël Draï evoked the 'educational genocide' to which his people were subjected in Algeria. By this he meant the numerus clausus that applied in schools from late June 1940 in Algeria – a practice also present in Tunisia and Morocco. In fact, from 1940 the special Jewish statute was extended to the French colonies and protectorates, and in October of that year the repeal of the Crémieux Law led to a collective loss of French nationality for Algerian Jews. The Allied landing in North Africa in November 1942, however, would soon change the framework for the better. Painful and distressing though the wartime fate of North African

Jews undoubtedly was, it evidently cannot be compared to that of their fellow-Jews in France and elsewhere in continental Europe. The expression of Raphaël Draï's involved a slippage in the language, but it revealed a kind of Sephardi 'complex' which the climate of insecurity in France in autumn 2001 made more discernible.

It had not been possible to call attention to the sufferings of exile, and possible only with difficulty to mention the pre-war or wartime humiliations in North Africa. But now the latest wave of 'Judeophobia' suddenly offered the Sephardis an opportunity to acquire the credentials of genuine persecution, and to share – if only in a minor and incomparably weaker mode – the fate of their Ashkenazi brothers and sisters. In fact, the most exposed to anti-Jewish violence in 2001–02 were the same Sephardis who still lived side by side with North African Arabs in the explosive suburbs. Suddenly, the memory of humiliation previously suffered in the lands of Islam could rise again to the surface; it was now possible to do more than share, rather abstractly, a common remembrance of the Holocaust. The Sephardi Sammy Ghozlan could say: 'We are taken for paranoids, but our collective memory makes us more vigilant … In August 1934, in Constantine, some places of worship were desecrated. The authorities reassured the Jews, and then for three days they endured murderous pogroms. Since 1954 I have always seen policemen in front of my synagogue. If France is not anti-Semitic, French policy is anti-Israeli.'[22]

Anti-Semitism and anti-Israelism are one and the same for the (often Sephardi) Jews who feel under fire from the attacks. And the frame of reference remains the history of European anti-Semitism and the genocide, so that even something like the Durban Conference can be compared to a 'pogrom'. This helps us to understand the repeated image of a new Kristallnacht – as if Sephardis in particular, and the younger Jewish generations in general, had suddenly lived through one such night of their own; as if this finally gave them access to the valued status of victims. The choice of vocabulary expressed and sustained the sense of panic. This extreme anxiety put people back in touch with a Jewish identity, now seen first of all in terms of participation in a history of persecution. In Israel the language was the same; there too comparisons with the genocide period abounded. The country's deputy foreign minister, Michael Melchior, distinguished for the sake of form between classical anti-Semitism, which attacked

Jews as individuals, and a new anti-Semitism which crystallized on the Jewish State. 'Auschwitz did not begin with Auschwitz,' he said. 'It is not that we are in the same situation today, but Auschwitz also began with the delegitimation of Jews and moved on to their dehumanization and finally their demonization.'[23]

In this field, however, the competition was tough: European Jews and Israelis met their match in North America. It was a question of who would issue the bleakest prognosis, whether or not the end of the Jews would coincide with the end of the State of Israel. In April 2002, in an article in the *New York Observer*, Ron Rosenbaum warned against the danger of a 'second Holocaust'. Nor was he alone: others followed suit in the *Village Voice* and the *Washington Post*.[24] An article published in New York used the term 'Kristallnacht' in its title, to characterize a terrorist massacre of Jews celebrating Passover in a hotel at Netanya in Israel. Binyamin Netanyahu described Arafat as a new Hitler – hardly a novel idea – but also as a new Stalin for good measure.

Now, although anti-Semitism has not totally disappeared, it can hardly be said that the Jews of Europe and the United States are in mortal danger or that the existence of Israel is currently in jeopardy – if only because of its military strength. So, in what way does the situation of Jews in Israel today recall that of the 1930s and 1940s? Some mystification, deliberate or not, is involved in such comparisons, which serve to blind people to the fact that what is taking place in the Middle East is not genocide but a war. The mystification also makes it possible to close one's eyes to what is happening elsewhere, to others, and justifies a retreat into one's own group. Do we Jews have a special tendency to frighten ourselves in order to recover our Jewishness? What a sad thought! In the columns of the *New Republic*, Leon Wieseltier, author of *Kaddish*,[25] recently spoke out against this taste for 'ethnic panic' and reminded us that 'Hitler is dead'.[26] As Hitler is dead, should we not look at the world differently? Should we not stop thinking of the Israeli–Palestinian conflict purely from the point of view of the threat of annihilation? Too often, unfortunately, such a change of vision seems out of reach of European or American Jews dulled by material comforts, but also of large numbers of Israelis, who are not sufficiently aware of the world of death and destruction in which the Palestinians are forced to live.

'Pessimism is an injustice we do to ourselves.' These words of Leon

Wieseltier are not difficult to make our own. Today, like yesterday, we refuse to give in to the morbid temptation of irrational panic. Today, like yesterday, we think it is right to pose the question of the future of the Jews – calmly, and in the knowledge that it can have a number of complex and qualified answers. But today, more than yesterday, we understand that our attitude might seem shocking to sections of the Jewish media, and that some of our fellow Jews might think it out of place to point up weak or labile aspects of contemporary Jewish identity, when in their own eyes the danger threatening them on all sides is immense. It still seems to us a futile and extreme wish, however, to present at any price to the outside world the image of a monolithic Jewish community in danger from virulent anti-Semitism, the image of an inescapably anxious and suffering Judaism. Is it really so difficult to recognize the existence of a plural Jewish identity, diverse, dispersed, in no way united, constantly repositioned, now self doubting, now boldly projecting itself into the future?

To avoid an excessive focus on the twenty or so pages we devoted to the Shoah and the transformation of the memory of genocide into a civil religion, and to ensure that this part of our reflections was not separated from the broader framework that gave it meaning, we originally deliberately refrained from dividing the book into chapters and maintained the fluidity of our dialogue. Wasted effort! All, or nearly all, the debate on the first edition concentrated precisely on those pages, thereby indirectly confirming our general argument. It really was that – death and persecution, suffering and mourning – which mainly attracted the attention of our readers, whether Jewish or non-Jewish, sympathetic or hostile. Were they really so oblivious to the main body of the book, to the winding path that has shaped Judaism and Jewish identity? Did our discussion of the long history of the Jews and the majestic unfolding of their culture, in all its rich detail, really count for so little?

In the same way that we were accused of downplaying the threat from anti-Semitism, just as it seemed to be growing apace and becoming a tool in the hands of sorcerers' apprentices, so were our warnings about the banalization of genocide misinterpreted. Alas, our fears took on flesh and blood before our eyes: banalization was progressing, and nothing could stop it. The exactions committed by Israel in the territories, at Jenin and elsewhere, became in turn the object of dubious comparisons. They were certainly not what some pro-Palestinians, blinded by passionate defence of their cause, claimed them to be; no 'genocide' was perpetrated there against the Palestinians. But a taboo had gone flying; ritual evocation of the genocide now put Israel and the Jews at an actual disadvantage. Others now systematically used the same language to measure every event, every act by this single yardstick. In a way, it was 'genocide against genocide' – the absolutist aberration.

The social and political circumstances of the time gave our argument an unexpected complexion and resonance. In times of crisis, in times of war, a balanced approach or even the entertaining of doubts is seen as an attack. You are expected to speak in clear-cut, radical tones: to classify people, to isolate identities, so that everyone knows with whom we are dealing. Our book made the mistake of presenting an unclassifiable voice that was still in the process of taking shape. We did this without simplistic prejudgement, being more concerned to raise questions than to fling out answers; we thought this more in keeping with the long Jewish tradition of learning. In emotional times, the detachment with which we approached the history of the Jews suddenly came to be suspected as coldness. Not everyone, of course, fell into this trap: prominent intellectuals and anonymous readers, both in France and abroad, agreed to participate calmly in the debate we had tried to open; the strong feelings to which part of the Jewish community gave way had left others with some scope for lucidity. Young people searching for a life oriented Judaism, as well as children of survivors who had opted for life themselves: many were able to find means of liberation in the approach for which we spoke – liberation from pessimism and anxiety, liberation from an obsession with victimization. Judaism was not only sadness and guilt, not only a burden. It was also about sharing. Judaism was a gay science.

We make no claim to be in possession of the truth, and we accept that some of the things we said may have disturbed others. But there is still a step between that and the view of us as Jews who had betrayed by not playing the community's game of instrumentalizing anti-Semitism – a step that some, alas, took all too easily. We could not be accused of being anti-Israel, since we were not anti-Israel, nor of being anti-Semites or 'self-hating Jews', since our personal histories, our current activities and our place in the community or the Jewish studies milieu (in France as well as Israel and the United States) proved the opposite. So what did that leave? We could still be accused of selling out to the media and of betraying our community for the sake of personal glory …

In fact, from our position on the inside, we had said to the outside world a number of things that Jews regularly say to one another. Even our thoughts about the Shoah are widely shared, at least among academics working on the subject. The uproar in some Jewish circles, relayed by organic intellectuals (new fighters against anti-Semitism) linked to the institutional community, was out of all proportion with the actual content of our book. In these times, when noble souls have some difficulty finding a noble cause, these intellectuals were glad to have discovered one. No doubt their extreme vigilance was worthy of esteem. But was it not risky, and much less noble, to feed the anxiety of Jewish groups – an anxiety most often expressed in unconditional support for Israel? Were we supposed to give up our own critical sense? Could we not argue that criticism of the Sharon government did not at all imply a wish to destroy Israel; or that peace, withdrawal from the territories and the advent of a Palestinian state with secure and viable frontiers were not just pious wishes but goals to be attained? We ourselves had never yielded to the temptation of naively presenting the Palestinians as innocent victims of the wicked Israelis. But none of this helped us in the least. One had to be either for or against Israel – as simple as that.

We do not in any way think of ourselves as victims. We were playing our role. As someone recently said about Edward Said, an intellectual is 'an outsider who is not affiliated to his affiliations, who cannot be summed up in his origins, his interests and his positions' – for 'there is no thought where there is not an effort at disaffiliation'.[27] For us, this 'effort at disaffiliation' never meant indifference or betrayal. It enabled us to look at things differently, without giving in to 'tribe' pressure, and to gather around us everyone, Jewish or non-Jewish, who also wanted to look at things differently in order to see better.

Even if the wounds were numerous, and especially painful when inflicted by our own people, the experience was rich in lessons for us both. For it allowed us to see that, in France, debate is often paralysed by those who think they have exclusive power over speech; that the scholar's scorn, a subtle form of populism, could be relayed by intellectuals themselves; that the emergence of 'specialists' whose ethic involves speaking only about what they know is likely to irritate others whose profession is to speak without knowing; that for some it is more important to 'slaughter' an opponent than to read him and to think oneself into what he is saying; that the Stalinist ways of disqualifying others have not entirely disappeared. Fortunately, however, we also know that there are still real intellectuals in France, who take the trouble to listen to what others are trying to tell them, and then subject it to criticism in order to move forward. Despite everything, words still count for something in France: they can still be expressed despite the barriers placed in their way. And it is still possible to exercise one's 'Jewish responsibility' without reducing it to 'raw tribalism'.[28]

After the first round of the presidential elections in 2002, French men and women showed that they were capable of mobilizing against Le Pen and racism and for democracy. When American Jews wanted to boycott anti-Semitic France, the president of the CRIF – who had made so much of the 'new Judeophobia' supposedly threatening the country – felt compelled to retract. In an attempt to persuade the main American Jewish organizations to call off their initiative, he declared his confidence in the new government and praised the French people for supporting the candidate hostile to racism, anti-Semitism and xenophobia whom the CRIF had backed in the election.[29] Will the community officials, by making a new turn, manage to calm the minds they have helped to inflame?

Today, in June 2002, denunciations of the anti-Semitic danger have lost some of their force, and websites devoted to the issue seem to be drying up. Has 'Judeophobia' disappeared now that the elections are no longer upon us? Has a period of dialogue with France's Arab community opened up? Will reason gain the upper hand, now that the first round of the presidentials has shown where the real danger lies? The president of the Union of Jewish Students, co-author of *Antifeujs*, told *Le Monde* on 1 June: 'With the elections and the mobilization against Le Pen between the two rounds, the tension has subsided again. It is as if the anti-racist idea has imposed itself in the country.' And he added: 'The parenthesis seems to have been closed.' Has optimism become acceptable again? Will the second edition of this book come out during a moment of respite? It is to be hoped that the discussion will finally take up all the things that hurt. There is no other way for the Jews to have a future – a future with Israel, with a particular history of light and shadow, but also with an opening to the world and to others. But let us not get too carried away …

E. B. and J.-C. A., Collegium Budapest, June 2002.

Notes

1 See the interview with Farhad Khosrokhavar in *Le Monde*, 12 April 2002.

2 *Le Monde*, 31 May 2002.

3 See Pierre-André Taguieff, *La Nouvelle Judéophobie*, Paris: Mille et Une Nuits, 2002.

4 *Le Monde*, 13 May 2002.

5 *Libération*, 2 April 2002.

6 *Le Monde*, 19 February 2002.

7 *Le Monde*, 11 May 2002.

8 See the article by Nonna Mayer in *Le Monde*, 4 April 2002.

9 Union des étudiants juifs de France and SOS Racisme, *Les Antifeujs. Le livre blanc des violences antisémites en France depuis septembre 2000*, Paris: Calmann-Lévy, 2002.

10 *Ha'aretz*, 21 May 2002.

11 *Ha'aretz*, 23 April 2002; *Le Monde*, 13 May 2002.

12 *Le Monde*, 14 May 2002.

13 *Le Monde*, 3 March 2002.

14 *Le Monde*, 22 February 2002.

15 Peter Novick, *The Holocaust in American Life*, Boston: Houghton Mifflin Co., 1999; *L'Holocauste dans la vie américaine*, Paris: Gallimard, 2001.

16 *Libération*, 2 April 2002.

17 *Le Monde*, 12 March 2002.

18 See Sylvie Strudel, *Votes juifs. Itinéraires, religieux et politiques*, Paris: Presses de Sciences Po, 1996.

19 *Ha'aretz*, 22 and 23 April 2002.

20 Let us make special mention of the following: Gilles William Goldnadel, *Le Nouveau bréviaire de la haine*, Paris: Ramsay, 2001; Raphaël Draï, *Sous le signe de Sion. L'antisémitisme nouveau est arrivé*, Paris: Michalon, 2001; Guy Konopnicki, *La Faute des Juifs*, Paris: Balland, 2002; and Shmuel Trigano, *L'Ebranlement d'Israël. Philosophie de l'histoire juive*, Paris: Seuil, 2002. The book by P.A. Taguieff that we have already mentioned does not belong to the same category; Taguieff is not an organic intellectual of the community, and the deeper reasons for his position are different. Nevertheless, his analyses bolstered the fears of part of the Jewish population, and gave the Jewish leadership the 'scientific' backing they might need.

21 See Henry Rousso, 'La guerre d'Algérie, la mémoire de Vichy', *L'Histoire* 266, June 2002, pp. 28–9.

22 *Le Monde*, 31 May 2002.

23 *Ha'aretz*, 5 May 2002.

24. See *Le Monde*, 26 June 2002.

25 Leon Wieseltier, *Kaddish*, New York: Knopf, 1998.

26 *New Republic*, 27 May 2002.

27. Interview with Edward Said in *Le Point*, 13 June 2002.

28 The expression is borrowed from Daniel Petter Lipstein (quoted in *Le Monde*, 26 June 2002).

29 *Le Monde*, 13 May 2002.

The Jews and Their Future

1 | What does it mean to be a Jew?

Jean-Christophe ATTIAS: 'Jew'? The word denotes a reality that appeared only quite recently, at least in the timescale of a people going back thousands of years. It comes from the Hebrew word *yehudi*, which means 'Judaean', a descendant of the tribe of Judah, or simply an inhabitant of the land or kingdom of Judah, or especially a 'Judaean in exile'. The book of the Bible in which the term *yehudi* emerges with a sense close to the one we know today is the Book of Esther, where it is used to refer to Mordecai, the cousin and tutor of the eponymous heroine. The story, which unfolds in Persia, tells of how Esther and Mordecai managed to save their people from extermination after it had been scattered through all the provinces of the Empire. The 'Jew' is thus clearly the Judaean in exile, a phenomenon that first came into being in Babylonia in the sixth century BC.

Esther BENBASSA: Other names established themselves in the course of time. In nineteenth-century France, for example, the term 'Israelite' came into circulation, no longer saddled with the deprecatory connotations of 'Jew' as the usurer of the popular imagination. Emancipated Jews no longer wished to be called Jews but described themselves as Israelites. In a kind of return to biblical origins, to an ancient Israel raised to the level of myth, the Israelite became a 'regenerated' Jew rid of the dross of history. He was, in France, an integrated Jew.

J-CA: This introduction of the term 'Israelite' was therefore a way of erasing the ethnic dimension that might be contained in the term 'Jew'. It was meant to be a denominational category, roughly equivalent to Catholic, Protestant or Orthodox.

EB: So, Jews no longer wished to be seen as belonging to a people apart. To become one with the French nation, they now had to define themselves in religious terms – and only in private, not in the public sphere. The term 'Israelite' was an indicator of this change. After the Six-Day War of 1967, however, it gradually dropped out of usage and acquired a pejorative force of its own. Some people, in good faith, feel

embarrassed to use the word 'Jew' because of the negative connotations that it still has for them; 'Israelite' gives them the impression of
being more neutral. But it is only rarely used today. Jews themselves
disown the term – with a special vehemence among the younger
generation, who thereby reject the anyway largely imaginary figure
of the nineteenth-century 'assimilated' Jew. It has become clear that
history was not like that; there was never total assimilation in France
– nor in Germany, for that matter.

J–CA: In current usage, then, 'Jew' has been rehabilitated and
'Israelite' has acquired a deprecatory force. The Israelite appears as a
Jew who has surrendered by agreeing to blend in with the Nations.

EB: 'Israelite' is a name that crops up when people do not know
what else to use. It is a prudish, hesitant term, whose very contrast
with the alternatives gives some idea of the ways in which Jewish
identity has been reconstructed over time.

J–CA: Nor should we forget our 'ancestors' the Hebrews! They
are the people in question in the historical books of the Bible: the
descendants of Abraham, the nation issuing from his grandson Jacob
and the latter's twelve offspring, the House of Israel, the people of
Israel. Theoretically, then, this biblical unity comprises twelve tribes,
but the tribe of Judah – or, more precisely, the Judaeans and Ben-
jaminites – were the only real or supposed progeny of the Hebrews
who remained on the historical stage after the destruction of the
Kingdom of Northern Israel in 722 BC and the deportation of the
Judaeans to Babylonia in 587 BC. The Judaeans thus appeared, and
Jews came to be perceived, as the last of an ancient Hebrew line. Evidently this is a historical construct: one should not imagine that a Jew
one happens to meet is a real descendant of the Hebrews. One never
knows, of course, and individual Jews may well imagine that that
is what they are. This kind of national and religious mythology has
enabled Jews to think of themselves as the sole rightful heirs of the
ancient biblical Hebrew tradition, so that a Jew becomes not merely
a repository of the original Hebrew message but an actual blood descendant of Abraham – which he is evidently unlikely to be in reality.
The very diversity of the Jews – at once ethnic, cultural, linguistic and,
if you like, 'racial' – is enough to prove that they do not all come from
the same 'national stock'. This is not to say that they do not constitute
a people aware of its existence and its unity. But there is no way of
demonstrating that a particular individual is a direct descendant of

Abraham, or of any other patriarch. Anyway, that is not what matters. What does matter is the way in which Jews think of themselves as the heirs and descendants of Abraham, the inventor of monotheism. Can it be shown historically that Abraham invented monotheism? Certainly not. All that can be said is that the Jewish tradition considers Abraham the father of monotheism, and Judaism the natural outcome. That is something quite different.

EB: But the fact that Jews are not what they say they are does not prevent them from being what they are. An imagined identity is already an identity.

J–CA: The Jews exist, of course. The Judaeans also existed in late antiquity, before and after the beginning of the Christian era, as a population both settled in Judaea and scattered throughout the Graeco-Roman world. Philo, for instance, was a Jew living in exile in Alexandria in the first century AD and writing in Greek. He wrote to vindicate Judaism, but at the same time he already managed to express all the ambiguity of the Jewish condition. He said that Jews have something special other peoples do not have: they have both a homeland (the country where they live and grew up, whether Alexandria or Rome) and a metropole (the land where their nation was born and built itself up – the land of Israel). The tension between the two was for Philo the sign of the Jewish condition, not so different in the end from that of many Jews in the modern world.

EB: So, in this way of looking at things, the break in 70 AD was not the founding moment that it might seem to have been?

J–CA: Indeed, I think we have to go a little further back. The reading of Jewish history which places the break in 70 AD (the destruction of the Second Temple by the Romans) certainly suits quite a lot of people, especially Christians. But the dispersal actually began in the sixth century BC, with the deportation of the Judaeans to Babylonia and the reformulation of their culture in exile. What did it mean to be a 'Jew' at that time? Already it meant to be capable of living one's culture, building one's community in exile, accepting the principle of defeat. In 587 BC, the question was whether the destruction of the First Temple and the Judaean exile meant that their god had abandoned them, that the gods of the Babylonians had irreversibly triumphed. The answer to this question, among the exiled Jews, was a clear 'no': both defeat and the expected reconstruction depended on the will of the god of the Judaeans, who became a universal god. It was thus in exile that a Jewish identity first constituted itself. The Roman occupation of Judaea, the destruction of Jerusalem and the Second Temple in 70 AD, certainly drew a line under the second attempt at an autonomous Jewish existence in the land of Israel. But although Judaeans were living in Palestine at the time of the Second Temple, there were already many more living outside. The destruction of the Second Temple put an end to the land of Israel as the principal existing centre of Jewish life, as a sanctuary or a goal of pilgrimage. But the exile had begun long before. It was exile and dispersion which made the Jew as such, and which explain why there are so many ways of being a Jew. To experience the world as a place where Jews are scattered around; to feel a sense of belonging to an ideal community, but also to be perfectly aware that Jews exist every-where, in very different social, cultural, religious and linguistic contexts; to live in exile but also to be in some way separated from one's own people: all this is part of what it means to be Jewish.

EB: It also means to live on the founding myth that a people once lived together in the land of Israel – a myth which has itself evolved through the ages, constantly fuelling the consciousness of exile. The mythical function of the land of Israel, as locus of origin and belonging, is at the heart of the Jewish religion itself.

J-CA: It is a central point of reference in the Jewish imagina-tion and self-characterization, but it operates as such only because of the exile. It is in this tension between the lost place and the place of present existence that the various forms of Jewish identity have taken shape. All the population transfers, all the exiles and expulsions, have kindled this consciousness of exile. One example will suffice. Moses ibn Ezra, a poet writing in medieval Spain, took up in one of his verses the famous words: 'If I forget thee ...' Of course, we im-mediately think of ' ... Jerusalem', as in Psalms 137:5. But, no, it is: 'If I forget thee, Granada', in Muslim Andalusia. Forced to take refuge in Christian areas, ibn Ezra transferred to Granada the nostalgia that the Jewish people feels for Jerusalem and Zion. Thus, each new exile has given new life to this condition or feeling of Jews that they are some-where other than at home.

EB: At Passover, the festival commemorating the departure from Egypt and heralding all the liberations to come, the words tradition-ally spoken are: 'Next year in Jerusalem.' Even today, Jews who have become Israelis and themselves live in Jerusalem continue to close the Passover ritual with: 'Next year in Jerusalem.' We are here inside the myth, as well as beyond it – a founding myth but also a ritualized myth. Through history, Jews have had such an extraordinarily complex relationship with that land of Israel which was lost to them that, in some periods, the great Jewish centres of the Diaspora set themselves up as new Jerusalems: there was Vilna, the Jerusalem of the East; Sarajevo, the Jerusalem of the Balkans; Salonica, the 'Mother City in Israel'; Tlemcen, the Jerusalem of the South; and Amsterdam, the Jerusalem of the North. The need was there, even in exile, to reproduce the founding myth and to make it the rallying focus. This explains why, much later, the early leaders of the Zionist movement finally ended their equivocation and opted for Palestine, not Uganda or Mesopotamia, as the site of their future state. Only the land of Israel had the necessary power to rally and unify.

J-CA: Nevertheless, the land of Israel was never the only point of reference, never the only lost land. Ancient Judaism – and, to a large extent, also medieval Judaism – encompassed a diversity of Judaisms. Jews never defined themselves simply as Jews: they were Jews from the country where they lived; Jews of the particular language they spoke; Ashkenazis from Central or Eastern Europe, with a mainly Yiddish tradition; or Sephardis originating in the Iberian Peninsula, mainly Mediterranean or Oriental. Moses Maimonides, who was born in Spain in 1138 and left for Egypt as a young man, spent his whole career in his new country and wrote there all his varied works: a philosophical summa, a revolutionary code of Jewish law, a commentary on the Mishnah, the first canonical compilation of oral law, and a number of medical treatises. But although he settled in Fostat, the old Cairo, he continued to characterize himself as a Sephardi, a Spaniard or even an Andalusian! In the Middle Ages, too, there were many definitions of being a Jew. The mere term 'Jew' remains abstract. To acquire greater content, it has to be fleshed out with that cultural and even religious diversity which has never ceased to grow over the centuries.

EB: This explains the various cleavages – even those which appeared at a much later date. In France, for example, on the eve of the Revolution, Sephardis living in the southwest did not recognize themselves at all in the image coming from the Ashkenazis of Alsace and Lorraine. There is no form of Jewish identity which has not been deeply marked by the conditions in which Jews have lived, by their particular relationship to the land and their past.

J–CA: Jews are Jews not only from the land where they now live, but also from the one where they used to be before.

EB: Yes. Still today, in Turkey, a Jew born in a village on the shores of the Bosphorus who has grown rich in the big city will come back to his and his father's home synagogue, at least for the great festivals of the cycle of life. He will use a car on Saturday and thereby breach the Sabbath, but he will also go and pray in the synagogue of the town of his birth. One always remains a Jew from a particular place.

J–CA: That is why Spanish Jews invented for themselves an ancient origin in Iberia. In the fifteenth century Isaac Abravanel, a favourite of Alfonso V of Portugal who was also on close terms with Ferdinand of Aragon and Isabella of Castile, followed many other Jews in claiming that a number of Spanish or Portuguese towns had Hebrew names, and that they had been founded by exiled Jews at the time of the destruction of the First Temple. Spanish Jews thus created a Hebrew mini-geography in the land where they were then living. After their expulsion from Spain in 1492, they spread all around the Mediterranean basin and entered the Ottoman Empire, where they were still known centuries later as Sephardim (that is, 'Spaniards'). In recent times, however, when these Sephardi Jews from the former Ottoman Empire have settled in Israel, for example, they have come to be known as Bulgarian Jews, Greek Jews or Turkish Jews – which they never were when they were living in the respective countries and among the respective populations. The names have always been 'one exile behind', so to speak.

EB: It was the same in France. Jewish immigrants from Eastern Europe organized themselves in Paris or elsewhere into *landsman-shaftn*, associations defined by country of origin. The process of uprooting strengthened their desire to sink roots, so that the previous land of exile now became a 'lost homeland'. In the United States, in Israel, one finds the same associations of people originating from a particular town or village. Even after their 'return' to the Jewish state that is supposed to mark the end of exile – but can there really be a 'return' to Israel in the sense of a mother country? – they continue to reproduce this model of origins. The problem is even greater when Jews living today in Israel, immigrants and especially the children of immigrants, make a trip back to discover the country that they or their parents left behind. Thus, for many Moroccan Jews – members of a poorly integrated community who have long been considered second-rate Israeli citizens – it is only after they return from a trip to their country of origin that they begin to see themselves as real Israelis; they need this time in the place of exile to reconstruct themselves as Israelis. Another enigma are those young people born in Israel, whether Ashkenazi or Sephardi, who serve a fatherland, their fatherland, by performing military service, then immediately go off on a long trip of perhaps six months or a year to the Far East or Latin America, before finally returning to Israel and again fully considering themselves to be Israelis. It is as if they must always go through the experience of leaving before they can really take on board the idea of a homeland. Others may return on a visit to their grandmother's or grandfather's village, especially in Eastern Europe. You see young people like that all the time. It is not nostalgia. There is an aspect of initiation, a passing through the place of exile as part of what it means to be Jewish – and, in their case, to be Israeli.

J-CA: But there is also a simpler and, if I may say so, more mundane side to this. What has made people Jews is their everyday life, their customs, language and food, just as much as the great canonical texts.

EB: Custom does indeed define the very substance, the ethnic-religious substance of groups of Jews. Take North African Jews, for instance, who are closer in time to the place from which they were uprooted than the immigrants who arrived from Eastern Europe between the world wars. They will say: 'We are Jews from Constantine', or 'We are Jews from Tunis', or 'We are Jews from Alexandria'. Too often it is forgotten that the texts are not the only thing; there is also the relationship with a place, or rather the social mores of a place, which always involves some degree of interaction with the surrounding milieu. It has also been through the particular customs of the micro-group that Judaism has perpetuated itself. North African Jews will tell you: 'We sing according to the rite of Tlemcen', or 'We pray according to the rite of Oran'. Even the reading and study of texts is heavily influenced by local specificities.

J-CA: That's true. The ritual chanting of scriptural texts, on Saturday morning in the synagogue, differs from one community to the next. The Hebrew is not pronounced or chanted in the same way. And it is that special way of chanting, eating and attaching oneself to a place or a custom which makes people Jews.

EB: Even among the ultra-Orthodox. For someone coming from

outside, all the 'men in black' seem the same. But they do not all belong to the same group: there are the Galicians, the Lithuanians, and so on. Their dress also functions as a distinctive sign enabling others inside the group to identify them. From the outside, they may appear to form a seamless whole; Judaism may give the impression of a cohesive unity. But to believe in such a unity would really be to miss the reach and the fluidity of Judaism.

J–CA: That diversity is the flesh and blood of exile: it is what gives it pungency and meaning.

EB: But there's exile and exile; it can be forced and it can be freely chosen. Exile today is chosen exile, since all Jews can opt instead for an *aliya* (literally 'ascent') to Israel. But the real truth is that all Jews can and cannot opt for it, as they are tied to the 'land' where they live, where they have their children, friends and work. You don't have to plough the land to belong to it: you are just as much bound to it by colours, odours and atmosphere. Exile is a difficulty reality to fathom.

J–CA: That is because exile is also a representation. Even if a Jew makes the *aliya* to Israel, he or she will still be in exile from somewhere, still separated from something.

EB: Yes, even in Israel you are a Jew from somewhere – a Jew from France, a Jew from Poland. Jews carry their exile with them. When they emigrate to Israel, they arrive with the Diaspora in their baggage. Israel is also a land of exile, the land that groups together multiple exiles.

J–CA: The very fact of exile, and even the awareness that Jews may have of successive exiles, has certainly varied. Clearly Jews did not feel exiled in the same way in Babylonia a few centuries BC or in Rome during the Second Temple period or within one of the medieval Jewish communities (whether in a Christian or Muslim country). The differences were even greater in the nineteenth or twentieth century, between the various points of dispersal. What has been constant, through the many different forms, is that to be Jewish is to be an outsider in a particular world – and sometimes, within a certain religious tradition, to be an outsider in the world in general, the broken, alienated world below that awaits redemption.

EB: At the same time, it is that which makes the Jew part of this world, which makes the world his fatherland, even if for many today that belongs only to the realm of theory.

J–CA: What is true for Jews is also true for Judaism, including

in its religious definition. Judaism presents itself, and is often perceived, as a force which has remained faithful to its original message,
preserving its wholeness and authenticity in the face of millennia of
history. What a mistake! Judaism was not born in a day: it has shifted
more than many would care to admit, and is not the preordained
guardian of some unchanging initial spark. Judaism is the product of
its own history and of the particular contacts it has had through the
ages. It has fed on those contacts. Jews do not think of or live Judaism
in the same way in Islamic countries, Christian countries and India.
It is true that there is a certain homogeneity in Orthodox practice, in
the sense that a number of rules are everywhere observed. But there is
huge variety in the ways in which they are applied.

EB: Perhaps that is the source of the richness of Judaism. It has
been in constant contact with the so-called dominant religions, and in
spite or because of the asymmetry there have been numerous areas in
which exchanges have taken place between them. Those who identify
Judaism with closure, with an unchanging world turned in on itself,
are clearly on the wrong track. The minority status of Judaism may
actually mean that it has been more open to outside influence. Contrary to what some people think, there has been no time in the history of Judaism when it has been 'pure' or 'integral'.

J-CA: The rabbinical authorities themselves are well aware of this
variety. They may see it as a sign of dispersion carrying the danger
of fragmentation for the Jewish people. But they certainly keep it in
mind.

EB: The literature on rabbinical consultations demonstrates this
profusion as clearly as one could wish. Issues subject to litigation may
be referred from one community to another, so that in difficult cases
a rabbi may end up consulting another rabbi thousands of miles away.
The picture is always one of extraordinary fluidity. The kaleidoscope
of law, schools and local traditions is constantly producing new for-
mations. Texts are not enough to settle everything; it is also necessary
to read and interpret them.

J-CA: Large-scale migrations have also led to new contacts and
made it necessary to reconsider a number of legal problems. Different traditions have suddenly found themselves directly facing one
another: for example, Sephardis expelled from Spain and Jews coming
from a Greek tradition were suddenly thrown together on the soil of
the Ottoman Empire. Although the rabbinical authorities deplore it,

they have always legitimated the diversity by means of two principles in tension with each other: the principle of remaining faithful to the tradition of one's fathers ('Do what your father did, what your grandfather did!'), and the principle of always valuing local customs higher than those of newcomers to a particular area.

EB: Nor should we forget the importance of local laws and the prerogatives of non-Jewish authorities as factors pushing towards adaptation and differentiation. One Talmudic formula expresses this succinctly: 'The law of the realm is the law.' In some fields, at least, Jewish law must therefore bow to non-Jewish legislation.

J–CA: Apart from normative Jewish law, then, we can see the authority of local variants, paternal tradition and state legislation.

EB: Exile, dispersion, custom and law: our discussion so far has mainly revolved around these concepts. But what of the specifically religious dimensions of being a Jew?

J–CA: Is that really the right way to pose the question? At least in the medieval world, being-a-Jew was fundamentally polymorphous: there was a religious aspect, a cultural aspect and a linguistic aspect. No doubt the religious definition of medieval Jewishness was strong and central, but it was not this which mainly distinguished Jews from others in the world around them; much the same could have been said of Christians and Muslims. The really crucial difference was the Jewish emphasis on precise conduct, on rigorous practical observation of the commandments. This, perhaps, is what has been forgotten in modern times. To be Jewish is to live daily as a Jew within a community, to attend a synagogue, to observe the chief rites of Jewish life: circumcision, marriage and burial.

EB: It was here that the full force of the Law made itself felt. Jews married and inherited in accordance with the rules of their law. But this was not a static phenomenon. In times of crisis, they might also be tempted to escape from their own jurisdiction. Sometimes, in inheritance matters, they might prefer to appeal to non-Jewish courts; Jews living in Muslim countries, in particular, often turned to the cadi, if only to ensure that their community did not know the exact size of their assets and impose too heavy taxes on them. Historians of the medieval period stress the juridical and organizational autonomy of the Jewish communities, and such autonomy did indeed exist. It rested upon a tacit agreement with the non-Jewish authorities, which were always in a position to cancel or circumscribe it. But the degree of autonomy should not be exaggerated: in both the Christian and the Muslim world, non-Jewish authorities did intervene in the running of the Jewish community, the raising of its taxes, and the appointment of its civil and religious leaders. Similarly, even when both parties to a dispute were Jews, it was sometimes in an individual's interest to withdraw from the jurisdiction of the community and to turn instead to a non-Jewish judge. (When one party was non-Jewish, this was of course compulsory.)

J-CA: That undermines a little more the idea that medieval Judaism was turned in on itself. There seem to have been many kinds of interaction with the outside world.

EB: Recently, in certain circles, there has been a tendency to imagine that Judaism developed and had moments of true glory only when it was turned in on itself, that outside influences merely debased or diluted Jewish creativity and identity. This is a far cry from the truth. We should not forget that the leaders of the Jewish community were usually laymen, not clerics; it was they who negotiated with the non-Jewish authorities over the future of their fellow-Jews and the smooth running of the community. In the premodern era, this situation gave rise to the figure of the Court Jew, the privileged mediator between the Jewish and the Christian world. For a long time he would embody this Jewish duality, which went well beyond the religious field.

J-CA: What distinguishes the premodern organization of Jews is not closure or absolute autonomy, but the fact that the individual Jew's relationship with the state – if we can speak of a state at that time – was mediated by the community and its leaders. That is all: there was never closure at a cultural level. The most disturbing feature about the way in which some Jews today look at their past is that they try to find in it an absolute Jewish authenticity, an absolute Jewish identity that is simply not there to be found. In fact, they invent one for themselves. At a cultural-linguistic level, too, there is countless evidence that the frontiers were porous both among scholars and among the population at large. The great Jewish thinkers were always in contact with what was happening outside; they adapted it and took it over for themselves. This was true both in the Christian world and in the Muslim world (where Maimonides, for example, in his famous *Guide for the Perplexed*, re-examined the truths of revealed tradition in the light of Greek and Arab philosophical thought). History shows no trace of the kind of 'pure, authentic' Judaism that is supposed to have been lost since the seventeenth century.

EB: Faced with the contemporary break-up, people seem to have a nostalgia for some single past identity. Yet, even before emancipation, the Jewish world displayed a quite remarkable multiplicity of conditions, self-perceptions and cultures. In medieval France, for instance, there was the division between the Jewish culture of the North, with its traditions of eleventh-century exegesis centred on Rashi and his disciples, and the Jewish culture of the South, which, under the influence of Spanish and Italian Jews, was more concerned with the sciences and philosophy. A Latin culture prevailed in the South, while the Rhineland was the dominant influence in the North. Nowhere do we find that ideal simplicity, that withdrawal and purity which are conjured up today. The very term 'identity' is too modern. Jewish 'identity' before the emancipation did not present the clearly defined features that are so fondly ascribed to it.

J-CA: What is true of the Middle Ages also applies to antiquity. One of the founding texts of Judaism is the Mishnah, the first great systematization of oral law, which was first published in Palestine around the year 200 AD. But the language of the Mishnah is not 'pure Hebrew'; there is no 'pure Hebrew'. The language of the Mishnah is clearly influenced by Greek and Latin, and by the ways of thinking which they disseminated at the time when the text was compiled. Only arbitrary and largely mythical reconstructions can come up with some originally intact Jewish identity on which to re-found contemporary Jewish identity. Yesterday and today we do not find the same religion, the same culture: that is what is so fascinating. The further back we go in time, the less Judaism resembles what we know today. We should not forget that there was a Judaism before Maimonides, a Judaism without Rashi. The image that certain traditionalist circles wish to convey is of a flattened, unhistorical Judaism in which all authors, texts and compilations, the Bible and the Talmud, codes and commentaries are somehow contemporaneous with one another, as if they formed an inseparable and perfectly consistent whole.

EB: So, you have no answer to propose to the question 'What is Jewish identity?'

J-CA: What a typically modern question! It is meant to force us into saying that to be Jewish is to be this or that. The problem is that Judaism is not necessarily defined in terms of an essence. To be Jewish is also to know, to learn and to act. For a long time, to be Jewish was to practise the Torah, to study the Law, to observe the festivals. It was not necessarily a question, not necessarily a problem. You were Jewish, and you did not even need to tell yourself that you were.

EB: In my native region of Turkey, and more generally the Muslim East, it is true that the question was scarcely ever posed. You were born a Jew, you lived as a Jew, and if you were lucky you died a Jew in the place of your birth. A Jew was Jewish because others saw him or her as such, and because Jews had always seen themselves as Jews. They had had no choice. Not to be Jewish, or no longer to be Jewish, was not an option. From this point of view – and only from this point of view! – I could say that I grew up in a premodern context. In the Middle Ages, in Muslim as well as Christian lands, Jews were simply what they were. In a world organized around religion, they had their place – a place open to debate, of course – and that was the Jewish condition. Jews were, in a sense, condemned to be Jewish. After emancipation, in the West, the question was no longer posed in the same way – or, to be more precise, it was truly posed at last. When Jews were integrated, non-Jews had difficulty detecting their Jewishness and even came to forget their Jewish origin. When a Jew was no longer in a place set out for Jews, the non-Jew's questions became more and more complex. Is he Jewish? Is he still Jewish? In what respect is he Jewish?

J-CA: These trends have forced us to recognize – if we needed to – that Judaism did not fall from the sky. No doubt Jews are defined by Judaism, but it is equally true that Jews themselves define Judaism. What is new today has to do with the fact that Judaism now presents itself in contrasting, opposite forms, and that the differences appear sharper than in the past. Perhaps, in the end, it is only a difference of degree, or at least as much one of degree as of nature. Judaism has never been a body of frozen doctrines or a set of frozen practices. Ancient Judaism, we should remember, was made up of a mass of conflicting currents. To some extent, the catastrophe of the year 70 solved the problem by handing power to the Pharisees – power which lasted for nearly two millennia, even if it was never able to impose itself everywhere in a monolithic manner. In Judaism there have always been centrifugal as well as centripetal forces. Thus, eighth-century Babylonia witnessed the emergence of Karaism, a 'deviant' current that called for a return to Scripture and radically challenged the power of the rabbis and the legitimacy of the oral tradition they claimed to defend. Medieval Karaites were nevertheless generally seen, and certainly saw themselves, as being Jewish.

EB: To insist on a rigidly one-sided definition of Judaism is to lapse into utopianism, for the reality of Judaism constantly eludes any such determination to pin it down. Those who 'return' to Judaism often imagine it to be strangely rigid and closed, and to involve rejection of others who are not, and do not wish to be, like themselves.

J-CA: What, then, is the 'hard core' of Judaism? We are not the first to ask this question, which has long haunted people's minds. Take, for example, that famous would-be convert who once asked the first-century sage Hillel: 'Teach me the Torah, in the time it is possible to keep standing on one leg.' Hillel's answer came straight back: 'No problem, we'll soon convert you. The Torah is nothing other than: "Do not do to your neighbour what you would not have him do to you." All the rest is commentary.' But we should not read this story too hastily, and especially not conclude from it that Judaism is all about ethics. What does Hillel actually say? That all the rest is commentary! Personally, I am not far from thinking that it is the commentaries which make Judaism. And what does Hillel add, before sending his proselyte away? 'Now go and study.' That too is Judaism: 'Go and study.' It is impossible to condense Judaism into a formula. That is its weakness today, but also what still constitutes its wealth.

EB: What is the way out of ambiguity?

J-CA: The point is not at all to break out of it: ambiguity is at the heart of the Jewish condition. Either you are born a Jew because you have a Jewish mother – which is what the Law says – or you become a Jew by converting to Judaism. That immediately implies two modes: either you are a Jew through the genealogical continuity of blood and family; or you become a Jew when the Jewish community agrees to open up and receive you as a foreign element. These two dimensions are to be found throughout the history of Judaism. You can be a Jew as a descendant of Abraham, from father to son or mother to son. But you can also become a Jew by subscribing to a body of knowledge, practising the Law, and becoming a disciple of Moses. That ambiguity is a constant. You find Jewish thinkers tending more towards Abraham or more towards Moses, but the tension persists. The two options are in conflict, but they never cancel each other. Not by chance has rabbinical Judaism set up great masters among those who have handed down and fashioned oral Law, presenting some as descendants of converts and others as themselves converts. Thus, tradition has it that Rabbi Meir, one of the second-century architects of what would become the first great code of Jewish law, had as one of his ancestors none other than the Emperor Nero, the man initially entrusted by God with the destruction of Jerusalem, who refused to carry out his mission and subsequently became a Jew. Similarly, Rabbi Akiba, who died in the first great revolt against the Romans, in 135 AD, was supposed to be descended from Sisera, the commander of the Canaanite army defeated by the prophet Deborah. Thus, rabbinical tradition tends to replace a flesh-and-blood genealogy with one based on knowledge, a spiritual, intellectual and cultural genealogy more open to outside elements. To make the descendants of non-Jews such important figures in the transmission of the Law is to demonstrate a real capacity to welcome the Other into the fold.

EB: Might we say that one genealogy eventually eclipses the other?

J-CA: No, both are always there, in a relationship of tension or complementarity. Even the convert, who begins by being a disciple of Moses, will be given a substitute line of descent and symbolically called a son of Abraham and Sarah. The two dimensions must be combined to produce a sense of completeness. But let us not stop at this legal, rabbinical definition of Jewishness; let us not place that much trust in the rabbis. The Law as established states that one must be born of a Jewish mother to be a Jew, but the texts have retained traces of an older rule that makes the father decisive in defining who is a Jew. Moreover, in today's France or the United States, there is a Reform Judaism which accepts the Jewish identity of children of Jewish fathers and non-Jewish mothers, without really demanding that they convert to Judaism. We can see that the matrilineal principle has not always been valid, and that it is today strongly contested in certain milieux. Nevertheless, genealogy has remained a powerful element in the Jewish tradition, which insists on the value of a line of descent. Jews define themselves by their ancestors, because it is ancestors – first and foremost, Abraham, Isaac and Jacob – who accumulated certain merits and handed them down for the benefit of their progeny. This model too is constant.

EB: This genealogical principle is taken by religious circles as the very basis of Jewish legality. Yet the legalism that characterized the Jewish condition in the premodern period was coupled with more diffuse and no less powerful elements. Some families, especially Sephardis, cultivated a tradition according to which they were descended from King David or a particular tribe, thereby gaining an aristocratic status in comparison with other Jews. Thus, in the Jewish imagination, other elements existed together with the legalism. One was a Jew from somewhere in particular.

J-CA: And also a Jew from somebody in particular – always with a strong touch of openness.

EB: Does this not take us back to the beginnings of Judaism, when it actively sought to convert others?

J-CA: That is the subject of debate. Complacent references are sometimes made to a few great collective conversions: the Edomites in the second century BC, or the Khazars, a people of Turkic origin, whose empire in southern Russia was at its height between the seventh and tenth centuries AD. There is a lot of myth in all that, and a dearth of hard evidence. We do not really know what the Khazars converted to – was it rabbinical Judaism or the Karaite splinter? – nor whether the whole Khazar people or only a few princes went over to it. Judaism is always ready to defend itself against the accusation of particularism, and a few fine examples of conversion can help to serve the cause. Although it is true that the option existed, the fact is that from late antiquity until the modern era the examples even of individual conversion are few and far between. I would add that, throughout the medieval period (in both Islam and Christendom), the conversion of a non-Jew to Judaism exposed both the convert and the welcoming community to the gravest of dangers. Decision-makers certainly posed the relevant questions: What must someone do to become a Jew? What should be demanded of a non-Jew seeking to convert? But they remained largely theoretical. And what is really symptomatic is that they continued to be posed.

EB: At the beginning of the Christianization of Gaul, when Christianity did not yet have a solid body of dogma, the Church seemed to fear Jewish proselytism – and we find that fear appearing again from time to time in history. All those rabbis and sages to whom tradition assigns a non-Jewish ancestry also make us wonder whether it was not quite late in the day that Judaism gave up attempts to convert others, and whether it finally did this to escape the wrath of the surrounding world and the Muslim or Christian authorities.

J-CA: Until now there have been two contradictory replies to that question. One is that Judaism made a virtue of necessity: there was a period in antiquity when Jews made great efforts to convert the Gentiles, but they abandoned missionary work when the rising power of Christendom made it too dangerous. The opposite view is that Judaism has no intrinsic vocation to convert others and does not naturally go looking to meet non-Jews; it may welcome converts but it certainly does not seek them out; and the proven cases of conversion, though quite numerous in antiquity, were not necessarily the result of active missionary work. Now, the problem is that people often support one or other of these two positions not so much because of any scientific evidence as because of an ideological parti pris and an implicit desire to convey a particular image of Judaism. But there is a simple solution to that. All we have to do is look at the photos of Jews on view at the Diaspora Museum in Tel Aviv, or go and meet Jews in their various communities, or go for a walk on the streets of Israel. The diversity of ethnic types is so striking that one can hardly think for a moment that there has not been mixing and therefore conversion.

EB: This fear of incurring the wrath of the authorities is still present. One day I happened to go into the rabbinical archives in Istanbul and – I'm not quite sure how – got as far as the place where the registers are kept. Jews in today's Turkey are citizens, but of a rather special kind, enjoying integration that is, shall we say, problematic. So, at that rabbinate where they usually never leave anything lying around, they had rather curiously forgotten to place one file in a safe place: the file on conversions of Muslims to Judaism. There were certainly not thousands of cases on record – in fact, there were only a few. But, when I asked about them, I was told quite clearly that it was better not to divulge such things. Since, in Turkey, Islam is passed down by the father, while Jewishness is passed down by the mother, any children born of a Muslim father and a Jewish mother are not admitted to Jewish schools. The reason is the same: not to get on the wrong side of the authorities.

J-CA: In the case you mention, the Jews are abandoning a strong rabbinical norm. The transmission of Jewish identity through the mother is a constant principle of rabbinical Judaism, although, as I said before, it has to be put into perspective. But it is also true that, in the premodern period, the problem was scarcely posed.

EB: And that is the big difference with the contemporary world. In the medieval period, there were no mixed marriages: Jews were defined by their religious observance and by a Jewish social fabric that fitted tightly around them; they were always more or less in compliance with the Law; a Jewish man married a Jewish woman, and his children were Jewish. Things did not go usually much further than that. The Jew remained in his place, even if it was at times very restricted.

J-CA: Here too, though, there was a slight difference between Christendom and the lands of Islam. After all, the Muslim world was more multicultural and multicommunal; Muslims and Jews did not face each other in a mutually exclusive encounter. The Ottoman Empire, for instance, contained Christians of all denominations and all ethnic groups, Arabs as well as non-Arabs, Armenians, and Europeans with all manner of origins. The situation was different in the Christian West, where things tended to be settled much more on a one-to-one basis. As an exogenous minority, or anyway perceived as such, Jews played an emblematic role in Europe.

EB: But when Jews ceased to be identifiable as Jews – with the appearance of the Marranos in Iberia and later, after emancipation, the 'Israelite' whose language, dress and customs no longer differed from those of Christian compatriots – a new kind of mistrust developed in the surrounding society which was no longer of a theological or ideological nature: it was a simple fear of the invisible Other.

J-CA: It is undoubtedly right to stress, as we have done, the variability of the relationship of Jews to others and to themselves. Amid exile and dispersal, this diversity of experience has certainly been integral to Judaism. Yet we can still say that Judaism has been *one*, or, at least, that it has always sought to establish its unity once again. Relations have always been maintained among groups of Jews: business relations, the circulation of manuscripts, exchange of letters, voluntary or forced movement of individuals and groups – the instruments have been many and varied. An emissary from the land of Israel, an Ashkenazi, travels through the Sephardi communities in the Muslim world to collect money for a Talmudic academy in Palestine. All these people get together and recognize one another, but at the same time they periodically discover again that they are different. We learn from travellers' tales that there is sometimes nothing more exotic for a Jew than another Jew. Nevertheless, there remains the awareness of a common destiny.

EB: There were numerous commercial and intellectual channels of communication. An Ashkenazi might study Maimonides, or a Sephardi read Rashi. A book printed in Vienna might be skimmed in Smyrna, or one published in Leghorn might be read in Amsterdam. Great though the distances often were, the separation was far from total. The Jewish world never stopped moving, as one community intervened in the life of another and knowledge continued to circulate.

J-CA: That is a fundamental point. The Ashkenazi–Sephardi polarization is a contemporary construct, and a false one at that. The truth is that everything was more diverse and more volatile.

EB: Besides, in the premodern era Jewishness was not reducible to what the Law had to say on the matter; it was not just a legal status but a condition, which varied with people's attitudes in the surrounding world. In the Middle Ages, that condition was regulated by the 'royal alliance'. When sovereigns had need of the Jews, to settle new areas as well as for economic reasons, they sometimes entered into an unwritten alliance with them. But it could be broken off at any moment, and when that happened it was because the Jews were no longer considered useful. The Jews thus naturally became a target for the nascent bourgeoisie, but also for all anti-royalist forces, wherever they were seen as allies of the regime under attack. The Jews' own degree of openness depended on the strength of the royal alliance: when the alliance broke down and left them as pariahs, they tended to withdraw again into themselves.

J-CA: Instability, persecution and expulsion could have contradictory effects. They were likely to cause some individuals and communities to withdraw together into attitudes of self-protection, but at the same time the great population movements helped to change the points of reference by promoting cultural recomposition. Thus, at the end of the Middle Ages, groups of Jews who had not previously been in contact were suddenly pushed up against one another as communities spread around and created a new Jewish geography. No doubt withdrawal was a constant temptation: the presence of danger brought out a spontaneous desire to preserve what might be lost. But to preserve, to hoard, was also to create and to innovate. That is a leitmotif of Jewish history. If the first codification of the Law was published in the late second century, if the Talmud (the commentary on this code) was eventually composed, if various syntheses and anthologies were later put together, if, after the expulsion from Spain in 1492, an anxious kabbalistic world tried to formalize and gather together traditions under threat – in each case, it was because of the presence of danger. There was always this conservative dimension in the face of a new spectre of fragility. Each time, however, the Jews in question completely reconstructed their world.

EB: The first and second generations of immigrants, though impeded by exile and the problem of sinking new roots in their adopted country, often proved to be creative. This was also due to interaction with the surrounding world. Isolation behind the closed gates of the ghetto was a later phenomenon, which really appeared only in the sixteenth century. Before, there had certainly been Jewish districts, but mainly because Jews chose to live there. Christians might also live in Jewish streets.

J-CA: There is nothing surprising about the fact that Jews lived together in a particular district. For their lives were organized around shared services: the synagogue, ritual bathing, ovens for unleavened bread, the burial society and so on.

EB: In eastern France, Jews continued for a long time to live in villages where non-Jews were mixed in with the Jewish population. Everywhere you can find Jewish streets, Jewish concentrations, but not ghettos in any real sense of the word. The Fourth Lateran Council of 1215, coming after other councils that restricted the place of Jews in society, undoubtedly represented an important break. From then on, Jews could no longer pass unnoticed: they had to wear a special sign that marked them out from the world around them, a physical token of their Jewishness. They had become the Other, by law. This was the beginning of their marginalization – and, in the end, of their demonization. It is in this process of marginalization, combining demonization and anti-Judaism, that we should locate the Jewish condition from the thirteenth century onwards. We start to find all those stories of poisoned wells, of Jews spreading the plague. It was also a period when attitudes were hardening more generally in Europe, with the launching of the war against the Cathars, not to mention the Crusades. Jews were not directly affected in France, but already in the eleventh century the Crusaders' advance through the Rhineland brought unprecedented acts of anti-Jewish violence. The thirteenth century was the century of expulsions, from England, France and more or less everywhere, and then came the large-scale persecution in Spain in 1391. This progressive hardening and isolation forced Jews into a number of crucial choices. For some, at certain moments, the solution was to convert to Christianity – which made it possible to escape the executioner and, above all, to remain in the adopted land where they had sunk roots. Jews had been in France and elsewhere from time immemorial, and the attitude of those with the power kept shifting backwards and forwards. Jews in the kingdom of France were expelled, then brought back, then expelled once more. Meanwhile, in the French seigniories, they managed to get by in the service of the local lord, even if they had to pay a high price for it. It was against this backdrop of difficulties and suffering that a culture nevertheless developed.

J-CA: In Champagne, the main force were Rashi and his disciples, with their commentaries on the Bible and the Talmud. In Provence and Languedoc, a whole army of translators from Arabic to Hebrew, such as the famous family of the Tibbonides, acclimatized on French soil the classics of the Greek and Muslim philosophical and scientific tradition: Aristotle and Averroes, as well as the great masters of medieval Jewish-Arab culture, Bahya ben Joseph ibn Pakuda, Judah Halevi, Maimonides and others. You are right: the picture should not be painted too black. Even the later Middle Ages were not a dark age for Judaism; there was both black and white. In the Muslim world there were also other shades, and Christendom itself was a fragmented world where Jews were not everywhere treated in the same way.

EB: So, the end of the Middle Ages was marked by the birth of ghettos. In 1555, the papal bull *Cum nimis absurdum* recommended their creation, and the first ones appeared in Italy. But later on we also find them in France, where expulsion decrees had not already ended the Jewish presence: in the east and the south-east, and of course also in the papal territories. For, despite the marginalization and the general hardening of attitudes, the papal lands remained receptive to the Jews, whether in Italy or in France. In the latter case, we may even say that Jews enjoyed a certain prosperity, having fled from Spain before or after the expulsion decree of 1492 that represents an emblematic break in Jewish history.

. J-CA: The process leading to the break was gradual, however. From the late thirteenth century and, as you pointed out, even more clearly from the late fifteenth century, the centre of gravity of Judaism shifted eastwards – both to Eastern Europe and to the Ottoman

Empire. Something changed then, as Western Europe became, so to speak, impoverished of Jews. But the whole history of medieval Judaism, in Christendom as well as the Muslim world, was rich in cultural production: in rabbinical writings, poetry, philosophy and science. Between periods of persecution, and in areas that escaped persecution, such activity flourished. Even in the harshest times of violent rejection, and even after the formation of ghettos, cultural links continued to exist between Jews and the world around them.

EB: Contrary to the situation in the nineteenth and twentieth centuries, when there was a shift from east to west, the Middles Ages ended with a movement towards the east. This concerned Jews first from northern Europe and then from the Iberian Peninsula: the former migrated to the eastern marches of Christian Europe, while the latter gravitated to the lands of Islam. We should not forget that Spain had long been the nerve centre of world Judaism, which therefore lost one of its key bastions in 1492. Nevertheless, all these population movements were also the fermenting agent of a new dynamism.

J-CA: There was indeed a real recomposition of Jewish culture around these new axes of mobility. In the end, however, the eastward migration seems to me to have produced an ever greater uncoupling of Jewish culture from that of the surrounding world. Jews who had spoken Judeo-Spanish in Spain spoke more or less the local language. And when they continued to speak their old language in the Ottoman Empire, this linguistic particularity could not but reinforce their closure. The same was true of Judeo-German. The fact that Jews went on speaking Yiddish in a new Slav context did not at all mean that they had no links with it. But the linguistic discrepancy with their surroundings was a new element, which favoured the relatively autonomous development of Jewish life and culture, at the same time that the weight of Hebrew was increasing as a scholarly language.

EB: I think it is important not to project our own models of interpretation on to the history of the Jews in antiquity and the medieval period. Few people avoid this mistake. They speak too easily of anti-Semitism, for example. It is certainly possible to speak of anti-Judaism in that period, but not of anti-Semitism. Anti-Judaism did not involve the aim of eliminating the Jews as a race; even the Christian hope of theologically converting the Jews did not entail forced conversion. To take the Jews along the path of conversion was, of course, one imperative, but it existed in a tense relationship with another imperative: namely, that the Jews must continue existing as evidence of the truth of Christianity. Even at the apogee of anti-Judaism, these elements did not disappear. The Jews were granted Roman citizenship in 212 AD, and for quite a long time afterwards they actually did live as Romans, with no ghetto and no differentiation in everyday life. With the rise of Christianity, of course, and especially after it became established as the 'state religion', a new, increasingly critical attitude to the Jews developed and became institutionalized. Nevertheless, when Christianity was installed in Rome, the Jews went to live in Gaul and continued to use Roman names; their religious services were not always in Hebrew; they wore a Roman style of dress; they were still considered Roman citizens; and they retained more or less the same privileges under the Franks. This enabled them to live in the same way as all their neighbours. It is true that, from the fourth and fifth centuries on, one Church council after another restricted the place of Jews in society, always on the grounds that they should be prevented from mixing too closely with others. The very repetition of these injunctions, however, shows that Jews went on living in the midst of Christians.

J-CA: We should not imagine either that it was Christianity which invented anti-Judaism. There was an anti-Judaism in antiquity before the rise of Christianity, and it was far from being an anti-Semitism *avant la lettre*. I think there were a number of reasons for it. Apart from the fact that the Jews were a people whose turmoil threatened the *pax Romana*, their monotheism could not but appear strange, or even troubling, in pagan eyes. Nor should we forget the various inter-religious, inter-ethnic tensions, particularly in Hellenistic and Roman Egypt. For example, we have traces of anti-Jewish texts to which Flavius Josephus famously replied in his first-century *Against Apion* – an illustrated defence of the Jews, of Moses and the Hebrews, against the prejudices and attacks coming from various quarters in Alexandria. So, there were forms of hostility to the Jews, in the ancient as well as the medieval world, which should by no means be equated with the convulsions of modern times.

EB: A distinction should also be drawn between Christendom and the Muslim lands. In the latter, the condition of the Jew was defined in quite a different way. There too, of course, we should be wary of a myth that has been gaining momentum in the last few decades: the paradise lost of the Muslim world, where Jews supposedly lived in peace and prosperity. If we make an overall balance sheet, it is doubtless true that Jews fared somewhat better in the Muslim lands than in Christian Europe: they had a measure of autonomy, and their condition was governed from above by the *dhimmah*, a covenant of tolerance attributed to Muhammad but actually dating from somewhat later, which guaranteed real status and protection to Christians and Jews, as 'peoples of the Book'. In return for a head tax, Jews and Christians were able to live relatively independently in accordance with their own rules and religion. We should note in passing that similar opportunities were occasionally allowed in Christian lands as well. Thus when, following the Reconquista, Spanish Jews passed from Muslim to Christian rule, their new masters granted them almost the same privileges as before, in order to keep them and to make them allies. In the lands of Islam, however, the existence of a real set of rules (albeit apocryphal in origin) meant that Jews were directly given some free space of their own. In Muslim Spain, then in Christian Spain, the Jewish condition was therefore quite tolerable. Under Muslim rule, the Jews flourished to an extraordinary degree and even occupied functions within the state. Of course, waves of fanaticism could also sometimes sweep the Islamic lands, and this explains why many Jews periodically moved to Christian areas. For, in Christian Spain too, the position of Jews remained generally favourable until the fourteenth century and allowed a remarkable cultural efflorescence. Only when the re-Christianization of Europe became harsher and more exacting did Jews suffer negative effects more or less everywhere in the West. The Jewish condition, whether in Christian or Muslim lands, cannot therefore be reduced to a single model. As to the distinction between anti-Semitism and anti-Judaism, it is a great pity that many people think they can simply dispense with it. In the context of anti-Judaism, as I have already said, Jews remained as witnesses for Christianity; it was not thought that they should be eliminated.

J–CA: Yes, although there certainly was a Christian anti-Judaism, the existence of the Jews was also recognized as necessary. On the one hand, the Jews were bearers of the Book; they had passed down the written tradition upon which Christianity was based. They did not understand it, of course, but at least – as Augustine put it – they were faithful librarians for Christianity. On the other hand, their history, their status as scorned and humiliated second-class citizens, and even their very survival were visible proof of the antiquity of Revelation, the authenticity of prophecy, the fulfilment of that prophecy, and the messianic character of Jesus. Their inferiority, a punishment for their blindness, testified to the truth of Christianity. Though deprecated, the Jews had to be kept alive.

EB: They were certainly on the wrong path, but conversion offered them the means of returning to the right one. Everything was done to lead them there. But the Popes strongly disputed the validity of forced conversions.

J-CA: There were instances of forced conversion, of course, but it was not the recommended course and it raised doubts about the sincerity of what was done in a state of panic. Even the principle of voluntary conversion was a disputed issue in the history of Christianity, as some argued that it would lead to the disappearance of the Jews as such and prematurely end their function as witnesses. Such reservations had a dampening effect on the ardour to win new converts. Medieval Christianity thus had its nuances and partial contradictions – in a way, it ensured the survival of the Jews as Jews.

EB: The strongest memories, of course, are of violent paroxysms such as the large-scale forced conversions of 1391 in Spain. But it cannot be stressed too much that the Jews were not always separated or excluded from medieval Christian society. Above all, we must not fall into the extreme view that the Jews were persecuted 'from time immemorial' in the lands of Christendom.

J-CA: Changing attitudes in the Latin West, in and around the thirteenth century, also had to do with the discovery by the ecclesiastical authorities that the Jews were not Hebrews, were not strict observers of the Law of Moses, but were loyal to the different, oral law of the Talmud. In these conditions, the Jews could no longer play their role as witnesses to the truth of the Old Testament, since they themselves had turned their backs on it. It was then that harsh campaigns were launched to convert the Jews, and the status that Augustine had granted them itself came under question. This brought about a massive upheaval. In any event, forced or sincere conversions and the apostasies of the late fourteenth century would lead to new paradoxes, by creating the issue of the Marranos.

2 | Modernity and Jewishness

EB: Indeed, with the Marranos, the whole issue of identity
was posed in a new and peculiar form, involving transgression of
the principle of Jewish law as well as the principle of Christian
distinctiveness. 'Marrano' was a pejorative term, not the name that
the Marranos gave themselves. A Marrano was a crypto-Jew, a Jewish
convert or descendant of converts to Christianity, who outwardly led
the life of a good Christian but in secret continued, or was suspected
of continuing, certain Judaic practices. These crypto-Jews obviously
muddied the waters. Whether their adherence to Christianity was
sincere or not, *conversos* occupied an important place in Spanish
society. All the restrictions weighing on the Jews were lifted in their
case, yet the surrounding society persisted in its refusal to see them as
genuine Christians. Some new converts fully subscribed to their new
faith and, once baptized, thought of themselves as Christians from
every point of view. But others, behind closed doors, did still adhere
to a kind of Judaism; these were the Marranos, the crypto-Jews. In the
sixteenth and seventeenth centuries, when some of these Marranos
fled the Peninsula to escape the clutches of the Inquisition, they
returned to the essential norms of Judaism, and the problem once
again exploded with all its force. Were they really Jews? Who was their
father or their mother?

J-CA: Still, I think that in late-medieval Spain and Portugal
endogamy mostly remained the rule: 'old Christians' married among
one another, and so did the 'new Christians'. Cross-marriages were
seen in a bad light. To have 'pure blood' status, one had to show that
no such misalliance had stained one's ancestry.

EB: But there was El Cid, after all: Rodrigo and Jimena, he a 'new
Christian', she an 'old Christian'.

J-CA: Maybe. Anyway, it didn't work out as well as all that.

EB: Let us return to less theatrical issues. In the medium term, the
Jewish traces of the Marranos faded away – or else they underwent
profound transformation. Especially in Portugal, where they were
converted en masse in 1497, the Marranos actually produced a new
religion – Marranism – which was not the same as Judaism, since they
no longer had any real contact with normative Jews. Marranism drew
inspiration from Judaism, but also from the practices of the surrounding Christian world. I think we can say that it established one of the
first radical splits that lie at the origin of modern Judaism.

J-CA: I agree: Marranism is an excellent example of that powerful tendency. Personally, though, I would approach it in a different
way, as a phenomenon that raises questions for historians and others.
The implicit issue for many is whether the Marranos continued to
be Jews. If they did, there was no loss of Jewish identity – which
means that Jewish identity is so strong and so constant that any such
loss is impossible. The rabbis also asked this question. Does conversion to Christianity ultimately have no effect on Jewish identity?
Do even several generations of heteropraxis and heterodoxy leave it
unchanged? Did all those forced or voluntary converts indisputably
remain Jews? Behind such questions lies a strongly essentialist drive
to affirm the absolute continuity of Jewish identity, its fundamentally
resistant nature. But is this not to blow up out of all proportion a
number of groups that were actually rather small in size?

EB: There is also another way of asking the question. Whereas, in
certain Jewish circles, late attempts were being made to use Marranism as proof that Judaism has the capacity to survive anything, might
we not ask whether those Marranos remained or again became Jews
because of the Inquisition? After all, it was the Inquisition which
went on telling them they were Jews, even when they had become
Christians (sometimes good Christians), and which never stopped
hunting for vestiges of Jewishness that would justify their persecution.
Did that persecution itself not create the new Jewish consciousness? I
think this brings us to the heart of the matter. When those Marranos
returned to Judaism in the late sixteenth century, they often practised for a long time no more than a lax Judaism. For Enlightenment
thinkers such as Voltaire, moreover, they became a model of the Jew
who was capable of being integrated. One ideal Jew, the shipowner
Gradis of Bordeaux, ate at the king's table – evidently not kosher on
that occasion. The Judeo-Portuguese of the French southwest long
kept their distinctive characteristics, especially their flexibility in religious matters, and elsewhere, when the Marranos returned to Judaism
within well-established Jewish communities, they encountered many
problems of adjustment.

J-CA: This brings us to the other side of the question. No longer:
'Is it possible to become a Jew?', but 'Is it possible to stop being a Jew?'

EB: We know from a reliable source that many of these Marranos
were no longer clearly aware of their Jewishness. Here I am tempted
to make a brief digression. All the force of the persecution came from

the fact that it did not simply take aim at the Jews but invented (or reinvented) them. This was also the case when, during the Second World War, Jews were rounded up who had no connection with Judaism and nothing 'Jewish' except the label given them by the authorities, in accordance with laws and decrees quite alien to their previous experience of life. Could we say that certain difficult periods in history have pushed some Jews into an awareness of themselves as Jews, in a way against their will?

J-CA: I would go even further. Even if it is not necessarily spelled out, no one will deny that some community leaders and rabbinical authorities consider a bit of moderate ostracization on the part of the dominant society to be perhaps a necessary evil. In their eyes, Judaism certainly has within itself the resources to survive and develop. But the Other's gaze of rejection, or let us just say a little distance, may ensure the necessary minimum of cohesion. What Orthodox or 'fundamentalist' Judaism fears most is an open, slightly over-tolerant society.

EB: That is not quite what I meant. When the Inquisition was established in Spain and Portugal, the secret transmission of 'Judaism' in Marrano circles did not take place on normative paths; it was not achieved in and through the synagogue. The process was not controlled by Jewish elders, nor even implemented by male members of the community. Rather, the responsibility fell to women, to the family cell, where the emphasis was on kitchen practices, the changing of clothes on Friday evening, or the compulsory bath before the Shabbat. Personally, I am quite convinced that it is not only persecution which makes people aware of their Jewishness; I do not see what the advantage would be if that awareness dawned only negatively. What I meant to say was that Marranism may serve as a model for our understanding of how the legal paths of transmission became clouded over.

J-CA: Perhaps it heralded certain modern forms of Jewish identity.

EB: At the same time, the 'clouding over' also applied to Christianity. The stubborn distinction between 'old Christians' and 'new Christians' was designed to separate – to establish a hierarchy between those who had always been Christians without any mixing, and those who brought the clouds of confusion into Christianity itself.

J-CA: The parallel between Christian and Jewish Orthodoxy is most enlightening on this point. The Inquisition accused the 'new Christians' of still being Jews, but for its part the rabbinical world was sometimes inclined to wonder whether the Marranos were still really Jews. This was the beginning of something new: the old points of reference were breaking up. There was a mixing, a blurring of boundaries, which later (without the duress, or anyway without such violent constraint) became a characteristic feature of modernity.

EB: Today, an aura of romanticism envelops the Marranos. Pilgrimages are made to remote villages in Portugal – to Belmonte, for instance, where people were found practising Marranism after centuries had gone by. Emissaries were sent to them from Israel; and they were so often and so forcibly told that they were Jews that they began to believe it, and to construct a new history and identity for themselves. What comfort it was for some that Judaism had persisted despite all the adverse circumstances! Meanwhile, Marranism also acquired a new status in the Christian world. It is said that Portugal is one of the few countries in the world where there are more self-declared Jews than actual Jews; the number of people who have described themselves in recent censuses as Jewish is greater than the number of officially recognized Jews. It is apparently good form to present yourself as a descendant of the Marranos. Clearly, on both sides, this is part of the modern concern with the reconstruction of identity. The Christians want to stand out from the run-of-the-mill Christianity around them, to give themselves an original identity, to set themselves up as an exception in this age of globalization.

J–CA: That is true of Portugal, as of the whole of Western Europe. To be a Jew is also quite simply a way of being, even when one is only a psychological Jew, an emotional Jew, a fantasy Jew. It is a way of standing out from an indistinct mass that is no longer either Christian or Jewish.

EB: What a modern way of seeing oneself! Don't you think that, for many rabbis, it would be preferable to be a Jew in eleventh-century Cordoba than a Jew in Berlin in the nineteenth century or Lisbon or Paris in the twenty-first century?

J–CA: No, not really. For a certain Orthodoxy, the Spanish 'golden age' of Judaism was also a problematic period of *conversos*, philosophers, rationalists, even antinomians! I myself would feel very good at some of those medieval times when the models were cracking up. The Middle Ages to which I feel closest are not a sinister or frozen period. At certain times and places, Jewish intellectuals were assured of a freedom of creation and thought that I sometimes find enviable.

EB: You are not entirely wrong. It is no accident that German Jews in the nineteenth and early twentieth centuries thought they could see something like a model, or a precedent, in the Judaism of the Spanish golden age, with its cultural renaissance and its virtual political emancipation. It is true that there were no state Jews at that time, but Jews did reach the highest echelons of power – even if they ran the risk of disgrace or other misfortune.

J-CA: Still, let us not surrender to the spell. That Spanish Judaism is also largely a reinvention of the modern 'science of Judaism'. Let us return to the rabbis you mentioned a moment ago, and to Judaism as a rabbinical construct.

EB: In the premodern Jewish world, rabbis often engaged in another activity as well; they might have been tradesmen or artisans, for example. Strictly speaking, there was no such thing as ordination. As the community evolved, however, their status gradually changed: what was originally the man of knowledge and religious transmission, the guardian of worship, acquired in modern times alongside these emblematic functions the quite different role of psychologist or social worker, in a context where Jewish life was increasingly atomized.

J-CA: The weight of the scholar or rabbi in medieval Jewish communities should not be exaggerated. It was not rabbis, or even religious leaders at all, who were in charge. The communities were regularly shaken by disputes between secular and religious leaders, and the latter were often paid employees of the community subject to the power of rich Jews and notables. The rabbi's influence was therefore often limited, more to do with personal charisma or moral authority than with any real institutional weight.

EB: The most important people in the community – especially the treasurer, who collected taxes for the sovereign – were in fact laymen. The head of the community was always secular. All the conditions were therefore present to trigger disputes over precedence.

J-CA: Strangely enough, the coercive power of community leaders over their flock derived more from their relationship with powerful non-Jews than from the community itself. If you were a notable close to the non-Jewish sovereign, perhaps his counsellor or financier, if this gave you access to spheres of power outside the community, you could exert strong pressure over the way it was run: you could directly influence the appointment of its officials, or the means used to raise taxes or to stamp out a particular violation of the norms governing community life.

EB: Such individuals exercised real political power. After emancipation, it was mainly the lay head of the community who gradually lost his power; the rabbi already scarcely had any to lose.

J-CA: The emancipation was actually prepared, within the Jewish elites, by an upsurge of intellectual activity and a desire for social reform linked to the Enlightenment. There was a Jewish Enlightenment in the eighteenth century, when demands were raised for an improvement in the position of Jews and a change in their legal status. We should not trace everything back to a few progressive Marranos or suggest that Jewish modernity owes everything to them. There was not only Spinoza, the excommunicated philosopher. Spinoza did, of course, become a kind of obligatory reference for many Jewish and non-Jewish modernizers, both those who were favourable to Judaism and those who were hostile to the Jews. Moses Mendelssohn, in Germany, is the most frequently cited example, but he was not alone. In enlightened Jewish circles, a whole new way of thinking took shape in parallel with, and drew sustenance from, what was happening among non-Jews.

EB: Nevertheless, Spinoza was the model of a Jew who broke out of the confinement that his community tried to impose. In a Jewish society that preached withdrawal and conformism, his was a voice raised high and loud. Other former Marranos such as Uriel da Costa moved in the same direction, and like them Spinoza too was rejected.

J-CA: Spinoza was a central figure, but can he serve as a model? In some respects he anticipated the condition of modern Jews, although the point about real Jewish modernity is that it exposes no one to excommunication. A tension persisted in the Amsterdam of Spinoza's time. Later, that tension disappeared: if someone moved away from the community, it never dreamed of excommunicating him.

EB: Yes. After emancipation, the community could excommunicate as much as it liked; Jews always had the option of quietly integrating into the surrounding society. Excommunication lost its power and therefore all justification when Jews were fully able to integrate and their quasi-organic link with the Jewish community grew slacker. Membership of the community then became strictly voluntary, and anything like the Spinoza affair was no longer possible. The severity of the Amsterdam community had also been partly due to the fact that it was made up of Marranos returning to Judaism, who, like all recent converts, tended towards exceptional zeal. Spinoza was a natural victim.

J–CA: To what extent did Spinoza feel himself to be a victim? Maybe he actually felt liberated. I would agree, though, that the Jewish community in Amsterdam was out of the ordinary, and its fierce battle against heresy and intellectual or religious deviation may even in a way have been a legacy of persecution. It demanded the same kind of purity of faith and morals as that which had been expected of 'new Christians' in Spain. The Spinoza affair also demonstrates that the premodern past was still hanging on in Europe at that time.

EB: In the Middle Ages, every Jewish community existed by virtue of tacit agreement among its members and explicit recognition by the non-Jewish authorities. Before emancipation made Jews citizens – which came in 1790–91 in the case of France – the communities applied the principles of Jewish law and had a legislative power that enabled them to issue edicts to regulate their own affairs. They organized, judged and punished. But they could do this only because of a tacit agreement between the governing Jewish bodies and those they administered. If too many people broke the rules, the community itself would be in danger – for its autonomy was quite limited and had not really been given written expression. To make as much use as possible of its weak means of coercion was thus a way of protecting its existence. Besides, it could be very dangerous to give others an image of disorder that might give grounds for outside interference, with all its associated problems.

J–CA: The coercion could work because there was no place in medieval society for a Jew excluded from his community. Excommunication was equivalent to social death, unless its victim converted and fully integrated into the surrounding society. That is what changed with emancipation. You could now be a Jew and not a Jew, or a Jew one day and a non-Jew the next, according to the situation and your mood at the time. Jews thus acquired a twofold legal status: on the one hand, there was the old rabbinical legality that had lost all its power of coercion; on the other hand, there was the legality of the non-Jewish authorities to which every citizen had to submit. When did this make its appearance? In fact, it did not appear everywhere in the same way, or at the same moment in history.

EB: It was certainly a long process, but the founding event was the emancipation of the Jews in France. For the first time, a decree was issued which (theoretically, at first) made Jews equal with all other citizens.

J-CA: It made the Jew an individual, defined not by membership of a community but by citizenship.

EB: Yet the Revolution passed almost unnoticed: you won't find much trace of it in the writings of the Jewish religious authorities of the time. They did not all immediately grasp how important the Revolution, and the emancipation, would become.

J-CA: Can we not see a certain ambivalence, though, among Jewish representatives who negotiated with the revolutionaries? Did they not sometimes seem to be saying that they would like to be citizens yet still keep their communities?

EB: It is certainly true that, with emancipation, it gradually became a matter of choice whether you were a Jew or not. The existence of that choice gave its shape to modern Jewish identity. In the premodern era, Jews in the Ottoman Empire were certainly Ottomans. But what was an Ottoman? It could mean a Muslim, a Christian or a Jew. But the Jew and the Christian could not climb to the highest rungs of power. When Jews occupied key positions before the emancipation, they usually did so in their capacity as middlemen: they were the bankers or doctors of the sovereign. Then emancipation brought for Jews the new problem of choice, and a wrenching choice it could often be. You can see this at various times and in various regions. One example will have to suffice. In the countries of Eastern Europe where Jews were not emancipated by law but many yearned to achieve it, a whole autobiographical genre describing the torments of the modern Jewish condition blossomed during the nineteenth century. For the writers in question – children of Orthodox families who wanted to break with their milieu – the desire for emancipation was mixed with feelings of guilt. Fascinated with Western ideas and the promise of liberty, they described themselves as incontinent, sick or impotent. These physical blemishes were but an expression of the dilemma of their condition, since they belonged to the first generation that dared to call into question the accepted standards. There is no comparable literature for the periods and the countries of the Jewish emancipation. But, if we look at how these nineteenth-century East European Jews describe their existence, we gain some idea of the painful conflict that any break with old models inevitably provokes.

J–CA: At the end of the premodern period, in the eighteenth century, the references of Jewish culture and identity, as well as those defining the situation of Jews, were becoming more complex. Jews might share a common Hebrew and religious background, but they also had the culture, language, ways and customs of their latest exile: Ladino for those settled in the Ottoman Empire, Judeo–Arabic for those in North Africa, and Yiddish for those in Central and Eastern Europe. In addition, a third reference had emerged: the surrounding culture of the West. There was a radical change, however, only when a new legal perspective opened up, only when a hope of integration and emancipation came to the surface. This was the real turnaround, even and perhaps especially in countries where emancipation was not yet possible: Eastern Europe, the Ottoman Empire and the Muslim lands. Something fundamentally new was taking shape in the West that would hold Jews everywhere spellbound.

EB: The date that needs to be kept in mind is still that of the emancipation in France – the late eighteenth century. But, of course, each region had its own distinctive evolution. In the case of Muslim countries, emancipation was placed on the statute books only when the Jews left: one piece of legislation after another was put forward in the nineteenth century but was never really followed through in practice. In Western Europe, the variable rhythm meant that legal emancipation occurred as early as 1791 in France but that the process extended into the 1860s in the case of Germany. Of course, the Napoleonic conquests in Italy and elsewhere went together with various measures of emancipation, but the gains were often subsequently challenged and the general picture was still one of diversity. German Jews did not experience the same evolution as French Jews: although already integrated in large cities such as Berlin, they were not yet emancipated. In France, on the other hand, Jews were first legally emancipated and given equality. Integration was one thing, but the act of legal emancipation was an event of incomparable significance.

J–CA: Emancipation actually had two dimensions: it granted equality and made the Jew an individual; it directly threatened community ties. That was the novelty. And it was typically French.

EB: Even before the Revolution, though, there was a trend in that direction in Europe. Under Joseph II, in the 1780s, a series of decrees liberalized the status of Jews. And in France even the letters patent of 1784 – considered restrictive towards the Jews – were part of the same current of reform that heralded the sweeping changes of the Revolution. Many prominent Jews were working in the same direction. First, there were the bankers and other notables who engaged in talks with the authorities; then there was a man like Cerf-Barr, who pushed through the letters patent of 1784 that followed hard on the heels of the measures introduced by Joseph II. Jewish intellectuals stimulated and advanced the debate, as did Enlightenment figures such as Moses Mendelssohn or Salomon Maimon who left Eastern Europe to settle in Berlin. Many saw that city as the symbol of a different kind of Jewish existence, with an integrated bourgeoisie. Mendelssohn, a precursor of the Jewish enlightenment in Europe of whom Kant had a high opinion, as well as a translator of the Bible into German, served as Theodor Lessing's model in his play *Nathan the Wise*. But, although Mendelssohn pleaded for an improvement in the Jewish lot, he still had fears that emancipation would eventually lead to the loss of Judaism.

J–CA: As we see, what was happening outside the Jewish world did not fail to make an impression on Jews. In the eighteenth century they too gave birth to an Enlightenment movement, and in the next century this spread to Eastern Europe in a modified form. The ferment agitating the Jewish world meant that it was able to position itself for what it would actually become some fifty years later. Laws were not enough to change attitudes. But the Jewish secular elite, in particular, prepared itself for the citizenship and integration that eventually transformed the condition of Jews and gave rise to an ambitious reformulation of their identity.

EB: Emancipation in France, with its superimposed Jacobinism, kept religion confined to the private sphere and ruled out any permeation of the public sphere. In Germany, by contrast, where emancipation took a long time to come, the already integrated Jewish elite sought ways and means of speeding up the process. At first they thought it important to purge the Jewish religion, so that the surrounding world would not automatically think of it as saturated with 'superstition' and therefore out of keeping with modernity. In this context, Abraham Geiger and a number of other German Jews created the Reform movement in the early nineteenth century and tried to gain acceptance for Judaism within German society. Their aim was to make Judaism more easygoing and better adapted, enabling Jews to assume both their Jewishness and their new condition as people integrated into non-Jewish society. This involved an explicit drive for religious modernization.

J–CA: The German Jews who went to the United States exported the Reform with them. Indeed, it was there that Reform Judaism reached its highest point.

EB: German Jews also tried to give a universal dimension to the teaching of Judaism, as Reformers stripped the liturgy of any reference to the return to Zion, or of any messianism that was too particularist in character. In a parallel movement, a number of scholars (often themselves Reformers) created what they called a 'science of Judaism', a *Wissenschaft des Judentums*. Whatever its ideological assumptions, this science rendered extremely important services by placing at the heart of Jewish learning (and thereby ensuring the survival of) a whole literature that was in some cases very little known. In opposition to this, however, Germany saw the growth of Samson Raphael Hirsch's neo-Orthodox movement, whose goal was to maintain Jewish tradition intact against radical modernism, to make Judaism viable without reforming it, to fit it solidly into modern society without destroying it from within. Neo-Orthodoxy certainly expressed a toughening of attitudes in response to the opening up of Reform Judaism, but both currents should also be seen in the more general framework of a reformulation of identities. On either side, Germany provided the image of a Judaism that met the challenge by turning to *Bildung*, to a process of self-education that would enable German Jews to resemble Germans without ceasing to be Jews. This attitude was the very basis of the Enlightenment; and when it was later taken over by German nationalism, Jews remained alone in preserving an open, cosmopolitan conception of *Bildung*. In the Jewish theatregoers and collectors of books or paintings, there is this same idea of culture as the force that should alone make it possible to overcome differences by absorbing them into something higher. Thus German Judaism, broadly differing in this respect from French Judaism, deeply identified with German culture but did not for all that lose its Jewish dimension. The proof of this is that, amid the great cultural effervescence of the nineteenth century, there were nearly four thousand German associations devoted to Jewish issues.

J-CA: It was precisely because they were not emancipated that German Jews reinvented Judaism. There is no equivalent in France, where emancipation came all at once and Judaism became a private matter, so that it was not necessary to rethink Judaism to make it part of modernity or to offer a positive image of it to the outside world. Germany's delay in emancipation was thus productive at a cultural and religious level, and in terms of Jewish identity.

EB: Although assimilation was quite marked in the German-speaking world, there were also people like Franz Rosenzweig who rediscovered their Jewish past. This rich diversity of identities, ranging from assimilation through neo-Orthodox and Reform Judaism to Zionism (whose thinkers were also, of course, German Jews), was expressed just as much in the writings of a Hermann Cohen as in those of a Walter Benjamin. Germany constituted a veritable reservoir of Jewish identity. It was between 1800 and 1850, at the height of the integration process, that 33 per cent of those four thousand associations were founded. Judaism, then, was by no means thrown overboard in the frenzy of acculturation. According to one common preconception, German Jews are to blame for abandoning their identity. But nothing can be further from the truth. In Germany, where emancipation took a long time coming, Jews struck out on a number of side paths. A German like Heine or an Austrian like Mahler converted to Christianity to force their way into Germanic society – by no means always successfully. German Jews made up 0.5 per cent of the population, but 10 per cent of them went to university. For those sons of traders, the crowning success would have been to become Herr Professor, but they were not able to set their sights that high. Mahler could not become director of the Vienna Opera as long as he remained a Jew. The rate of conversion to Christianity between 1800 and 1871 averaged 6 to 7 converts per ten thousand in Germany – which gives a total of some 11,000 conversions for that period. In France, the comparable figure was no more than 700.

J-CA: What is the reason for the difference?

EB: In France, the separation of the private and public spheres meant that you could both be a Jew and a patron of the Opera. Fromental Halévy, for instance, the composer of the opera La Juive, as well as other musicians such as Meyerbeer or Édouard Colonne, rose to enviable positions without ceasing to be Jews. And, of course, there were also those 'state Jews' who were appointed to important functions in the French civil service. Emancipated Jews were fully fledged citizens: they did not have to justify the high quality of their Judaism in order to assume office. This, no doubt, is why Reform Judaism was officially created in France only in 1907, after the separation of Church and State, when the Consistory lost its political prerogatives. Even today, Reform Judaism in France has by no means reached a point comparable to what we can see in the United States. Nor did French Jews feel the need to create a 'science of Judaism' to demonstrate the greatness and universality of the Jewish texts. The itinerary of modern Jews has thus been closely dependent on the policy of the country in which they have lived.

J-CA: The Jewish voices that spoke up amid the intellectual ferment in Germany put new life into Judaism and started a process of fresh reflection. You don't find any echoes of similar demands among French Jews in that period. Of course, there were people like Joseph Salvador, who tried to work out a universal system of belief (a kind of fusion of Judaism and Christianity that ended up as a doctrine of progress); or Bernard Lazare, the stubborn defender of Captain Dreyfus; or the writers André Spire and Edmond Fleg. But Lazare was rather a marginal figure. In general, we may say that there was no French-Jewish thought comparable to German-Jewish thought.

EB: That is easily explainable.

J-CA: We should not be unjust, though: French Jews were behind the original combination which has been called, rightly or wrongly, Franco-Judaism. Strong links developed in France between the Republic and Jewish elites: the Republic emancipated the Jews and was dear to their heart; and a Franco-Jewish discourse took shape which consisted of saying that the ideals of the Revolution of 1789 were the culmination of messianic Jewish hopes and models. The messiah was the Revolution. That intellectual construction appeared at quite an early date.

EB: Yes, in the second half of the nineteenth century, the Jewish orientalist James Darmesteter theorized a synthesis of Jewish and French progressive values. Franco-Judaism consecrated the passage from 'Jew' (whose negative connotations went back for centuries) to 'Israelite'; it thus seemed to end up abandoning the very notion of a Jewish people with a collective culture and identity beyond strictly religious rituals and beliefs. The Jews of France were now Israelite Frenchmen and Frenchwomen, and as such they tried to repay their debt to the Republic by going one better than anyone else in patriotic fervour. One may well wonder whether assimilation was not the logical result, and it would certainly be wrong to deny that strong choices were sometimes made in that direction. Nevertheless, the assimilation in question was gradual and multiform. Too often there has been a tendency to place an equals sign between acculturation to the values of France and outright assimilation.

J-CA: The ideology of Franco-Judaism turned out to be a quite radical reformulation of Jewish values. Skating blithely over such monuments as the Talmud, whose fussy legalism was a source of embarrassment, its main emphasis in the end was on the universal message of the prophets and the biblical heritage common to Christianity and Judaism. Kabbalah, the mystical and esoteric tradition within Judaism, was considered too irrational or superstitious or peculiar to find a place within the system – notwithstanding a few exceptions such as Adolphe Franck, professor of philosophy at the Collège de France, who wrote the first great works on kabbalah in the French language. Franco-Judaism, then, involved a redefinition of Judaism that stripped it of all its rabbinical traits, a veritable mutation that could not but shock upholders of a more Orthodox tradition. On one side of the Rhine Jews longed for emancipation, while on the other side their aim was to justify and consolidate the emancipation they had already obtained, and to strengthen their integration into French society.

EB: Integration proved to be a lengthy process. Whereas emancipation was the work of one year – between 1790, when Sephardis and Avignonnais from Bordeaux gained citizenship, and 1791, when the turn came for their fellow-Jews in the East – integration stretched in instalments over nearly a century. Nor should we forget that the reform of religious worship was slowed down by quite strong traditionalist tendencies originating mainly in Alsace and Lorraine. The Consistory, for its part, was in the hands of laymen, bankers, such as the Rothschild family, who called for liturgical modernization and gallicization, including the introduction of choirs and an organ in the synagogue, as in Christian churches.

J-CA: The state also exerted strong pressure in France. In 1807 Napoleon assembled a new 'Sanhedrin', reviving for his own purposes an ancient Jewish model. The rabbis and community figures gathered together in Paris had to decide on a number of highly delicate issues

– but under pressure from the state for Judaism to normalize itself and give up such peculiarities as the insistence on endogamous marriage. Do Jews authorize Jews to marry non-Jews? The answers to this and other questions were sometimes pretty convoluted – for a good reason. Despite resistance from the rank and file, the state was trying to force the notables to accept a reformulation of Judaism more acceptable to itself.

EB: But sometimes modernity used gentler constraints.

J-CA: What is true is that no form of Judaism escaped the compulsion to adapt, or at least respond, to modernity. All formulations of identity, all types of religiosity or non-religiosity that we know today – Reform or liberal Judaism, cultural or psychological but also Orthodox Jews – revised their conception and practice of Judaism to meet the challenge of modernity. In their special way, today's Orthodox Jews are – if I may put it like this – as 'modern' as the most reformed or liberal Jews. No doubt they would not admit it, but that is beside the point.

3 | From anti-Judaism to anti-Semitism

EB: There is a fairly widespread idea that the golden age of integration and successful accommodation ended with the Dreyfus affair, and that this already heralded the genocide and other catastrophes to come. This version of history, however, involves a great oversimplification. Unquestionably there were broken contracts between the Jews and the authorities of the countries in which they had settled. But the Dreyfus affair was only one such case, and all the breaches of contract did not lead directly to extermination. For the same reason, we must take care to situate the emergence of anti-Semitism in its proper context, as an opposition to the modernity that Jews were supposed to represent, and as part of a theorization of racial hierarchy in which Jews, afflicted with visible physical signs of inferiority, did not occupy the best position. Once again, certain distinctions need to be made. When we read Jewish texts from the nineteenth century, we find that Jews themselves said that they belonged to the Jewish race. The word 'race' had not yet acquired the strongly negative connotation that derives from the uses to which it was later put. Moreover, we should remember that anti-Semitism developed in the Christian countries: it did not really exist in the Middle East, in that form, when the new ideology was beginning to emerge in the nineteenth century. This does not mean that there was no hostility between Muslims and Jews, or Christians and Jews, nor that the new forms of anti-Semitism were not being gradually introduced through the ports of Smyrna and Istanbul. Indeed, the European powers used these locally by setting Jews and Christians against each other, as a test of the Ottoman rulers' capacity to repress revolts and to confront minorities. The calumny of ritual murder, completely forgotten in the West and still virulent only in Eastern Europe, was now imported by Westerners into the Middle East, where conflicts broke out between Jews and Christians, and especially between Jews and Greeks. In the East, then, new versions of anti-Semitism advanced through early forms of anti-Judaism. In the nineteenth century there were dozens of cases – the most famous in Damascus, in 1840 – where the approach of Passover brought accusations that the Jews had used the blood of a Christian to prepare unleavened bread. Meanwhile, in Central and Eastern Europe, the similar Tiszaeszlár affair shook Hungary in 1882, followed by the Beilis affair in Russia in 1911–12.

J-CA: So, we are not talking of a Christendom sullied with anti-Judaism and anti-Semitism over here, and a fairy-tale Muslim world over there.

EB: Definitely not. But I would like to stress again that anti-Semitism, though drawing inspiration from an older anti-Judaic tradition, is itself a modern phenomenon; the word appears for the first time, in Germany in 1879, in a pamphlet published by the political agitator Wilhelm Marr. This anti-Semitism, when looked at closely – and even if it was inspired by anti-Judaism – marked the beginning of a new phase. As to the connection with what came later, only a teleological conception of history could claim that German anti-Semitism led directly to extermination. As I said before, nineteenth-century anti-Semitism drew mainly on the racial theories of the age and a rejection of modernity, within still traditional societies that feared modernity and saw the Jews as its fiendish instruments. This was the case not only in France but also in Germany. Finally, in these lands of nationalism and neo-romanticism, the fact that Jews seemed devoid of any national demand was interpreted as another sign of their inferiority. Anti-Semitism has had its peaks and its quieter periods; it has even been able to outlast the disappearance of Jews from a particular country, as in Poland where there are today no more than 3,500 left. Since the fall of Communism, it has remained endemic in Eastern

Europe, ready to be taken up and used by politicians. One can also find a sort of anti-Semitism without Jews – as in Japan, where virtually none exists. On the other hand, it is perfectly possible to imagine societies that have never known either the reality or the concept of anti-Semitism. Indian society, for example, has managed to escape it.

J–CA: It is not present there because of India's social structure, the recognition of group diversity, and the sealed frontiers between groups. But, in my view, we should also bear in mind that nothing has really been at stake in India as far as anti-Judaism or anti-Semitism is concerned; that the cultural and religious divisions which so strongly marked the Christian West, and to a lesser extent the Muslim world, have not been an issue in India. As far as modern anti-Semitism is concerned, I think we should be wary of two dangers. The first is to see it as something radically new, a legacy of the Enlightenment, the culmination of the rising power of science and a certain kind of rationality – although it is true that Reason can be the road to hell as well as heaven, that its universalizing tendency makes it inclined to sacrifice the particular to the universal, and that its penchant for classification involves a tendency to draw up rigid and exclusive hierarchies. The second danger is to see in modern anti-Semitism no more than a natural continuation of Christian anti-Judaism and of a more general anti-Judaism running through the history of the Jews in their various host countries. The fact of the matter is that two new problems make themselves felt in modern anti-Semitism: on the one hand, a questionable relationship to cultural and religious particularism that does stem from the Enlightenment; and, on the other hand, a perception of the Jews as a transnational reality. 'There are Jews everywhere,' anti-Semites think. 'They are not attached to any territory and do not have the same relationship to the idea of the nation.' All that is thoroughly modern, and induces two types of reaction: either forms of 'moderate' anti-Semitism which aim to integrate or even assimilate Jews into the surrounding society, with the idea that they will gradually fade away as such; or the opposite perception of Jews as a foil to be set against the nation-building project to which they can never be assimilated.

EB: It is true that, in the distant past, anti-Judaism sometimes led to massacres or violent attacks, creating a real physical sense of danger among Jews. At other times, however, Jews tried to develop strategies of accommodation that would allow them to go about their lives. Not all epochs were hostile: if they had been, there would have been no Jewish culture and no survival of the Jews as such. Strong outbreaks of anti-Judaism occurred only during periods of aggressive re-Christianization of Europe, when the power of the Church was strengthening and attitudes were hardening. It must also be recognized that, in modern times, a particular kind of hostility to minorities swept the Muslim world, affecting Christians as much as Jews, and sometimes the former more than the latter. In the nineteenth and especially the twentieth century there were certainly pogroms in North Africa – but in the Ottoman Empire, where this hostility to minorities remained intense, the fate of Christians was more harrowing. Jews were considered loyal subjects, with no territorial claims up to a certain moment, and they were not affected too much; but Christians were seen as the real transnationals, resting on the support of Europeans. In Eastern Europe, anti-Semitism had a wide range of physical expressions: from the pogroms of the nineteenth and early twentieth centuries (1881–82 in Russia, 1903 and 1905 in Kishinev) to the restrictive laws in Romania. In Western Europe, where Jews were emancipated or in the course of emancipation, anti-Semitism appeared as a turning back of the clock that was deeply humiliating to them, a slap in the face at a time when integration was in full flow. The accusation of ritual murder in Damascus in 1840 was a good example of this. The affair seemed to be unfolding a long way from Europe, but Western Jews discovered that anti-Jewish persecution had not disappeared and that its primal forms were still capable of manifesting themselves. It was in response to the Damascus affair that Jews in Europe organized themselves on a footing of what we would call modern solidarity and established the first Jewish periodicals: the *Jewish Chronicle* in Britain, the *Archives israélites* and *L'Univers israélite* in France, and many others in various parts of the West and even the East. They also set up modern institutions such as the Alliance israélite universelle in France (in 1860) or the Anglo-Jewish Association in Britain (in 1871). Suddenly realizing that a medieval image could still be held against them, Jews were surprised at the nineteenth-century emergence of anti-Semitism in France, Germany and elsewhere in Europe, with its stream of anti-Jewish manifestations. All that was unexpected. It brought a dawning awareness of the fragility of integration.

J–CA: The Jews of the West were a little wrong about the significance of the new hostility when they thought that it represented a survival or resurgence of medieval ways of thinking. At first they found it difficult to grasp the novelty of modern anti-Semitism, and the radical danger that it might involve. Believing that the march of progress must inevitably lead to the disappearance of anti-Semitism, they harboured a simple illusion: 'The Ottomans have lagged behind; it's a hangover from the Middle Ages that must be fought.' This explains the institutionalization of a new Jewish solidarity in relation to the Damascus affair, an aspect of a new Jewish identity detached from the religious practice that had been characteristic of Judaism prior to integration.

EB: It is sometimes forgotten that the Damascus affair produced a real sense of shock and represented a challenge to the fine old optimism. In 1840 a monk, Father Thomas, disappeared in Damascus together with his servant; neither was ever found again. At the instigation of the French consul, the crime was blamed on the Jews, who were rounded up and tortured in large numbers. In fact, the affair took place in the context of Louis-Philippe's imperialist ambitions in the Near East. No one, except for the Jewish notables who mobilized in protest, cared about the fact that the people thrown into prison were innocent – and Thiers himself, then head of the French government, lent his authority to the thesis of ritual murder. Some sixty years later, the Dreyfus affair produced similar amazement among the Jews of France, but it was not only, or even primarily, a Jewish affair, even if the army captain at the centre of it would not have been put through everything if he had not been Jewish. It was an affair that concerned France: the birth of intellectuals, the rise of its Right and its Left.

J-CA: Can we return to what we were discussing a moment ago: whether there was not another dimension liable to associate anti-Judaism and anti-Semitism as two moments or types of hostility to the Jews: namely, the dimension of demonization. This demonization of the Jews was an invention not of the modern epoch but of the late Middle Ages, when it could already be seen gradually developing in popular imagery (not necessarily in everyday relationships). The figure of the Jew was endowed with non-human physical characteristics such as horns, claws and a tail. This may, however, be thought of as prefiguring a thoroughly modern form of racism, in which the Jew is dissociated from the human race. The 'pure blood' statutes in the Spain of the Inquisition were also perhaps another pointer in this direction: conversion to Christianity was no longer enough to solve the problem, even after a number of generations.

EB: Yes. On the other hand, it would be a mistake to suggest that the beginnings of genocide appeared in the late nineteenth and early twentieth centuries. A number of different elements were mixed up in the hostility towards the Jews, but as yet there was no clear sign of the ultimate form of extermination. The decision for the Final Solution was taken in late 1941, and the logistics put in place in January 1942, at the Wannsee Conference, although it is true that the butchery had already begun in June 1941 with the invasion of the USSR. That cannot be traced back to the dawn of time; nor can it be said that it was a result of the Church's anti-Judaism, or that the anti-Semitism of Edouard Drumont led directly to it, or that the Dreyfus affair ushered in an exterminatory anti-Semitism. There can be no doubt that modern anti-Semitism has been racial, but the exterminatory form of anti-Semitism in the dark years of the twentieth century should also and mainly be placed in the context of world war.

J-CA: We should not forget, though, that there is what might be called an exterminatory tradition in the West. The Jews were not the first to be exposed to extermination: Native Americans came before them. Two traditions exist alongside each other in the West: on the one hand anti-Semitism; on the other a readiness to remove others from the human race and to make them objects of extermination. The twentieth century saw these two traditions come together against the Jews. Anti-Semitism does not necessarily result in extermination, but was the latter not a conjunction of two traditions of which the Jews bore the brunt?

EB: Do not let us pass too quickly over the distinctive feature of modern times: that genocide and modernity are actually inseparable from each other. The twentieth century was the century of the major genocides. The new aspect was that modern racial theories saw the Jews as belonging to an inferior species. The Church said only that they were not Christians, that they had not followed the genuine message, that they had therefore to suffer the consequences in the shape of theological and social inferiority. If they had to wear a sign and be subjected to various legal incapacities, this was not because they belonged to a particular race but because they were not on the right path. The Church never said that the Jews must be eliminated because they did not recognize the messianic and divine nature of Jesus. What is so distinctive about modern anti-Semitism is that it does make Jews irredeemably part of an inferior race, so that they have no way of 'catching up' through conversion and entering the domain of the Other, of the superior race. Should anti-Judaism and anti-Semitism be seen as an outcome of Christianity? Maybe. Should Christianity be seen as inevitably leading to the Final Solution? Certainly not. It was also Christians, sometimes Christians driven by their Christian faith, who joined the Resistance battalions and saved numbers of Jews. Let us avoid reducing anti-Semitism to Christianity, or vice versa.

J-CA: There is another point about the Church that is often overlooked. At certain crucial moments in the history of anti-Jewish persecution, the Church defended the Jews against popular riots – always with the idea that the Jews must not disappear. During the Crusades, many prelates gave their protection to the Jews.

EB: Nor did the shift take place from one day to the next. The chronology of events in the nineteenth century is rather surprising in this respect. In 1840 the Damascus affair erupted with the accusation of ritual murder. In 1845 Alphonse Toussenel, a disciple of Fourier, published his *Les Juifs, rois de l'époque: histoire de la féodalité financière*, with its anti-capitalist emphasis on the Jew as a capitalist figure: to be anti-Jewish was to be anti-capitalist. In 1853 Gobineau published his classic *Essai sur l'inégalité des races humaines* and racial doctrines began to take off. In 1858 we come across anti-Judaism again, with the Mortara affair in Italy where a Jewish child was forcibly converted to Christianity. Thus, during those years, the distinction was not yet absolutely clear. Shortly afterwards, in 1869, Henri Gougenot des Mousseaux brought out his *Le Juif, le judaïsme, la judaïsation des peuples chrétiens*, then in the 1880s pogroms broke out in Eastern Europe, and in 1886 Drumont's *La France juive* appeared. All this was part of a pattern. The word 'anti-Semitism' itself crystallized in Europe in the final decades of the nineteenth century, in a political context for which pan-Slavism and pan-Germanism formed the backdrop. Central Europe now in turn became fertile ground for anti-Semitism. After a long period of ambiguity (ambiguity which persisted, moreover), the century slid from anti-Judaism into anti-Semitism.

J-CA: The ambiguity, and the variety, of fin-de-siècle anti-Semitism …

EB: Anti-Semitism certainly took a variety of forms. It reached its acme when it turned into collective violence, when it served as a weapon of political struggle or a safety valve for rising social pressures, or when it became state anti-Semitism as a fundamental element of the ideology and politics of a strong state (as in Germany or France). This is not to say that America was spared, only that there anti-Semitism was not relayed by the state (a concept that anyway scarcely exists in the US) but remained present among popular layers or even in fashionable society. The damage it caused there is well known, but it did not take the extreme forms visible elsewhere. Once again we should draw some distinctions. There was anti-Judaism. There was anti-Semitism as a reaction, either as anti-capitalism or as anti-Bolshevism (since Marxism was invented by a Jew, even if Marx's relationship to his Jewishness was altogether problematic). These kinds of demonization involved real and intolerable aggression against the Jews, but in so far as they were not exploited by the state they did not acquire the dimensions later seen. State-led incorporation takes place at precise historical moments. Today, it is easy to treat anyone as an anti-Semite. But we should be careful to use words in the right way, to avoid the kind of banalization that tends to occur today.

J-CA: People did not everywhere have the same awareness of the phenomenon. Until the time of Vichy, and in the teeth of ideological anti-Semitism, French Jews enjoyed the protection of the law in a society which accepted their integration and recognized that they had a full part to play. For Jews living in the Russian Pale of Settlement, conditions were truly abysmal and involved a constant threat of pogroms. For Jews in Muslim countries, their subject condition might have been difficult to bear but did not necessarily lead to continual or large-scale acts of violence. The situation varied in accordance with their legal status, the ideological environment, and the power and attitude of the state. Another general question we may consider is whether an awareness of the relative hostility of the Nations has troubled Jews throughout history. I think that such an awareness has not been a constant feature, even in the medieval period. Jews have certainly been aware of what is called in Hebrew *sin'at Israel*, hatred of Israel, on the part of the Nations. But there is also the evidence of cultural works that have brushed off such hostility, or made no reference to it. There is no uniformity in this respect, even at one and the same time in history.

EB: Images have kept changing on either side. In the nineteenth century, Rothschild became the very symbol of the Jew in popular mythology. And, for those who know what the Jewish world was like in those days, it is clear that most of the Jewish population was not rich but mainly consisted of poor layers and a middle class, and not only of bankers, whose numbers have often been exaggerated. In the anti-Semitic campaigns of the nineteenth century, the point about the Jews was that they had no roots, no link with the soil that was the mainstay of national identity among the rising forces of nationalism. To be without roots meant to be fragile. At the same time, however, the Jew was seen as the man of capital who exploited the people – a perception that was part of a certain continuity. On the eve of the French Revolution, the Jew was already the usurer; he had been condemned to play that role in the Middle Ages, because of the restrictions that weighed on him at certain times, but he had also been able to engage in other activities when the context permitted – medicine, for example, or even viticulture (like the contemporaries of Rashi). The identification with money-lending became more widespread when Europe's need for liquidity increased. The Jews, not having the right to own real estate, were the ones who had the liquid assets.

J-CA: We may say that the old medieval distrust of 'Jewish money' was reactivated and reformulated in modern times. Jewish tradition has not looked upon money in a hypocritical or essentially reproachful manner, and it is sometimes forgotten that, in the face of threatened persecution, it enabled many communities to purchase a degree of (often short-lived) peace and quiet. Later, some came to see money as a means of getting even, of gaining access to social respectability and family security. But, at the other end of the spectrum of anti-Semitic denunciation, there is also the tradition associated with Voltaire and the terrible pages he wrote on Judaism.

EB: It is true that Voltaire has been attacked for being anti-Semitic. He was anti-clerical and anti-Christian, and his anti-Judaism basically stemmed from that, even if, here and there, he did fly off at a tangent. But the same clichés and the same hostility would later be found in the International and other revolutionary circles – on the Left, then, as well as the Right. It was fairly natural that the lender of money with interest in premodern times turned into the banker in the modern epoch; people generally choose trades with which they have some familiarity of tradition. The Jewish banker thus became the modern emblematic figure of an ancient prejudice, so that the bitter legends in relation to money that had such strong roots in Christian lands persisted in new forms. Yet it was too easily forgotten that the Pereire brothers, those illustrious bankers of the mid-nineteenth century, were followers of Saint-Simon and helped bring about his dream combination of railways, telecommunications and industry – although, of course, some harboured the same animus against the Jews as pioneers of modernity. At a somewhat later date, it was in Marxist and socialist circles that the Jew appeared as the symbol of capitalism. This too had its contradictions. For Jews were also often among the first to join these movements – especially children and grandchildren of bourgeois capital-owning families who, above all in Germany, were unable to satisfy their dream of an academic career. They chose intellectual professions on the margins of academia, such as journalism, which enabled them to join the new movements that were seeking to change the world and therefore, as they saw it, to change the Jewish condition. So we see the contradiction: many Jews were to be found among the ranks of Marxists, socialists or anarchists, but at the same time Jews were looked upon as representatives of capital.

J-CA: In its way, this anti-Semitism was conservative in its inspiration; the development of banking and the explosive spread of machinery filled it with fear. Lacking roots, Jews could enter the new structures and were for that reason seen as a threat to tradition and the foundations of the nation.

EB: The second half of the nineteenth century, which witnessed the powerful surge of modern anti-Semitism, was also a period of Jewish social ascent, of great Jewish composers, playwrights and actresses, the consolidation of the Jewish presence in the universities (at least in France), and the extensive participation of Jews in great ideological movements and debates. It was the era of the theorization of socialism, and soon afterwards of psychoanalysis.

J-CA: It was the era when Jews, fully in tune with their host societies, worked alongside their non-Jewish contemporaries to lay the foundations of modern thought. Today, with our temporal distance, we have the impression that it was mainly a period of anti-Semitic ferment and growing dangers for Jews. But the Western Jews of the time experienced it as a great moment of liberation.

EB: It was not even a period of growing dangers. Jews were no longer discernible as Jews and modern anti-Semitism made it a point of honour to track them down. Though no longer visible, Jews were not forgotten because they were a presence in society. Thinking of themselves as full citizens, they were present in every stratum of society – but they were not accepted as such. They made endless efforts to achieve integration, sincerely believing that they had a role to play in the society which had accepted them and to which they felt a sense of gratitude. On the other hand, although the society was hospitable, it did not always look favourably on this process of acculturation. The combination of lesser physical visibility and great social visibility disproportionate to their numbers may be seen as another factor in the rise of anti-Semitism that Jews themselves do not always take into account. The Jews of the time saw themselves not as Jews succeeding in a non-Jewish society, but as full citizens – French or German, Austrian or Hungarian – succeeding within an undifferentiated society.

J-CA: You are right to stress that Jews no longer had a special rhythm of life, no longer observed Shabbat, dressed like everyone else, ate the same food, and were beginning to speak perfectly the various national languages. All the distinguishing features that history had heaped upon them were in the course of disappearance. Nothing clearly distinguished a Jew from a non-Jew: all that remained was 'race'.

EB: The danger represented by Jews was all the greater for their no longer being tied down by any restriction. At a time of widespread shock and fear in the face of the rise of modernity, non-Jews frequently came across Jews at the École polytechnique or École normale as well as in the wheels of the state bureaucracy; the Jew was beginning to be seen again as the Other, but without any distinguishing marks of the Other. Newspapers claimed to see Jews everywhere, piling up inordinate riches. Drumont's *La Libre Parole* went into a frenzy, and the Left was not free either from the surge of hostility. But this was not the hour of persecution – at least, not in the West.

J-CA: We should not forget that in the end Dreyfus was rehabilitated, in opposition to a certain idea of the nation and the army. The affair may be seen as traumatic, yet its conclusion seemed to confirm the march of progress.

EB: Jews told themselves that they had succeeded, but that they needed to keep a low profile. Still, this was one of the most dazzling periods in the history of the Jews in the West; their sense of being in harmony with France did not involve an abandonment of their own identity, but rather a will to fuse with the surrounding culture and to match those who had shown confidence in them.

J-CA: This debate on anti-Semitism in its various forms makes us realize that no one escapes it. But our main concern here is with the

Jews themselves, and we should not reduce the whole Jewish experience of their relations with the Nations to anti-Semitism.

4 | Jewish nationalism and Zionism

EB: Nor can anti-Semitism exhaust how Jews related to themselves, or to their own idea of the nation. It was not only hatred of the
Jews that pushed certain intellectuals towards Jewish nationalism; the
Jewish nationalist idea first arose because nationalism was building
itself up all over Europe. Jews did not remain outside this trend. First
of all, in Germany and elsewhere, neo-Romanticism was in the air. As
attempts were being made to root national cultures in a remote Greek
or Latin past, Jews also thought it best to search out roots of their
own. Not by chance was it at that time that debates began to take
place (first among people with a utopian approach to nationalism)
about the possible return of the Jews to the land of their ancestors.
The first Jewish nationalists of the nineteenth century were mostly
religious figures such as Zvi Hirsch Kalisher, Judah Alkalai or Eliyahu
Guttmacher: that is, Europeans living in border areas in a multi-
national context (Sarajevo in the case of Alkalai, or Poznania in that
of Guttmacher and Kalisher). Their view was that Jews should return
to the land of Israel because it was there that the Redemption would
take place; an earlier return would mean an earlier Redemption. For
the first time, such people began to develop actual projects or even
well thought-out plans for a return, but other, non-religious figures
such as Moses Hess or Marco Baruch also came under the influence
of nationalist ideas then in vogue in Europe. Curiously enough, the
theoreticians of political Zionism came from Central Europe, one of
the regions where Jews had integrated (or appeared to integrate) so
well and closely identified with the nations among which they lived.
Herzl was Viennese, and the great Zionist ideologues were German.
Despite everything, integration did not prevent these Jews from retaining a certain Jewish identity. There was also, I think, a failure of the
ideal of a cosmopolitan culture, of a Judaism fully inserted into the
surrounding society.

J-CA: We should also add the great waves of persecution in
Eastern Europe. The first nationalist nuclei, which later gave rise to
practical Zionism and trained the early pioneers in Palestine, built
themselves up after the pogroms of 1882. They realized physically that
no emancipation or decisive improvement was to be expected there.

EB: Zionism is clearly a modern idea, a post-Emancipation idea. It shows that Jews were not cut off from their environment, as it is only a variant of the nationalist ideas current in the nineteenth century.

J–CA: Yes. Zionism was a nationalism that emerged at the same time as other nationalisms and drew its inspiration from them. Jewish particularism, then, is an expression of the harmony of Jewish thought with its environment: that is the first paradox. But there is also a second paradox: namely, that Zionism was theorized and conveyed by people living in countries where Jews were integrated if not emancipated. Moreover, Zionism often built itself up in opposition to the model of emancipation, integration or acculturation, and to the dilution of Jewish identity. In a way, however, among the Zionists as well as those who pinned their hopes on emancipation, we find the same goal of normalizing the Jewish condition. In both cases, there was at least a partial rejection of bi-culturalism, of a position both at the centre and at the margins of society. Either one became French through and through, or one became a Jew in exactly the same way that others were French: that is, a member of a nation settled in its own land. Either one was a citizen of the French state, or one was a citizen of the Jewish state.

EB: In the early period of Jewish nationalism, a state of one's own was still a utopian aspiration. The idea of a state for the Jews emerged at a later date: it was not part of the expectations of the precursors of Jewish nationalism. Very soon, however, the desire for normality began to appear, since it was an anomaly in Europe not to be nationalist, not to long to be part of a nation. It was felt necessary to be a patriot in relation to something specific. And integration, as it was developing at that time, did not satisfy all Jews. We should also distinguish between the two Europes. In Eastern Europe, Jews did not experience emancipation and never would – or only much later, under Communism, and we know the difficulties that communist-style emancipation brought. Thus, given the lack of emancipation and the strength of persecution, the national idea and nationalism became a veritable refuge for Jews in those countries; it was a retreat born of disappointment with an unchanging situation, and disillusionment with the Enlightenment and a Europe that could not come up with a solution to the Jewish question. Those who opted for socialism had the same wish as those who opted for Jewish nationalism: to find a means of profoundly improving the lot of Jews. In both cases, and in Central as well as Eastern Europe, there was a clear objective for many Jews: either to give another meaning to their Jewishness, or to change their condition. In France, on the other hand, the Jewish national idea did not catch on.

J-CA: That is because in France another kind of normalization was possible. The general choice facing Jews seems to have been between becoming citizens among other citizens (as in France) and aspiring to become a nation among other nations (as in Zionism). In this respect, modernity clearly meant rejection of the exceptionality of the Jewish condition – exceptionality that could be distressing, especially in Eastern Europe.

EB: In France, where their lot had greatly improved, Jews did not want to risk being accused of a dual allegiance, which might serve as a pretext for others to turn the clock back. It was only during the Second World War, in the Jewish resistance, that French Jews really became familiar with Zionists and Zionism.

J-CA: But Zionism was also built on other ambiguities. In a way, it advocated a break with the passive attitude of the Jews, who for too long had expected their liberation to come from heaven, for too long awaited the Messiah. Instead, it called for Jews to take their fate in their hands and to realize here and now, through human means, something that had previously been a vague horizon dependent on God's will. While breaking with this religious tradition, however, Zionism still needed all the emotional charge conveyed by that past, all the images of hope, of the gathering of exiles, of the return to the land of their ancestors, of the final Redemption. It wagered on a more or less secular idea of redemption, but, in order to attract and move the masses, including the still traditional masses of Eastern Europe, it took over the themes and vocabulary of religious Redemption. Zionism was thus built upon a contradiction, and that contradiction has kept periodically re-emerging right down to the present day.

EB: Nevertheless, the pioneers of Jewish nationalism were themselves religious; there was even a religious Zionism, especially the current inspired by the teachings of Abraham Isaac Kook. The year 1902 saw the founding of the Mizrahi movement – an abbreviation of a Hebrew expression meaning 'spiritual centre' – whose slogan was: 'The land of Israel for the people of Israel in accordance with the Torah of Israel'. This religious Zionism, driven by sometimes very strong messianic expectations, allied itself with secular socialist Zionism and accepted that pioneers who were mostly non-believers could be valued as the architects of the indispensable first stage of Redemption.

J-CA: Nevertheless, let us not downplay the importance of the militant, radically anti-religious Zionism of yesterday and today. Similarly, there are Orthodox and ultra-Orthodox milieux which, being aware that the project of secular liberation poses a serious break with tradition, are still resolutely hostile to Zionism and the very principle of a Jewish state, seeing them as a veritable profanation of the religious ideal. Zionism thus appears both as the pursuit of the same struggle by different means and (for certain Orthodox Jews) as a movement of betrayal.

EB: The theocratic character of today's State of Israel is bound up with this paradox. Here we have a resolutely democratic state, resolutely turned to the West (or rather to America), which is also a theocratic state, at least in its foundations.

J-CA: Anyway, a state that has never been able to propose a non-religious definition of what it means to be Jewish, independent of any religious norm. That too is a legacy of the past.

EB: Palestine, as we have already said, was the only place that had a symbolic charge capable of bringing Jews together. Until Herzl's death in 1904, there were still a number of different projects: one thinks of Mesopotomia, Uganda and other possible locations. But then the World Zionist Congress opted for the settling of Jews in Palestine, and the decision would never be reversed.

J-CA: It was not easy, however, to claim rights to a land for a people that was not even living there; the longing for normality was from the outset contradicted by the objective situation of the Jews. In this respect, Jewish nationalism could scarcely be the same as that of other nations: whereas European nationalism was also the nationalism of a language and a territory, in the case of the Jews the territory itself had to be invented, and linguistic unity was for the time being out of reach. Everything had to be re-created by drawing upon an ancestral heritage. For a long time, Hebrew was not the language that came most readily to the lips of Zionists.

EB: At that time Jews spoke either the language of the country in which they were culturally integrated or their own Jewish language (Judeo-Arabic, Judeo-Spanish, Yiddish etc.) or both. Hebrew was little more than a scholarly, religious and liturgical language, spoken by small numbers of people. On the other hand, the religious precursors of Zionism stated that the land of Israel was the land of our ancestors, as well as the place where the Messiah would come and the Redemption take place. Political Zionism only gradually came round to the view that the centrality of the land of Israel was self-evident. But, when it finally threw itself behind the Palestine option, it did so in the name of the historical right of the Jewish people to the biblical lands.

J-CA: This kind of Zionist focus on biblical precedent, which now functioned as an absolute model, also involved a break with Jewish tradition. To return to the Bible, to place all the weight on a few centuries in which the people of Israel lived more or less autonomously and more or less together on its own land, was to jump over 2,000 or 2,500 years of exile and diaspora. To return to the biblical model was, of course, to remain faithful to certain of the inspirational sources of Judaism. But the very priority given to those sources meant breaking with everything that subsequently came to form Jewish civilization: Talmudic Judaism, the Judaism of the ghettos, the multilingual culture of the Diaspora. The return to the biblical language, biblical lands and the Bible itself was an obvious sign of modernity. Still today, the Bible is an integral part of the Israeli syllabus, including in the state sector and in the most secular schools, because Zionism reinstated it as the founding text. But the Bible never so clearly played that role in the history of Judaism before the nationalist awakening.

EB: In the same way, before 1967 the frontiers of modern Israel by no means coincided with those of biblical Israel, which were, it is true, themselves highly mobile.

J-CA: Indeed. The State of Israel created in the aftermath of the 1948 war lay outside the historical territories of Judaea and Samaria. The war of 1967, which ended with the Israeli conquest of the West Bank (the biblical Judaea and Samaria), brought a dramatic turnaround, introducing a confusion between the Israel that had actually been constructed and the mythical Israel inherited from historical memory and dream. A land then empty of Jews thus became an absolutely critical issue.

EB: It even aroused strong emotions among the most secular Israelis. Wild hopes were born in certain Orthodox milieux, and the most religious Zionists used the 'territories' to reclaim all the constitutive elements of the Zionist ethos. They created new settlements and demanded a return in Judaea-Samaria to the Zionist ideal of work on the land, or at least occupation of the land. As people started leaving the kibbutzim, and the Zionist ideal was exposed to criticism or scaled down, it was these religious Zionists (the base of the Gush Emunim, the Bloc of the Faithful) who aimed to take up the torch. The ambiguity of the Zionist relationship to religion re-emerged here in all its intensity.

J–CA: There is, to be sure, a fundamentally secular Zionism which may be understood as a kind of secularized messianism – and that, in the eyes of a certain Orthodox tradition, is a defilement of messianic expectation, which can never be secularized. Yet a coming together or overlapping of secular Zionist ideology and religious ideology is always a possibility, when political action, occupation and work on the land – which are secular, earthly objectives – are invested with a hyper-religious and hyper-messianic significance, when the act of settling down in a West Bank backwater acquires a value at once political and messianic. That kind of political-religious messianism is not shared by all tendencies within contemporary religious Judaism; on the contrary, it may be seen as a deviation from the messianic ideal. And we should not forget that some Jews have always been anti-Zionist, either out of solidarity with the oppressed Palestinian people, or in opposition to the actual policies of the State of Israel, or as a way of rejecting a Jewish particularism that they consider unjustifiable, or out of internationalism. Today, however, I think we are in a period when the debate, at least among Jews, is not really between Zionists and anti-Zionists. Rather, we are in a post-Zionist configuration, in the most ordinary sense of 'post': that is, Zionism has broadly speaking become reality, and once it becomes reality it loses its reason for existence. The State of Israel exists, and even if most Jews in the Diaspora are prepared to show some interest or to lend it unfailing support it is accepted that they never for a moment think of going to live there. The discourse of militant Jewish anti-Zionism is mainly found among a small and quite marginal minority of ultra-Orthodox. But another sign that we have entered a post-Zionist phase is the fact that a number of sociologists, historians and philosophers in Israel are rehabilitating the experience of exile. On the other hand, in France and elsewhere in the Diaspora, we see ways of returning to Judaism that do not mainly focus on identification with Israel. The revalorization of strict observance, the fascination with the Kabbalah, the fondness for the study of texts: all this crystallizes a way of identifying with Judaism that fairly easily dispenses with any reference to Israel or political activism.

EB: At the same time, you cannot deny that there is still a strong Zionist rhetoric and ideology in Israeli society; we should not imagine that the whole of Israeli society has gone over to post-Zionism! But is true that, despite the bitterness of recent difficulties, what is now taking shape will force Israel to go beyond the utopian principle of Zionism. The contradictory nature of the utopia already in place, confronted as it is with the constant tension of the Israeli–Palestinian conflict, is beginning to appear more and more clearly to the Israeli population.

J-CA: In any event, the new man of Zionist dreams is not fundamentally new. Zionism has had to face a major difficulty: that is, to admit that Jews made do for two millennia with living in the Diaspora, but to try to get round those two millennia by linking up with a biblical ideal of rootedness – and to achieve this precisely with Jews from the Diaspora! What was to be done in these conditions? For Zionism the solution seemed to be to develop a historiographic and ideological discourse which highlighted everything in Jewish life, imagination and literature, even in dispersion and exile, that could be held to indicate a profound, constant and unshakeable attachment to the lost land. What was the new Jewish man? A Jew in good health, vigorous, athletic and sun-tanned. It was necessary to find in the past, including the darkest centuries of the Diaspora, an element of continuity that would be this attachment to the land of Israel. 'Jews were not on their own land,' it was said, 'but they never stopped thinking about it. They might have been sick and persecuted, but at least they had that to keep them going.'

EB: Don't forget that the Zionists also had a discourse close to that which the earlier advocates of emancipation had deployed in dreaming of a new Jewish man who had broken with the ghetto, learned new trades and rebuilt his health: a 'regenerated' Jew. The Zionists imagined their ideal in much the same way: a new Jew who, though originally from the Diaspora, would break with it and live in the new state, regenerating himself on the soil of his ancestors, in touch with the land of his dreams now become a reality.

J-CA: But that was possible only if one assumed that the Jewish people had always kept its loyalty to the land of Israel.

EB: And we know that such loyalty was not constant but went

through a number of phases. Zionism was therefore driven, first, to write a history of the Jews entirely centred on key moments in which the Diaspora Jew appeared close to the land of his ancestors, and, second, to articulate a veritable ideology of negation of the Diaspora. This could not but give rise to a further paradox. The Jew who came from the Diaspora to settle on the 'land of his ancestors' was expected to make a clean break with the past – a situation likely to favour the kind of schizophrenia which anyway comes quite naturally to Israelis today, unable as they are to base their identity on anything other than a return to, or a detour via, their roots in the Diaspora.

J–CA: You are right to compare the Zionists' aspirations to those of the 'regenerators' who were pushing for emancipation. In the end, that is what characterized the nineteenth and early twentieth centuries: a striving for emancipation. The only little difference is that on one side it was a question of emancipation and on the other a question of what Leon Pinsker, the Russian Jewish nationalist, called self-emancipation. Emancipation from what? In either case – integration into a Western society or into a newly created Jewish state – the aim was to emancipate Jews from subjection to the Nations or submission to an alien power, as well as from a model of Diaspora life that was rejected by all. Here the two discourses came together, in the ideal of creating both a new Jew and an emancipated Jew.

EB: These discourses were typical of the age, and their numerous variants always tended to converge. Thus, the Jews of Western Europe developed rather similar projects for their brothers in North Africa and the Middle East – projects that involved creating a new Jew in Muslim lands, along the lines of the European model of the emancipated Jew. Modern Jewish identity has been built around this superimposition of discourses.

J–CA: But that is no longer really where we are at today. What we are witnessing are a number of spectacular reversals. Post-Zionism is one of them.

EB: And it has many different aspects. Look, for example, at what is happening with those Russian Jews who began to emigrate to Israel right at the end of the 1980s. In a country they think of as a diaspora, their homeland continues to be Russia – you can hardly get more post-Zionist than that! In their everyday lives, without theorizing it, they have inverted the whole Zionist discourse for which arrival in Israel meant a return to the motherland and a break with the

Diaspora. The Russian Jews of Israel are Russians in exile, and remain faithful to their country of origin. In their case the model really has broken down.

J-CA: But the singularity of those Russians does not cover all the questioning that post-Zionism involves. To keep things in proportion, we must recognize that post-Zionism as an ideology or a way of thinking concerns, in Israel, only a small number of intellectuals.

EB: Unlike their predecessors in the 1970s, who had no other wish than total integration, the Russian Jews arriving in the late 1980s and 1990s immediately experienced the upheavals associated with the Intifadah, in a country that was beginning to question itself and to distrust the rhetoric and ideology of Zionism. Their reaction, in that rather changed Israel, was to keep their own identity, not to give up what they were. At that same time in the late 1980s – even if the Russians in question were not aware of it – the first post-Zionist discourse was making itself heard. It was a symptomatic coincidence in time. In their own way, and without exhausting its content, the Russian Jews symbolized quite well the new phase of Zionism which, for want of another term, I call post-Zionist. In practical terms, their attitude ran counter to all the foundations of Zionism.

J-CA: Precisely. Let us remember that, long before it was pounded by post-Zionism, even before it was watered down into a rather weak ideology widely shared by Jews, Zionism ran into a number of obstacles. For a long time Jewish communities around the world were mostly hostile or indifferent to it; this was a general attitude, not a peculiarity of French Jews. Time was needed to raise people's consciousness. Here, the trauma of the Nazi extermination played a quite fundamental role: it became difficult, for many Jews, to remain aloof from – or *a fortiori* hostile to – Zionism.

EB: Shelter had to be found urgently for all those Jews in transit camps. But the real dawning of a new consciousness, the widespread leap of affiliation to the Zionist or Israeli ideal, dated from the year 1967. Let us recall that in the 1920s a Zionist was a utopian. France, under the terms of the Sykes–Picot Agreement of 1916, had found itself allocated a part of Palestine. Why, then, did it finally take such little interest in the region? How are we to explain the fact that the Cambon Declaration of 11 June 1917 – a letter from Jules Cambon, secretary-general of the French foreign ministry, to Zionist leader Nahum Sokolov, which officially backed the Zionist project and precipitated the publication of the much weightier Balfour Declaration – eventually sank into oblivion? No doubt there was more than one reason for the hesitation waltz. But it is clear that the attitude of French Jews influenced the Quai d'Orsay, and that neither the Jewish community nor its institutions then really believed in Zionism. Why run the risk of being accused of dual allegiance, or of disturbing the comfortable existence that had been won in Western Europe with such difficulty? At most, Palestine might offer a safe haven for the persecuted Jews of Eastern Europe.

J-CA: We need to situate all this, though. At the end of the nineteenth century, when Jews had no common territory or language and had been living in exile or diaspora for more than two thousand years, how could anyone have imagined for a moment that they could form a nation on one land, with a state of their own? Any sensible person would have seen that as madness.

EB: Yet France too did have its 'Palestinophiles': one of them, in the nineteenth century, was Chief Rabbi Zadoc Kahn, although this does not mean he thought a Jewish state would ever actually be built in the land of Israel. Edmond de Rothschild supported the new Jewish farming settlements in Palestine, without himself being a Zionist. And, although he surrounded himself with as much discretion as possible, he became known as 'the generous hand'. One of his ideas in doing this was to show Europe that Jews were not interested only in commerce, that they were capable of the kind of authentic regeneration that the champions of emancipation had demanded. Jews knew how to work the land, and so the Jews too could have roots.

J-CA: That was another link between the emancipation movement and pre-Zionism. For French-Jewish notables such as Rothschild, support for the settlements in Palestine was also a way of rehabilitating the image of Jews through labour, especially labour on the land.

EB: As we see, Zionism built itself up in a typically European climate in which Europe occupied the central position. The European discovery of the Sephardis came at quite a late date. It was with colonization that the Jews of France discovered the North African Jews and tried to 'regenerate' them in turn, with a discourse highly similar to that which the leading theorists of emancipation had once used in relation to themselves. The Zionists also experienced the Sephardis as an exotic element: it took them some time to grasp their significance and the potential they represented – with the exception of a few regions, such as Bulgaria, where Zionism would really catch on. Between 1948 and 1949, a total of 50,000 Jews left Bulgaria for Israel – a mass emigration unique in the history of Zionism, since it was usually the poor and the persecuted who left, not intellectuals or rich people. The Zionist encounter with Sephardi realities was more down to earth in the case of the Middle East. At a very early date, after the Young Turk revolution of 1908, the World Zionist Organization tried to use local Jews to advance its negotiations with the Ottoman government over Palestine (which was, of course, part of the Ottoman Empire until 1917). This was the context in which the Zionists discovered the descendants of the Jews who had been expelled from the Iberian Peninsula. As early as 1908 they set up a Zionist agency in Constantinople – the first of its kind in a Sephardi area. Their hope was to find more sympathetic interlocutors among the Young Turks, as Herzl had previously failed in his talks with the Sultan. But they saw their new contacts with the Sephardis mainly in ad hoc, instrumental terms; they did not think that Zionism could catch on in those regions. Meir Dizengoff, the future mayor of Tel Aviv, even declared: 'In Turkey there are Zionists without Zionism.' It was not expected that the Sephardis would make a real contribution to the building of the future state. In fact, the Zionists did not do any real Zionist work there in Constantinople.

J–CA: As you said, a Sephardi is mainly defined as a Jew originating from the Iberian Peninsula, and many Jews from North Africa have nothing Iberian about them. Yet the word is also used today to denote all Jews who are not Ashkenazi. This bipolarity is a little absurd, as it arbitrarily erases a number of distinctions among highly diverse groups. It is the fruit of recent history, especially of Zionist and then Israeli history. This exoticization of the Sephardis, this perception of them by many a Zionist as an indistinct mass, has weighed quite heavily on political developments.

EB: At first, the Sephardis were not at all a major concern for the Zionists. Only later, especially from a demographic point of view, did they become an important factor. Thus, after the creation of the State of Israel, talks were held with the North African communities to promote the immigration of at least the poorest layers from those countries. But in the earlier period, the Zionists certainly did not have them in mind as the population of the future state. Even Istanbul, with its quite large community of Iberian origin, was seen only as the gateway from Odessa – a port of transit for Russian Jewish immigrants! It was the so-called 'practical' Zionists of Russian origin, belonging to a current that emphasized work on the land in Palestine more than negotiations with the Great Powers, who became the leaders of the local Zionist movement. But a number of Germans, such as Richard Lichtheim, were also sent down to Istanbul. Even Vladimir Zeev Jabotinsky – father of the 'revisionist' (that is, right-wing) tendency that appeared in 1925 through a split in the World Zionist Organization and eventually gave rise to the Likud Party now headed by Ariel Sharon – was parachuted into Istanbul shortly after the Young Turk revolution. His talent for languages was especially useful for his mission of creating newspapers. The Zionist Organization even went so far as to buy up a number of Turkish nationalist periodicals so that they would favour the creation of a Jewish national home in Palestine (without mentioning, of course, any idea of the founding of a state). It also tried to purchase Jewish newspapers, linked to the Alliance israélite universelle, which backed Westernization and the official discourse of French Judaism: 'No to dual allegiances, no to Zionism! The Ottomans must not be antagonized. The aim should be to Frenchify the Eastern Jews, to teach them new trades, to make them productive, and to trust in their emancipation.' Jabotinsky was the linchpin of this vast press operation, even founding and writing for papers in French, the language of the Sephardi intelligentsia and bourgeoisie in the Ottoman Empire. But this level of activity did not survive the dismemberment of the Empire and the Balfour Declaration of 1917, since not much use could be made any longer of the Sephardis.

J–CA: Meanwhile, in parts of Central and Eastern Europe that would become a demographic and activist pool for Zionism, there was sometimes very strong resistance to the new movement. This was especially true of Orthodox Jews, for whom the Zionists were pork-eating renegades with an idea of Jewish identity that made no reference to God or the Torah and a project that seriously endangered the mission of Israel in exile. In the eyes of the Orthodox, Israel was in exile not only as punishment for its sins, but also so that it could assume an ethical, mystical and redemptive function *vis-à-vis* the nations of the world. Had not Judah Halevi, the medieval poet and thinker, already argued that God's design for Israel was similar to that which he had for a seed? A seed falls to the ground and undergoes transformation: it appears to become one with the soil, water or manure, but in reality it becomes a plant or a tree and thereby transforms the soil or water; it imparts its nature to them, gradually transmuting the elements into something akin to itself. Such is the mission of Israel in exile: scattered and even humiliated, it is everywhere present to redeem this world. It is not in its power to end its exile, and even to attempt it is an act of betrayal.

EB: The Orthodox Jewish world was not monolithic, however. As we have seen, a religious Zionism began to develop which, though sometimes hesitating to recognize a fundamentally religious value in Zionism, did see something positive in it and which would accompany it along the way.

J-CA: A formula that has become part of the Israeli synagogue ritual testifies to the nuanced way in which a trend within Jewish Orthodoxy has approached Zionism. In a blessing bestowed on it, the State of Israel is called 'the beginning of the burgeoning of our salvation'. So, there are stages after all: it is not salvation, not the Messiah, but something that is going in that direction.

EB: There have also been certain events or circumstances which have shaken great masters of the Orthodox tradition. The catastrophe that struck European Judaism during the Second World War brought about divergent reactions: on the one hand, acceptance of the principle that Jews must be saved in a land of their own, or – going beyond that – actual affiliation to moderate Zionism; on the other hand, even firmer rejection of Zionism as a modern heresy, a scandalous imitation of the path of the Nations, with the catastrophe itself as punishment for the heresy. So began the age of increased fragmentation of the Jewish religious universe, into mystical-Zionist, compromise-Zionist, non-Zionist and openly anti-Zionist religious people.

J-CA: Zionism and the reactions to it have certainly been highly complex. For all the incredulity, rejection and conflicts, Herzl's dream became a reality. But was it truly his dream which became reality? He tried to neutralize and tame the religious dimension, and turned a blind eye to the gravity of the Arab question. Would he recognize his work today, if he were to make a little trip to the country that makes use of his name?

EB: Perhaps he would tell himself that he failed to understand anything about it all. Ahad Ha'Am, the Russian-Jewish essayist of the late nineteenth to early twentieth century, had already warned the theoreticians of Zionism about pitfalls that sometimes proved insurmountable. The intensity of the Israeli–Palestinian conflict and the comeback of aggressive religiosity are both things that might well have surprised or shocked Herzl.

J-CA: Still, he would perhaps recognize one trend he hoped for in Israel: the development of a hi-tech country. Did he not dream of an ultramodern society, within a Middle East that would somehow have been reborn from the ashes?

EB: You forget the growing 'Levanticization' of Israel. Would not he, the Viennese Jew, be astonished at the music you hear in all the cafés and public places? Did he ever really appreciate that Palestine was in the Middle East?

J-CA: That is not the most serious thing, either. He would have to note that Zionism had neither the time nor the means to avoid the most terrible persecution in the history of the European Jews. Was not the main purpose of Zionism to offer a safe haven to the persecuted Jews? Worse: he would discover that the catastrophe had been needed to convince so many doubters of the legitimacy of the Zionist enterprise. And he would be stupefied that, for many people in the twenty-first century, the very creation of the State of Israel would appear as a consequence of the Shoah and have the strange value of a 'compensation'.

5 | Remembering the genocide: a new civil religion?

EB: Israel was evidently not the 'result' of the extermination of the Jews of Europe, as the idea of a Jewish state emerged long before. Nor is that tragedy sufficient to explain why the state was created in 1948. How could we treat so lightly more than half a century of Zionist research and theoretical and practical work? Today, it is no longer just Israel but the Jewish reality as a whole which is being seen through the prism of the Shoah. It is true that a lot of documentaries, as well as historical and literary work, have been devoted to the Shoah. People like Elie Wiesel, with their work and their personality, have played an invaluable role by informing and sensitizing a public that knew little about it. To sensitize the public is a perfectly legitimate thing to do. But what can and should be done then? I am not interested in the accusation that Wiesel and others promoted a kind of 'holocaust industry' – we need mention only Norman Finkelstein's recent book with that title. I don't know at what point people start to conduct a business. After all, business is involved in everything, so why should the Shoah be an exception? The real problem does not lie there. Wiesel played the role of sensitizing people. Perhaps he did not know when to stop. That is a different matter, and I don't think I could really settle it. Actors know that, at a certain moment, it is a good idea to make up your mind to stop. But that is not the most important thing either; other questions are more fundamental. For example: is it possible to think differently about the uniqueness of the genocide of the Jews? Perhaps, somehow or other, we must agree to keep together what was unique and what was universal in it. Each genocide is specific; each takes place in a particular context. Whether their roots are racial, ethnic-religious, political or religious, they all come down to the mass murder of human beings. So, uniqueness? Yes, the uniqueness of all the genocides, and therefore of the Jewish genocide as well. It is important that the specific nature of that catastrophe should prepare Jews to be sensitive to the genocide of others, to the tragedy of others. No doubt it is that passage from the particular to the universal which will be at the heart of the debate in coming years. Has the important place of the Judeocide in contemporary Jewish and Israeli consciousness been sufficiently universalized to make Jews open to the tragedies of others? That is the question. The painful conflict in the Middle East places it at the heart of a problematic which is not only mine but is more and more the subject of debate. I think it raises us to a new level of reflection. Is Wiesel, having sensitized the world to the suffering of the Jews, capable of going on to sensitize Jews to the tragedies of others? Perhaps that is not his role, but it is where we are at today. It is one of the reasons – not the only one, of course – why we should not forget the Shoah. For, to forget it would inevitably mean to close our eyes to what is happening to others, to humanity. Let me repeat, emphatically, that the Shoah must not be forgotten. But the much-asserted view that the Jewish genocide was, or should be considered, absolutely unique has no meaning.

J–CA: The widespread idea of God's silence or absence at Auschwitz proves in this respect to be highly significant. It is a non-theological, or anti-theological, discourse which is itself a new kind of theology – a theology of the silence or absence of God, a theology, moreover, that calls for silence about the Shoah. In this still largely prevalent conception, it is not possible to say anything about the Shoah: neither to justify it, of course, nor to explain it. In the face of absolute horror, at once incomprehensible and unjustifiable, there is indeed nothing. This discourse is as current among Jewish believers as it is among people indifferent to religion or actual atheists. Certain Orthodox milieux, however, have asked questions about the Shoah which generally remain within the traditional schemas. After all, it confronts Jewish religious consciousness with more than one question, and not all Jews consider silence an answer. How can it be explained that God so abandoned the people of Israel – his beloved people, his eldest child? And how can it be explained that the massacres hit indiscriminately at the most assimilated, the most irreligious, the most cut-off from Jewish roots, as well as the Orthodox mass of observant Jews from Eastern Europe, who were strongly attached to tradition? Neither belief in God nor fidelity to Judaism saved a single person from death. How can it be explained that the ones who were saved were rather the secular, anti-religious pioneers in Palestine? All these questions have been asked, and they sometimes go far beyond the noisy silence that is generally imposed. Lastly, to return to what you were saying, the extermination forces us to formulate in a different way the question of the uniqueness of the Jewish destiny itself. Was the Shoah one more instance of persecution in an intrinsically unique Jewish history? Or is it the Shoah, an intrinsically unique event in itself, which for ever defines the singularity of Jewish history? It is not the same thing. Or again: is the extermination mainly an event in human history whose significance can, or should, be universalized, and in which we find neither the uniqueness of a Jewish destiny nor the uniqueness of an event?

EB: Shoah … This Hebrew word, which may be translated as 'catastrophe' or 'destruction', has entered ordinary usage – at least in France – as a veritable proper noun. In the 1950s the Israeli authorities themselves anglicized it with the word 'Holocaust' – a term which, in English, had long before lost its sacrificial connotation. I accept that this word too, popularized by the American TV series *Holocaust*, is not entirely satisfactory. We can also use 'extermination' or 'Final Solution' or simply 'genocide'.

J-CA: The way in which the word Shoah is normally used tends to singularize the event in the extreme. A single word for a singular event, a word that cannot be associated with any other event. This is not true of genocide. As we see, every battle over words is a battle over meanings.

EB: In this connection, it seems very strange that the particularizing term has won out precisely in France, the land of universalism, because of Claude Lanzmann's powerful film *Shoah*. It happens that I use the word myself, since it has entered common usage. I also find 'Holocaust' useful enough. But my preference is for the word 'genocide', which has the merit of not cutting off the history of the Jews from that of other tragically decimated peoples, or from human history in general. However it is called, the event itself mainly poses for me the question of indifference, a question that makes it possible to move from particular to universal. What is the attitude of us Jews to the suffering of others? The example of the Armenian genocide is instructive in this respect. How did the Jews in Palestine conduct themselves during the massacres of 1915? The children of the first pioneers displayed a real sensitivity to the Armenian genocide, as we see in the case of the Nili group, a secret pro-British organization active between 1915 and 1917, and its leader Aaron Aaronson. Jews born in Palestine – the 'sabras', as they were later called – also reacted to the event. In France not all the Jews kept quiet: already in 1895 there had been the voice of Bernard Lazare, in particular. But the new Jewish immigrants in Palestine, mainly from Russia, yielded much more to the argument that the Ottomans, the Young Turks, had to be kept as allies, because it was with them that a solution to the Palestine question would be found. This kind of Realpolitik persisted long after the creation of the State of Israel. In fact, from its early days the Zionist movement had been on more or less cordial terms with the Ottomans, and Turkey later became the only Muslim country to have fairly harmonious relations with the new Jewish state. In recent decades, the principle of maintaining good relations has regularly prevailed over other considerations. Thus in 1978, when a film was due to be shown on the Armenian quarter of Jerusalem, it was decided at the last minute not to go ahead. Similar problems arose in 1983 in connection with the Holocaust Museum in Washington, when those in charge wanted to open it up to cover other genocides, especially that of the Armenians. This idea was endorsed in 1987, but we now know that because of outside pressure the space given to the Armenian genocide was more limited than in the original plan. The most significant development occurred in 1989, when US senators wanted to designate 24 April 1990 as a national day to commemorate the seventy-fifth anniversary of the Armenian genocide. (Similar proposals had already been rejected in 1985 and 1987.) Under the influence of the Israeli Embassy in the United States, and of the Jewish lobby in Turkey (where the Jewish community numbers no more than 20,000), this proposal was also eventually dropped. The Chief Rabbi of Turkey wrote to each senator explaining that the Turks had welcomed the Jews after their expulsion from Spain in 1492, that this was proof of Turkey's indulgent attitude to all minorities, and that there was no reason to describe as genocide the events in which the Armenians had been entangled. Such interventions were made in response to requests by the Turkish government, which, in its effort to gain entry into the European Community, was trying to remove the obstacle of the accusation of genocide. In that same year, the Turkish foreign minister himself approached the Anti-Defamation League (a powerful branch of the American B'nai B'rith, a Jewish philanthropic organization structured along the lines of a masonic lodge) and tried to convince it of the Turkish view that there had been no genocide. Turkish Jews, for their part, had an interest in their country's membership of the EC, at a time when Islamists were gaining ground, and their loyalty to Turkey could only have been strengthened by recent military and economic agreements with Israel. Not all American Jews fell for it, however. Reform rabbis opposed the manoeuvring, and the Anti-Defamation League did not add its voice to those hostile to the day of commemoration. In Israel, where the official argument was always that the long-standing relations with Turkey had to be preserved, a fierce controversy broke out over the state's intervention in the affair. On top of this, in 1990, came the cancelled screenings of the film *Trip to Armenia*. Each time the debates in Israel were very lively. And a certain evolution became discernible, so that in 1994 a film was eventually shown concerning the Armenians.

J–CA: We could also mention the position taken by Yossi Sarid, education minister in the former Barak government, who asked for the Armenian genocide to be taught in Israeli schools in the same way as the Jewish genocide. Clearly, public awareness has been developing on the issue.

EB: But why was there such protracted resistance to the idea that universal lessons could be drawn from the Armenian genocide? Why have there been so few books on the affair, in a country whose collective consciousness is partly based on the Jewish genocide? I would therefore stress that we have a duty to use the Jewish experience of catastrophe as the basis for a response, not only to the terrible ordeal of the Armenian genocide, but also to those of Cambodia or Rwanda and to everything happening today in the immediate vicinity of Israel. A number of Israeli intellectuals have been posing the question more or less in these terms. They are among the first to say: our own experience must help us change profoundly our behaviour towards the Palestinians.

J-CA: What you are raising is not only a moral or political question. When you say that the lesson must be universalizable, you imply that a connection or a comparison can be made between different incidences of genocide.

EB: That in no way removes the particularity of each genocide.

J-CA: Every event in history is by definition 'unique'; there is no absolute repetition. What you are advocating is an essentially historical approach to the event.

EB: Not only historical, but also political.

J-CA: A political message can come out of a historian's practice. What you also want is that those whose job it is to study the events, and who have seen the similarities between the Jewish and Armenian genocides, should also be given the opportunity to speak.

EB: That is why I think it more useful to stress the specificity, rather than the uniqueness, of the genocide of the Jews. The two are not really the same. The main aim is that people should become more aware of *all* genocides. To enclose the Jewish genocide in absolute singularity is to risk holding back a genuine receptivity to the suffering of others. In my view, such an extreme particularization of the Jewish genocide is detrimental to the Jews themselves.

J-CA: It also leads Jews to see their history in a fundamentally unhistorical way. Their history loses all universal significance once its message becomes somehow circular.

EB: If the lesson you draw from your history is turned in on yourself, how can it open your eyes and encourage a new way of seeing the world? Still, not all Jews can be simply lumped together. I have mentioned the Armenian genocide only because it is in a way the closest to the Jewish genocide, within a geopolitical context of which Palestine was an integral part. We should always bear in mind that until late 1917 Palestine was under Ottoman rule. Nevertheless, many Jewish voices were raised against the atrocities: Henry Morgenthau, for example, the American ambassador in Istanbul between 1913 and

1916, witnessed and denounced them; and Abraham Isaac Elkus, also a Jew, who succeeded him in that post from 1916 to 1919, took up where Morgenthau left off. There was no lack of discordant voices; the indifference was by no means total. Here too, we should not give in to a Manichaean view of things. But it is incumbent on us to understand the reasons for the indifference, so that indifference does not become the general rule.

J–CA: The extreme sensitivity to the Shoah that has developed in recent years may therefore have pernicious effects.

EB: Among Jews, certainly, but also among non-Jews. Can it be that, in being made to think of the Jewish genocide as unique, non-Jews too may become less sensitive to other genocides? The crystallization around the Shoah has clearly not served the cause of humanity, for it suggests that it was a unique event which struck only Jews, and which, in the end, can never be reproduced elsewhere in a different form. I would note in passing that debates about its uniqueness have been much more intense in the United States than in France. Here, the issue is not publicly discussed, even if it is implicit in the systematic use of the term 'Shoah'.

J–CA: The focus on the Jewish genocide has an opposite but correlative effect of banalization. Everything becomes genocide, everyone becomes a Nazi. In the daily sparring match, the words themselves lose their meaning.

EB: That is the case with Jews too. Just think of a few well-known amalgams, such as Arafat = Hitler. In Israel, such ideological simplification has also served as a propaganda weapon – though not massively, it is true, because you hear more dissident voices in Israel than in the Diaspora. Is it really possible to go on seeing enemies everywhere, or to say that the Palestinians are nothing but new Nazis, the new embodiment of an eternal enemy? No doubt the exacerbation of the Israeli–Palestinian conflict since October 2000 is unlikely to help matters.

J–CA: That kind of discourse can anyway be turned around and used by the other side, so that Israelis become Nazis and their leaders new Hitlers.

EB: The Western world has also played a role in this simplistic failure of judgement. The Christian West evidently wishes to pay off a debt and to rid itself of the crushing weight of guilt in relation to the Jewish genocide. We therefore end up in a perverse situation. Banalization is not the only consequence of the general outburst of pity, of the tearful and moralizing preoccupation with the genocide to be found among certain (fortunately not all) non-Jewish intellectuals. In all this, what becomes of those who experienced the Shoah in their own bodies, or of their offspring who have been marked for life by the tragedy? Do they really count for anything? There is more than banalization here. The emotional overload that seems to characterize certain groups of intellectuals today is not always as straightforward as it may seem. It is as if, by constantly dwelling on the Jewish genocide and hounding anyone who dares to strike a slightly different note, one hopes to extirpate all evil from oneself. Is the aim of this perhaps to create the fiction of a 'pure' society, wholly in the service of 'Good'? But what is the 'Good' in this case? Since when has the ideal of purity been accessible? What other turpitude is being hidden beneath all these fine sentiments? Is there an idea that the issue will eventually have a 'pay-off'?

J-CA: Is this collective contrition, this ceaseless confession of the fault, supposed to wash away the fault – all fault? Paradoxically, to see the Jews as eternal victims of total Evil and to see the Israelis as new Nazis are products of similar approaches. In both cases, the point is to free oneself of all blame, to absolutize evil as something completely outside oneself. Banalization goes hand in hand with self-purification.

EB: Alas, we are all the time in this circuit. This is why I would like to return to what I said before. The gravest aspect of the 'Shoah business' is not the business, but rather this polymorphous, mainly ideological utilization of the issue for questionable interests. We are familiar with the ideological uses to which the Jewish genocide has been put in Israel. But there has been an appropriation of the issue in the Diaspora too, since the Shoah now forms an integral part of Jewish identity. If Jews did not take refuge in the memory of genocide, would they still exist as Jews?

J-CA: I wonder whether there is not another aspect that might throw more light on the question: I mean the amazing contrast between the scale of the tragedy and persecution during the war years, and the daily life of Jews today. After all, we live in a time when a Jewish state is in existence, when there is no longer any destructive manifestation of anti-Semitism, when Jews generally live in security – even if they may be less secure these days in Israel. Rarely in their history have Jews enjoyed such freedom to claim and affirm their identity – without danger. Perhaps this is precisely what Jews find difficult to live out, or what they can experience only with a sense of guilt.

EB: No doubt that is why some are tempted see anti-Semites on all sides, or why the Jewish press gives so much space to incidents that are mostly not very disturbing. Anti-Semitism is certainly not dead, but I see no reason today why Jews should do their utmost to detect it more or less everywhere. The non-Jewish press also keeps the phenomenon going. I am not quite sure what to call it. An obsession? Which periodical lets a month, sometimes even a week, go by without publishing an article on the Shoah, or on the latest manifestation of anti-Semitism? This – we should stress – is all happening at a time when Jews have never been so remote from their Jewishness, from religious observance, Jewish learning and the transmission of Judaism.

J-CA: Nor so remote from the danger of persecution.

EB: The two seem to go together.

J-CA: It is also amazing that many Jews, without realizing it, participate in a kind of christologization of the destiny of the Jews. The reading of the Holocaust as a redemptive self-sacrifice – a reading that Mauriac, in particular, relayed as early as the late 1950s – experienced a certain vogue in Christian circles. Even today, some see the martyred Jewish people as a new Christ, but a completely secularized surrogate Christ, which does not even appear consciously as Christ in the minds of ordinary mortals. But it is none the less a Christ-like figure. It is as if, to be fully accepted and justified – in the West at least – the figure of the Jew had to end up merging with that of a Christ.

EB: For want of anything else, it is this history, this memory of shared suffering that binds together the Jewish world, in a period when it has been losing its sense of direction. What does it mean to be a Jew today? When someone asks me this question, I have little difficulty answering for myself. I do research work on the Jews, I modestly write their history, I am a kind of Jew by profession (though not only that, of course). So, the question does not really pose itself for me, even though I am not at all observant. But if I have to answer for others, or to suggest a possible path for them, things become more complicated. What does it mean to be a Jew today? To feel close to Israel? To share a memory of extermination? And what else? Sometimes, perhaps naïvely, I feel like adding that to be a Jew is also to live within a certain ethic, to have a love of life – not a passion for death. The cult of death surrounding the genocide certainly is a morbid passion. But what if it owes a lot to another 'death', the death of a certain form of Judaism, which is such a source of anxiety for so many young people with observant parents, grandparents or great-grandparents who are no longer observant themselves? The most tormented are usually those Jews who have been deprived of any transmission, not only of religion but also of learning, know-how and history; Jews whose only transmission has sometimes come in the shape of pathos or a vague nostalgia. But nostalgia cannot fill the void of Jewishness that some of them feel.

J-CA: Maybe I can expand on what you are saying by means of a brief Talmudic detour. How is someone received when he wishes to become a Jew? What questions are asked of him? The first thing he is told is: 'Do you really want to become a Jew? Do you want to join a people that is persecuted, dispersed, subject and tormented?' And what is the ideal answer a candidate can give? If he replies: 'I am not worthy', if he says he is unworthy of sharing the sufferings of the Jewish community, they convert him without further ado. But how do they convert him? By teaching him a little of the Torah (the positive commandments, the negative commandments), by explaining that there are rewards and punishments, by indicating that it is anyway not in this world but in the next that Israel will be rewarded. For the time being, Israel suffers – to earn its paradise. This elaborate ritual brings two elements into play: the community of suffering, real suffering, and the Law. What is left of these two elements for a Jew living today, for someone who does not become a Jew but is born one? No one comes and asks him any questions; he has to ask them of himself. But he has neither of the two elements: he no longer has the Law, and he no longer has the suffering. All he has left is the memory of suffering.

EB: By dwelling endlessly on anti-Semitism, by denouncing any discourse that slightly deviates from the norm, and by tirelessly hunting down the least sign of hatred, rejection or even indifference, it is certainly possible to create a community of imagined sufferings. To this is usually added a certain closeness to Israel, a solidarity with Israel. The closeness is often deeply felt and is not illegitimate in itself, but whatever some may say the long drawn-out conflict makes it more difficult to sustain and transmits an image of the country that is not at all easy to handle.

J-CA: If we return to the facts and figures, we may find that they explain or confirm this dominance of the imagination in

contemporary Jewish identity. What proportion of French Jews have
never set foot in a Jewish place?

EB: A study conducted in the 1980s put the figure at 60 per cent.
It is understandable that, for descendants who never lived through it
themselves, the Shoah does not only prescribe a duty to remember
but provides a substitute identity. This centrality of the genocide, in
memory, identity and representations, is quite a late phenomenon: it
first emerged towards the end of the 1970s. In the immediate post-
war period, Jews still spoke little of what they had been through, and
did not have much of an audience when they did speak of it. French
intellectuals took little interest in the Jewish experience during the
war, and their general picture of it hardly differentiated between racial
and other deportees. Only gradually did the awareness become widespread and verbal. Today, however, we are in a period of over-awareness
or over-verbalization. In the aftermath of the Six-Day War, and later
the Yom Kippur War of 1973, Jews started to search around for their
Jewishness. Alain Finkielkraut was certainly not the only 'imagined
Jew' of his generation. This return pointed in a number of different
directions: towards religion for some, towards culture for others, towards the remembrance of genocide for others again. But the weight
of the latter could not fail to increase as a result of the declarations and
actions of the French authorities themselves. It was all of a piece.

J-CA: We should also take into account a wider sociological
trend: the ever greater attention paid to victims in general. The late
twentieth century over valued the status of victim.

EB: That's certainly true. In the case of the Jews, however, the
quest for identity played an essential role and involved the simul-
taneous expression of a number of tendencies. Today, for example, the
return to strict observance is clearly one of these tendencies. Furthermore, Ashkenazis and Sephardis did not necessarily experience
things in the same way. The arrival of North African Jews in the late
1950s and after caused real upheavals in France: they had an assertive
and visible Jewish identity, while at the same time proving capable of
rapid and deep integration; they embodied a Judaism without complexes which did not have too many problems adjusting to the French
context. We should note, however, that in recent years the Shoah has
become quite a strong element in the consciousness of the descendants of these North African Jews; it is as if the only way of being
a good Jew were to appropriate that traumatic experience. Yet the

North African Jews were not directly exposed to the genocide, even
if they suffered from Vichy policies. So, what should be said of their
children? Can they still have their quality of Jewishness fully recognized without sharing in the memory of tragedy, if only abstractly in
their imagination? We can thus understand the ever growing place
of the genocide in the minds of this younger generation. They feel a
need to give some substance to their Judaism.

J–CA: Nevertheless, there has been a substitution of one religion
for another, of one cult for another, each with its distinctive cere-
monies.

EB: The genocide has been replacing the lost religion. It gives
rise to commemorations and a whole series of rituals that strangely
resemble religious ones. In fact, this religion is also accessible to non-
religious Jews and to non-Jews, and the more space it occupies, the
stronger the banalization will become.

J–CA: But a religion cannot revolve only around death. Remembrance of genocide erected into a religion is a religion without God
and without hope. We might accept that a religion can do without
God. But without hope? Is a religion not also a projection into the
future, a yearning for redemption and expiation, an overcoming of
guilt and suffering, a hope of resurrection? It is a strange religion that
Jews without religion somehow find themselves left with. In these
conditions, I find it rather hard to see what tomorrow holds in store
for us. But who is talking of tomorrow?

EB: I would add that this religion is entirely self-enclosed: it feeds
off itself; sanctification ends all debate. Hopefully, this is no more than
a critical moment that may be overcome with the passing of time. All
I wonder is whether the process of overcoming it will not involve
a return to ultra-religiosity. The picture is fortunately not the same
everywhere. Profound reflection on these issues is taking place today
in Israel, as well as in the United States. In France, where we are more
restrained, you have the sense of colliding with a brick wall, which
allows no way through and no possibility of debate.

J–CA: In fact, this religion is the very opposite of religion. It is an
imprisonment.

EB: That is why I see no salvation except through universalization. To universalize is not to forget. It is from an excess of speech that
oblivion and normalization flow.

J–CA: You must agree, though, that the religiosity is also there among non-Jews, where acts of repentance maintain a certain atmosphere and justify attitudes that sometimes border on the ridiculous. I have noticed that those who repent are not the ones who have done wrong, and that those who might forgive are no longer here to do it. Once again, I suspect that what is taking place is an empty ritualization. In true repentance, the one who repents is the one who committed the offence. If he or she dies before repenting, it is too late. It is time to move on to something else.

EB: To some extent we all feel this thirst for religion, but for a religion without too many burdensome practices. In the age of self-service, people take from religion only what might be of help to them, only what compensates for an absence.

J-CA: I would now like to raise another question. Is this the first time in history that the Jews have faced such an intense trauma? We have already spoken of the massacres accompanying the First Crusade in the late eleventh century, which inspired poignant Jewish chronicles in memory of the glorious martyrs. We might also mention the riots accompanying the Cossack revolt under Bogdan Chmielnicki, in 1648–49, which struck Polish Judaism full-force. But I am mainly thinking of some studies of Jews expelled from Spain and the first and second generations of their descendants. The despair among them was plain to see – the sense that God had abandoned his people, that Israel might be on its way to disappearing, that those who were not subjected to forcible conversion would perish at the hands of pirates or from epidemics in their new host lands. At the same time, however, a determination to hold on kept expressing itself, as well as an obsession that they must at all costs produce children for the future and for the survival of Judaism. In the face of despair, they continued to look ahead. The trauma might be either a punishment or an unjust and unexplained catastrophe, but it must not prevent them from building tomorrow and the Judaism of tomorrow.

EB: Today there is no faith to sustain the flagging, no genuine religion capable of nurturing hope in spite of everything. Individuals immerse themselves in the catastrophe, which becomes an element of their identity. But if they were suddenly to turn against this 'religion of the Shoah', this religion of those who have no religion, what would be left? Israel at war?

J-CA: There would still be Orthodoxy, to which more and more Jews eventually return. For some it even serves as a refuge – far from

Israel, far from the Shoah. But I would agree that this remains a minority trend.

EB: The irony is that this religious Orthodoxy, in its new forms, is coming to us largely from Israel. When we traced the historical rise of Jewish nationalism, we may not have sufficiently emphasized that for a long time its dominant socialistic wing rejected religion, while at the same time advocating a return to the ancestral land and claiming it in the name of roots going back thousands of years. This mobilization of the past was at the same time a secularization – at least it was in the minds of the socialist Zionists, who held the reins of power until the right-wing Likud victory in 1977. After that date, we began to see the first obvious signs of a return of the repressed: that is, repressed religion came bouncing back in its most extreme forms. Today I would say that Israel is living through a return of all the repressed. A return of the religious repressed and a return of the oriental repressed.

6 | Ashkenazis and Sephardis: exchanging looks

J-CA: The two things are to some extent the same, rooted in demographic realities. When a strong Oriental presence establishes itself in Israel, there is ipso facto a strong presence of quite traditionalist Jews unformed by Zionism.

EB: That is not quite what I meant. During the period when socialist Zionism was dominant, the Sephardis – long seen as 'traditional' – were also thought of as a non-Zionist population that had played no significant role in the foundation of the State of Israel. They were not exactly second-class citizens, but nor were they in the front ranks. And today the Shas, a religious party mainly recruiting among Jews of North African origin, best embodies the twofold return of the repressed about which I spoke a moment ago. Many of its members are Moroccans, the least highly regarded population among Israelis. They are the people who voted against the socialists and brought Likud to power. In the Shas, the religious repressed and the Oriental repressed have found the means to make a comeback, for it has become a major political force in opposition to the dominant Zionist wing, which has been left-wing, secular and Ashkenazi. From this point of view, too, Zionism in Israel has entered a new phase and will have to face up to its own repressions. One of these, of course, will be the repression of the Arabs.

J-CA: The prejudice and distrust between Oriental Jews and

Ashkenazis does not weigh only upon Israel. Stereotypes often threaten to poison relations.

EB: Here is one example. Recently I received separate invitations to two festivals of 'Jewish' music, organized by the same institution. The programme of the cycle of 'Yiddish' (in fact classical) music lined up Bloch, Shostakovich and a few famous names of the repertoire, while the publicity for the cycle of Judeo-Spanish music carried a photo of old ladies in nineteenth-century traditional costume and listed hardly anything more than love songs and other popular favourites. The intention was praiseworthy enough, and there was no wish to mar the image that people had of the Sephardis. But it was a striking contrast: on the one hand the Ashkenazis, aristocrats of culture identified with the values of the West; on the other hand the Sephardis, a source of folklore and objects of nostalgia. That, after all, is one part of the problem. It does not affect the United States, because most of its Jewish population is Ashkenazi. But in the case of France, the arrival of Jews from North Africa created considerable tension, as not everyone in the Jewish section of the population took kindly to their integration and rapid success. The well-established Ashkenazi community, with its intellectuals, its men and women of letters, its promotion of learning and its record of educational achievement, looked upon the newcomers not with contempt but with a degree of condescension. The barbarians had arrived. In fact, this was an old tradition repeating itself. For, in the nineteenth and early twentieth centuries, documents emanating from the Alliance israélite universelle (a French-Jewish organization that founded many schools in the Ottoman Empire and North Africa) already directed a thoroughly colonial gaze at the Orientals, describing them as primitive and superstitious, still dressed in their traditional costumes, with dirty fingernails and dubious hygiene.

J-CA: Let us note in passing that the 'Israelites' also looked with a degree of condescension upon their fellow-Jews who streamed in from Eastern Europe between the two world wars. In any event, certain Ashkenazi circles – whatever their origin – fully absorbed this colonial vision of the Sephardis.

EB: It was not only in France that it was rife. A new generation of Israeli historians and sociologists – the famous post-Zionists – are currently re-examining the origins and effects of this dichotomy between Ashkenazis and Sephardis, and are trying to find the reasons why the latter have not been successful in Israel. No doubt the fear of

'Levanticization' has played a role. There is also the prestige attaching to the German-Jewish founding fathers, and to Eastern Europe as the historical cradle of Zionism. The typical figure of the pioneer is that of an Ashkenazi. The Zionist militancy in North Africa has even been erased from the history books and the people's memory, so that the preferred image of the Oriental Jews who came to Israel is of poor people whom their community leaders were unable or unwilling to feed and therefore pushed into emigration. Very little on the positive side was said about them; their only merit, if it is one, would seem to lie in their traditionalism.

J–CA: Their other defect was that they did not speak Yiddish – as if it was necessary to speak Yiddish to be a real Jew. There is no lack of piquancy in this, for the Zionist tradition had promoted Hebrew against Yiddish, which it saw as a mere patois. Still, the question now was whether a Jew whose mother tongue was not Yiddish was really a Jew that Israel needed.

EB: They did not speak Yiddish and they were traditionalists. Since the dominant branch of Zionism was secular, it undervalued their religious inclinations as something negative to be erased or overcome. Today, the Orientals draw all their pride from this negative trait and do not hesitate to vote against the Left. All the humiliations have become politicized. The Mimuna, a typically North African festival closing the Passover period, has all but become a national Israeli festival. The Sephardis have laid claim to precisely the aspect that others held against them: their religiosity. They have converted it into something positive. Shas party sympathizers send their children to Ashkenazi Orthodox schools, as if they have absorbed the principle of the superiority of the Ashkenazi model, only this time on the ground of religion. Behind all that lie the wounds of emigration, of the period after the Oriental and North African Jews first arrived in Israel, when they had to remain in transit camps for years on end. The rancour now expresses itself without any sense of shame. Russian Jews arrive and are given apartments as well as financial assistance to settle in the urban centres. Moroccan Jews, by contrast, were sent far away into the development towns, which they have not since been able to leave. In France, the factors of distrust look rather different: the Sephardis may have succeeded but they did not live through the Shoah; and, in the eyes of Jews who settled in France before them, they do not have the privilege of culture.

J-CA: That does not correspond in any way to the reality, how-ever, since a huge part of Jewish Francophone culture since the 1960s has been produced by Sephardis.

EB: Sociologically, the French Jew is Sephardi. There are the Jews from North Africa, and the less numerous Jews from the Middle East. All of them are called 'Sephardi', even though the original meaning of the word, as we have seen, was simply 'originating in Spain'. The North Africans make up a majority of the Jews in France, and their social ascent has been spectacular. What is the explanation for it? Many were French citizens before their arrival, of course; those repatriated from Algeria, including a large number of civil servants, could therefore rapidly integrate into French society. This was the first wave of Jewish immigration to be spread throughout the country, not concentrated only in Paris. In particular, the accidents of civil service appointments meant that Jews ended up almost everywhere, even in places where almost none had lived before. Furthermore, some Tunisian or Moroccan Jews also had French nationality or belonged to the cream of Jewish society. The poor and uneducated went straight to Israel, while others wended their way to Montreal. In France, the newcomers brought all their dynamism to a Jewish society left lifeless by the war. Besides, they were Mediterraneans, and some found cause to regret that they were not a little more discreet.

J-CA: Let us not fall into caricature, though! *La vérité si je mens*[1] is all very nice and jolly: there are Jews like that, but there are others who are not at all like that, even among Sephardis living in France. The Jews in *La vérité si je mens* are Jews, not all Jews.

EB: You are right. The Sephardis also distinguished themselves in-tellectually after their arrival in France: the Jewish cultural renaissance of the 1970s and 1980s owes a lot to writers from North Africa. In the generally favourable context following the Six-Day War and the Yom Kippur War, young Ashkenazis naturally also found their way back to Judaism. Sephardis were not ashamed to call themselves Jewish – indeed, they turned it into a positive affirmation. But it is surpris-ing that, at the same time, they integrated into French society so easily that they were able to enter sectors often closed to newcomers: not only the medical profession, but publishing, journalism and culture. The Ashkenazis who came in the inter-war period had had to learn

1 A popular French film from 1997, with a sequel in 2001, focusing on competitive rivalry in Paris's Garment District. *Trans. note*

French, and it was rather their children who succeeded in life. Now, however, the social advancement was immediate. Even if it is true that it was a difficult challenge for many lower-middle-class Algerians, who had had to leave everything behind. Nor was everything rosy for the poorest Tunisians and Moroccans, some of whom did not have French nationality.

J-CA: To understand the origin of this supposed hierarchy of Ashkenazis and Sephardis, we need to go back a little in time.

EB: And to situate the problem in a long-term view of things. Ashkenazi culture came to be seen as 'aristocratic' only when Ashkenazis started emigrating to America and elsewhere. Great writers such as Bashevis Singer, or the various great composers and scholars, did not win fame and glory in the small towns of Poland. It is true that, in the same period, Oriental Jews did not have to face any challenge in the Muslim world, and that they did not feel themselves inferior to the non-Jews around them. In the West and in Central Europe, on the contrary, a desire to equal non-Jews on their own ground played a powerful role for those who set their sights on becoming an artist, writer or professor, or on owning a library or art collection. In the Muslim countries, the idea that Jews were not inferior to Muslims despite their second-class status may have contributed to a certain stagnation. But even that is not altogether true. For, in North Africa and the Middle East, eyes were turned westwards: people identified with Europe and, in areas of European colonization, with the colonizer.

J-CA: The spread of French culture occurred very early on – which is why France now has so many Sephardi intellectuals. Nor was it limited to North Africa.

EB: Indeed, the Judeo-Spanish from Turkey and the Balkans, who are only a minority in France, were at least in some cases Frenchified as early as the 1870s, at schools run by the Alliance israélite universelle. These people quickly turned their eyes westwards, and Bulgaria soon became a bastion of Zionism in Sephardi lands. This also explains the ease with which Ladino-speaking Bulgarian Jews acclimatized to Israel, where Balkan Jews generally appear as 'invisible Jews' because they have posed no problem of integration. Similarly, because they spoke French, the Oriental Jews who began to arrive in France in 1909 settled in the eleventh arrondissement of Paris and integrated harmoniously into their new environment. Nor had they previously experienced the problem of colonization, which, in North Africa, tended to distort relations between Jews and the surrounding world. A number of prominent French or French-speaking personalities have come out of this group, even if they do not all proclaim it. The novelist Albert Cohen was not a one-off case.

J-CA: You often present the Judeo-Spanish as the most Ashkenazi of the Sephardis. That is not without a certain irony.

EB: To be sure. I myself was born in Istanbul; my father had Bulgarian origins and my mother's roots were in Salonica. I feel Jewish first and foremost because I feel Judeo-Spanish: I speak Ladino, and I am conscious of being Sephardi in a different way from the Jews of North Africa – which does not imply any kind of hierarchy. But my surname, Benbassa, could pass as a North African patronymic, although that is not at all what it is. And, faced with the injustice of the gaze directed at myself and the Sephardi group, I feel solidarity with everyone within it.

J-CA: You described yourself a little earlier as a 'Jew by profession'. Are you not perhaps also a 'Sephardi by profession'?

EB: It is true that, at a certain point in my academic career, I veered off towards my origins, at first with nostalgia and then with all the strict requirements of a scientific attitude. Together with an American colleague, also Judeo-Spanish from Turkey, I have written the history of my vanishing group, simply because writing was a way for me to exist and to make my own Jews exist. And I claim all this as a special dignity solely in opposition to the deprecatory scrutiny that can still be found among some of the Ashkenazi intelligentsia in France. In their eyes, Sephardis are garment traders. When they write books, they easily become figures of fun or arouse disbelief.

J-CA: But the big problem for the Ashkenazis is that they no longer have the power.

EB: Indeed, a good part of this attitude – we are not rivals within the same camp – comes from the fact that the intelligentsia of Ashkenazi origin has on the whole been supplanted. The Sephardis, for their part, have ended up nursing a kind of complex. I am not speaking here of the Oriental Jews, because they have long seen their Iberian origin as an aristocratic privilege, and because they too have been through the ordeal of genocide. The North African Jews, on the other hand, developed a kind of guilt over the fact that they did not share the ordeal. The feeling of discomfort really does exist; it is almost as if, to be a good Jew when nothing much is left of religious practice, you have not only to be Ashkenazi but to have been through the experience of the Shoah. When their grandparents are dead and their family traditions extinct, what will the North African Jews be left with except religion? This makes it easier to understand why, in respect of 'memory duty', some Sephardis sometimes appear more zealous than Ashkenazis. Is it for all these reasons that we see some young Sephardis building their identity around the Shoah, organizing conferences on anti-Semitism, or writing dissertations about the genocide?

J-CA: Some signs of resistance to this overvaluation of the Ashkenazi experience are nevertheless beginning to appear among Sephardis. You sometimes get a sense of saturation, as if Sephardis have been denying themselves in adopting what is in the end an alien Jewish vision of the world. Although I do not look much like one, I myself am a Sephardi – in at least two respects. First, genealogically, my father was a Judeo-Spanish from Algeria; his family originated in Tetuan in Morocco, the equivalent there of what you were describing a moment ago in the eastern Mediterranean. Second, I am also a Sephardi through cohabitation. With you, I mean! Through my mother, however, I am neither Sephardi nor Ashkenazi, as she is not Jewish. Or let us say that my non-Jewish mother is in a way my Ashkenazi side! But, in the research topics I have chosen to take on, and in my personal way of relating to the Jewish world, the dominant aspect is Sephardi and Mediterranean. No doubt I found that climate more suitable, and the existence of the Sephardis greatly assisted my identification with Judaism, which began in early youth and became official through conversion. (The fact that my mother was not Jewish meant that I was not either in the eyes of Jewish Law.)

EB: People too often deny the vitality of Sephardi culture. They readily accept that it had its high point – the golden age of Spanish-Jewish philosophers and poets, and then the kabbalists. But that is all. Most ordinary Jews know nothing about the culture that developed in North Africa and the Orient beyond a certain date. You get the sense that everything more or less ground to a halt after Maimonides and the *Zohar*, the key work of Jewish mysticism, and that only Ashkenazis picked up where things had been left. What a simplification that is!

J-CA: Jewish reality is made up of all these cultural and even religious differences. These are a source of wealth as well as tension, and they must not stand in the way of a mutual encounter. Ashkenazis and Sephardis can very well pray together, even if their rites are very different! A Sephardi who has only ever practised Sephardi forms of worship, and who finds himself in an Ashkenazi synagogue where the Hebrew is pronounced in the Ashkenazi way, will be completely lost. He will try to find his bearings from central elements of the ritual – the removal of the Torah scroll from the Ark and the reading of it aloud – but he will find it difficult even to follow the spoken text. And yet, small communities exist where force of circumstance means that Sephardi and Ashkenazi believers have to worship together. Compromises involving a certain mixing of liturgies are worked out; Sephardis have the main say on one question, Ashkenazis on another. A modus vivendi is thus possible. The main requirement is that everyone should want to achieve it, should avoid hierarchical classification, and should recognize each other's Jewishness (whatever its expression) as full, real and legitimate.

EB: In the traditional Sephardi world, especially North Africa, the practice of religion sometimes seems to me less cut off from everyday reality. It is a matter of custom, family experience, sociability. Perhaps that is why you find fewer expressions of ultra-Orthodoxy in Sephardi milieux – except in Israel, where religion has become over-politicized with the rise of the Shas party.

J-CA: Perhaps, in the Sephardi context, religion has simply not been so much of an issue, and therefore not so highly ideologized. In the Muslim countries, the encounter with modernity is on the whole less conflictual, and more likely to favour compromise; people do not brace themselves into an anti-religious, hyper-secular position on the one side or an ultra-Orthodox position on the other. What you see instead are a number of supple formulas ever open to revision. We'll eat kosher at home, but not outside. We'll ritually bless the wine every Friday evening in the family, but we won't refrain from driving to the synagogue, or doing the shopping, by car on Saturday morning.

EB: For a long time in Eastern Europe, religion and everyday life were not separate from each other, but that region was also the theatre of major ideological and political confrontations. The history of Judaism in North Africa, by contrast, does not seem to have predisposed people to religious extremism – and even less so in the Orient.

J-CA: Let us not forget that before modernity there was no 'Orthodox Judaism'; it first appeared in the nineteenth century, in

Central and Eastern Europe. In fact, Orthodoxy emerged as such, in a form close to what we know today, at the very moment when it was ceasing to come naturally to many Jews, and when other different options were taking shape. In Hungary, in the face of Reform Judaism, an ultra-Orthodox reaction organized itself around Moses Sofer. In his view, there was no way in which the Torah could be reconciled with innovation, yet such determination to lock Judaism into a rejection of modernity was itself an innovation. We must not confuse this tendency with neo-Orthodoxy, which responded to the same challenges by trying to combine the Torah legacy and its strict norms of Judaism with modern culture. Ultra-Orthodoxy is a form of categorical – and modern! – rejection of modernity. It sees danger in the Jewish Enlightenment, in Reform Judaism, even in neo-Orthodoxy itself!

EB: This mistrust of the Jewish Enlightenment is far from having disappeared. I remember a student I once had from a rabbinical background who, after a lecture on that late-eighteenth-century current of Jewish cultural and social renewal, came up to me and said: 'But it was still the Enlightenment that killed Judaism, and you can talk about it in such an easygoing way. You should think about it more.' How can the Jewish Enlightenment still appear today to Orthodox Jews as a negation of Judaism? Is it the Enlightenment as such which frightens them? Moses Mendelssohn, the father of that current, never stopped being a practising Jew – although it is true that his descendants converted to Christianity.

J–CA: We should realize that, whatever they may say, contemporary Orthodox have invented a fundamentally modern Judaism to combat modernity, basing themselves on a selection of sources capable of providing authority for the imposition of certain norms of behaviour. Their reading of those sources is itself selective, involving a highly angled interpretation of the Jewish past. In fact, they refuse to face up to history: what they present to us as pure tradition is an invented tradition.

EB: Presumably you mean that a rejection of modernity is here combined with an undeclared adaptation to modernity. This is not the first time that Judaism has adapted, and changed itself in order to adapt.

J–CA: That's true. But when you speak of Jews or Judaism today, what do most people think of? Men in black with beards, women in wigs. But that is not contemporary Judaism. Such men and women are only a tiny visible part of it, perhaps inordinately visible. After all, Reform currents are also part of Judaism. In France they may still be considered rather secondary, but across the Atlantic they are accepted as quite ordinary and legitimate.

EB: When we go to New York to work at the Jewish Theological Seminary, which is part of the conservative movement, more or less halfway between Orthodoxy and liberal Judaism, we book accommodation on the site. And there we meet young female students wearing the skullcap traditionally reserved for men, walking like that in the corridors as if it were the most natural thing in the world. It does not raise any eyebrows. Some of those women will later hold responsible positions in the Jewish community. Some are even training as rabbis – a possibility that this current has accepted since 1983.

J-CA: What will ensure that Judaism survives? The large size of ultra-Orthodox families, turned in on themselves? Or, on the contrary, lively variants of Reform-minded Judaism, prepared to innovate while retaining traditional references of varying strength?

EB: I think we can say that it is in large part the Reform movement which has saved American Judaism.

J-CA: The opposite might also be said, of course. Orthodox would ask whether that kind of Judaism – which compromises over rabbinical norms, redefines the role and place of women in Jewish society, takes liberties with the Talmud, and affiliates to a pretty abstract congregation – can still be properly described as Judaism at all. Personally, I think it is absurd to pose the question in such terms. Judaism is what Jews make of it.

EB: Especially at a time when everyone is taking from religion what suits them, or what they consider vital.

7 | Judaism, Christianity, Islam: combining differences

J-CA: But is it still possible to speak of religion when it is lived outside any constraint, not as submission of a non-autonomous individual to a divine Law coming from outside that has to be accepted lock, stock and barrel? I do not know. Anyway, can we think of historical Judaism as a system, let alone a closed system? Clearly not. Historically, that is not how Judaism was constructed. Jewish Law itself, whose rabbinical tradition tells us that its main source was the revelation on Mount Sinai, was actually the fruit of a slow and complex process not without its frictions; it was always capable of innovation when the circumstances required. Nor did Judaism ever acquire a really elaborate set of dogma. Of course, articles of faith were knocked into shape in the medieval period, but we have them in quite a number of variants. Is adherence to a creed really central to Jewish religious fervour? It would not even appear to be formally demanded of believers.

EB: That does not mean that Jews do not believe in something. There are a number of points on which they are supposed to be agreed.

J-CA: No doubt. There is the belief in the unity of the one God, in Revelation, in the mission of Moses to pass on the Law to the Jews on Mount Sinai. Or there is the idea of a covenant which commits God in relation to his people (he will give it the land and promises to reward and keep faith with it), and which also commits his people, more or less under duress, to respect the divine commandments. In fact, the covenant lays down the priestly vocation of the entire Jewish people.

EB: So, a number of elements may be seen, or shaped, as dogma or a Jewish creed.

J-CA: But that is still fairly marginal, and when you think about it the main elements of this creed are found in other monotheisms, in Christianity and Islam. Is that what constitutes the originality of Judaism as a system? Revelation, a covenant, the one God, messianism?

EB: There is also the idea of election, of course.

J-CA: Election: hard to get away from it. It is both what Jews claim with a more or less good conscience, and what others are most tempted to hold against them. Yes, there is certainly the idea that God chose this people among all the peoples to be a people of priests; election marks Israel out from the other nations. And within sacred history, or history *tout court*, it gives Israel a special role that it alone assumes. This being so, the theme of election is used as the basis for accusations that it glorifies Jewish particularism, or even that it encourages Jews to see themselves as superior to other peoples. The danger is real. To some extent, however, Judaism wards off this temptation by admitting non-Jews to the Jewish people. There are no Jewish missions among the Nations, but Gentiles can convert to Judaism and a fairly well-codified procedure allows those who did not appear chosen to be chosen after all. They must truly wish it, and in general quite a few obstacles are placed in their way. But conversion is possible, and it does happen.

EB: But what of the Gentile who chooses to remain what he is, who never dreams of converting to Judaism? Is there any hope that he will be saved?

J–CA: Yes, there is. While Judaism confers on the Jewish people the status of God's chosen people, it also recognizes that other nations – especially Christians and Muslims – have a real status of their own. There are the children of Israel, but there are also the children of Noah. And the children of Noah – the whole of humanity – have a status within Judaism; they too are party to a covenant made with Noah after the Flood, which involves both divine commitments (especially the one never again to destroy all flesh on earth) and human obligations. Seven commandments were enjoined on the children of Noah: the obligation to establish a legal system; the prohibition of blasphemy, idolatry, incest and adultery, murder and theft; and a ban on the consumption of any limb torn from a living animal. Another point we should bear in mind is that, although Judaism sometimes does it with regret and not without some precautions, it partly recognizes itself in Christianity and Islam by assigning to each a relatively positive function in the history of humanity, a function of helping to spread monotheism and the knowledge of God. As a general rule, Jewish scholars concede that belief in the *one* God is shared by Jews, Christians and Muslims. This is evident enough in the case of Muslims. Perhaps it is less clear in relation to Christians, because the Trinity, Jesus and the Incarnation seem to have some affinity with idolatry. But it is usually accepted that even Christians are not idolators or pagans but monotheists – if not perfectly, not as they ought to be. Thanks to Christianity and Islam, the Nations are slowly preparing to recognize the ultimate truth of Judaism as pure monotheism.

EB: That is a nice reversal of the Christian theme of evangelical preparation, which accepts that Judaism at least has the merit of having 'prepared' the coming of Christ.

J–CA: For a number of medieval Jewish thinkers – from Maimonides the rationalist to Judah Halevi the fideist – Christianity and Islam are both kinds of messianic preparation. They are leading the Nations to recognize the ultimate and authentic messiah, the Jewish Messiah, the Son of David. It is within this messianic perspective that Christianity and Islam have their legitimacy. They are debased, faulty forms of Judaism, still full of dross, but they play a positive role in history by assisting the religious development of humanity.

EB: The idea of election has nevertheless harmed Jews in the modern era. And you do find, especially among groups of integrated or would-be integrated Jews in the nineteenth century, a temptation to neutralize this aspect of Jewish identity by erasing any dimension of particularism.

J-CA: No doubt. But, if election is so often held against the Jews, it is because Christians claim to have dispossessed them of it. Do you know any people which, at one moment or another in its history, has not felt itself to be 'chosen' by God or destiny to accomplish some great task? Just think of 'France, the fatherland of human rights'! But, to return to the heart of our subject, let us recall that Christianity could do no more than try to take over the idea of election for its own advantage, even if it claimed to be 'universalizing' the enjoyment of this privilege. For a certain Christianity, Israel in the flesh is a fallen people; Israel in the spirit – that is, the Christian people – is the true inheritor of the biblical promises.

EB: But do you think that only Christianity is forced to think of itself in relation to Judaism?

J-CA: Not at all. Jews have never stopped thinking of themselves in relation to both Christianity and Islam. On the one hand, the fall of Constantinople to the Turks in 1453 and then the Protestant Reformation were seen as good news, in so far as they weakened the power of the Church and split the unity of the Christian world. Some thinkers even saw those events as heralding the end of time. But the main challenge was to justify the survival of Judaism as belief system and revealed Law, in the face of Christianity and Islam. A role in the religious history of the world could be allowed to the two rival mono-theisms. But the antiquity, excellence and legitimacy of Judaism had also to be affirmed against a Christianity or Islam that was triumphing by force of numbers or arms. Against all the evidence, it was necessary to demonstrate the grandeur of a weakened, impoverished and dispersed Judaism, without a state or territory to call its own.

EB: It was also necessary to argue, against all Christian teaching, that the Messiah had not yet come but was still awaited.

J-CA: On that point, though, we need to be clear about the meaning and the centrality of the messianic hope within Judaism. There have obviously been some periods when the level of messianic effervescence and expectation was higher than in other periods, but one also finds in certain thinkers a kind of desire to soften or neutralize the messianic expectation, on the grounds that such fevers end in catastrophe – for Jews at least. In this view, any intensification of messianic hopes threatens to encourage a break with accepted models, or needlessly to provoke the ire of the Nations. Judaism knows on occasion how to cultivate prudence. We should not reduce it to messianism: that is not all it is. We can even conceive of a Judaism that indefinitely postpones any idea of the coming of the Messiah. Paradoxically, however, medieval Judaism was capable of recognizing a messianic dimension in Christianity and Islam, of treating Jesus and Muhammad as imperfect messianic figures prefiguring the final revelation of the true Messiah.

EB: OK, but Jesus was given a pretty rough ride in one tradition of medieval Judaism.

J–CA: It is true that he appears in a rather unflattering light in the famous anti-Gospels, the roots of which go back a long way and which circulated widely in a number of versions throughout the pre-modern era. Nowadays, Jews do not want to hear too much about them, but the texts existed and were read. Nevertheless, even in these violently anti-Christian parodies or caricatures, there is not only hatred or resentment. Judas is given the role of the good guy, with Jesus as the negative character. Yet, beyond the virulence of the parody, one also glimpses a recognition of similarity in the Other. The whole problem facing the authors of these texts was to show as clearly as possible what distinguished Judaism from Christianity. At the end the figure of Simon Peter, founder of the Church, is curiously presented as a genuine Jew faithful to the Torah, who pretends to be a Christian, rises to head the new community, and does everything to ensure that Christianity distances itself as clearly and definitively as possible from Judaism, in terms of liturgy, theology and culture. That is a complete reversal of history. But it is also proof that the medieval Jewish authors and readers of the anti-Gospels were perfectly aware of the strange affinity between themselves and those who were all too often their persecutors. In these conditions, the Other could not appear as totally negative: he always had a chance to be redeemed, or even to contribute, without knowing it, to the Redemption already under way.

EB: But the Other was not always just an imperfect approximation to a perfection still to come. The Other could also function as a model, arousing a profound desire for imitation among the Jews. If we look closely at the past, what is so astonishing is the permeability of the cultural frontiers. In the Middle Ages, for example, it was possible for the Muslim world to serve as a model for Jews. The principles and rules of Arabic poetry were adapted to Hebrew poetry. People found sustenance in the Arab-Muslim rereading of the great scientific and philosophical classics of Greek antiquity. In periods of rare glory and efflorescence, when the world around them was full of stimulation, the Jews would be sure to identify with it. Not even the Jewish messianism you mentioned a moment ago failed to draw inspiration or sustenance from expectations in the wider world. Thus, the messianic movement that Sabbatai Zevi launched in Ottoman lands in the seventeenth century appeared at a moment when the Muslim world and the Christian world were criss-crossed by similar expectations. Even at this level, the interrelations were apparent; they are also observable in what later happened to the movement. Subsequently, a number of Sabbateans converted to Islam, while another sequel, in Europe, was the conversion of the 'Frankists' (followers of Jacob Frank) to Christianity. Such interpenetration with the surrounding society, which helped to weave the web of Jewish life throughout the premodern period, reached its apogee in the modern period.

J–CA: And that is when we see the emergence of a form of Judaism that places the main emphasis on ethics, on what has been called ethical monotheism, on the message of the prophets. In this way, certain Jews more or less openly rid themselves of everything that made rabbinical Judaism: the Law, the Talmud, practical observance, daily meditation and study of the 613 commandments underpinning the Jewish tradition, and that had been seen as a proof and token of God's covenant and a testimony to election. In the nineteenth century, as so often in the history of the Jews, this return to the Bible marked a break more than a continuity: it involved a modernization drive and, in this instance, a determination to place more emphasis on what linked Judaism to Christianity than on what separated them.

EB: Quite recently, at the oral defence of a doctoral thesis on the comparative integration of North African Jews in France and Israel, I witnessed a curious display of this typical attitude of nineteenth-century integrated Judaism. A number of people in interview material for the thesis had claimed that biblical references, and the universal values they promoted, played a central role in their own identity. When I pointed out to the candidate that this was perhaps an ad hoc response to what they saw as the expectations of a non-Jewish French researcher, rather than a true reflection of their everyday experience, a number of other scholars on the panel, themselves of Jewish origin, protested that in their families too the only subject of discussion had been the Bible! They undoubtedly grew up in integrated families, or ones with a strong desire to assimilate.

J–CA: The image of the Jews as the people of the Book is a rather exogenous representation of Judaism. One finds it among Christians: Augustine, for instance, makes it the vocation of the Jews to be bearers of a Book, the Old Testament, which announces and vouches for the truth of Christianity, although they themselves do not have the keys with which to understand it. One also finds it in Islam, where the legal-religious concept of 'peoples of the Book' affords special protection to Jews, Christians and Zoroastrians. But only Karaism, a current on the fringes of Judaism, placed the Bible at the centre and rejected the whole rabbinical heritage – and even it, in later periods of its history, was tempted to reclaim selectively some of the extra-biblical rabbinical teachings. It is true, though, that some Jews still under the influence of nineteenth-century 'Israelitism' or Franco-Judaism speak in the kind of way you evoked – unless theirs too is an ad hoc discourse, designed to present an acceptable and attractive image to the outside world.

EB: By eliminating everyday practice, traditional observance and the primacy of the Oral Law from the Jewish landscape …

J–CA: Whereas, according to the normative tradition, what constitutes Judaism is the Oral Law revealed on Sinai and passed down since Moses from master to disciple and generation to generation. Without it, say the rabbis, the Written Law itself would remain a sealed text. We should note here that our (real or fictitious) 'Israelites' are very selective when they speak of the Bible: they expunge four-fifths of the Pentateuch – that is, everything in the five books attributed to Moses which refers to the Law and the commandments – and retain from Scripture only the prophets, the tales, the history of the patriarchs, and of course Exodus, the great epic of liberation. It is a kind of neutered, de-Judaized Bible that can be shared with everyone else as a universal reference. When Jews stress their relationship to the Bible, it means that something is changing. You can see that clearly in the nineteenth century, when the Bible is a means of guaranteeing legitimacy in the eyes of Christian and even secular non-Jews, and when the French Revolution appears to 'Israelites' as neither more nor less than the messianic spirit on the march or even already fulfilled.

EB: A way of joining with everyone around the shared heritage of mankind.

J-CA: Yes, the Bible for all – with the Jews as the ones who produced it and brought it to the rest of humanity! In one go, Jews gain for themselves legitimacy, resemblance and the privilege of anteriority!

EB: And all that is combined with a traditional, if largely revamped, theme of the mission of the Jews among the Nations.

J-CA: And a strongly ethical recasting of the Jews' message to the world. In my view, those contemporary Jewish thinkers who have spoken out strongly against this trend have been right to do so. To lay so much emphasis on ethics is another way of putting aside that which essentially makes Judaism what it is: the Law. Is it true that ethics was invented by the Hebrews and disseminated by the Jews? I know nothing about all that. It also seems to me a way for the West to award itself a patent in morality. Ethics, the ethical imperative, is supposed to be the characteristic legacy of Judaism – therefore of Christianity, therefore of the West. Sometimes you hear it said that human rights are inscribed in the text of the Bible; others, more Jewish, find them in the Talmud. I see all this as a mere drift into apologetics. Human rights are the fruit of a history going back thousands of years, and an essentially Western product. Here there is a link between Jewish ethnocentrism and Western ethnocentrism. Judaism cannot be reduced to a system of ethics, but that does not prevent Jews from living their Judaism as if it were one. But that is quite a different matter.

EB: Let us admit that the diversity of definitions and references can easily confuse an observer external to Judaism. In the eyes of most Christians, the Jew largely remains a fantasy figure; there is nothing really new about that. But, when religion was key to the definition and self-definition of groups, at least everyone could find some bearings and insert the Other into a reassuring framework. Today the Jew is indefinable.

J-CA: There are two reasons for this: first, Jews have changed and no longer recognize themselves only in a religious conception of Judaism; second, non-Jews have also changed. The decline of religious culture, in the Christian West and especially France, prevents ordinary mortals from giving Jews the place they used to have in a general economy of the sacred.

EB: Yet there are staunch Christians who, although they may have broken with the more problematic aspects of the old theology, continue to allocate Jews a quite precisely defined place in the history of Christianity and the history of the world.

J–CA: A new kind of discourse is making itself heard in such quarters – especially in Jewish–Christian friendship societies, which (we should note) tend to involve more Christians than Jews. But this discourse is not at all a common heritage of French society as a whole; it appears in particular, deeply Christian milieux, which have accepted the idea that Judaism is the elder brother, still alive and still useful. This is one way of rehabilitating Judaism, of giving it a legitimacy that it did not really have before. But I also see it as a way of enclosing Judaism within a definition that is, broadly speaking, valid only for Christians, not for Jews. Whereas Christians still define Judaism in relation to Christianity, this is far from necessarily the case with Jews. It is certainly praiseworthy for Christians to give an honourable, indeed more than honourable, status back to Judaism. Yet this also encourages a perception of Judaism and Jews that is still as remote from reality. A Jew who does not know his Bible or his Talmud, who practises his religion faultily or not at all, is the kind of Jew that one is most likely to come across today. He does not see himself as anyone's elder brother. And he is all the more enigmatic for being a Jew none the less.

EB: Non-Jews simply wonder in what sense he can be described as Jewish. Since they do not manage to define him adequately in religious terms, they cling to (non-existent) external signs or to a status in society: the Jew as lawyer, doctor or dentist, never baker or farmer.

J–CA: Or sometimes an academic! But, to return to my previous point, the big issue for Christianity is to find a useful Judaism. There has always been one around, varying from epoch to epoch, ever since the first few centuries AD. Philo the philosopher, for example, or his near-contemporary the historian Flavius Josephus, provided ancient Christianity with a 'ready-to-use' Judaism, even as they themselves were disappearing from the cultural horizon of normative Judaism. We see the same phenomenon with the ancient Greek translation of the Bible, the so-called Septuagint, which was made by Jews. It served as the basis for the Christian reading of the Scriptures, before finally being rejected by Jews themselves. I sometimes wonder whether, for many Jews, even the best-intentioned and least co-optive Christian interpretation of Judaism is not always a little suspect.

EB: There is also Paul – especially Paul.

J–CA: Paul the enigma, whom Jews today tend to blame for every-thing. Jesus was still OK: he was not God, not the Messiah, not really a prophet, but he could easily pass muster as a vaguely non-conformist and generally likeable rabbi. Paul is another matter. He has to carry the can for the fracture, and at the same time it is difficult to recog-nize him as a Jew. There can be no doubt that Paul was a Jew. But what remains of the Jew in Paul? What can possibly be left of Juda-ism in that 'renegade'? It is by no means clear that this is such a major concern within Judaism; recognition of the Jewishness of primitive Christianity is much more a Christian preoccupation. Since the nine-teenth century, the Jewishness of Jesus, his disciples and his milieu has been more and more widely recognized: the idea may still provoke resistance here and there in the Christian world, but it is now solidly established. Among Jews, some may welcome it, while others feel discomfited because it blurs the frontiers.

EB: Is it not the case that the maximum blurring occurs in what is known as Judeo-Christianity or the Judeo-Christian tradition?

J–CA: 'Judeo-Christianity' is a concept that has been taken up by contemporary historians. The term refers to a moment in Jewish and Christian antiquity when the line between the two religions had not yet been clearly drawn, when there could still be Jews faithful to Jesus who continued to subscribe to the Law. As to the 'Judeo-Christian tradition', it involves an ideological view of a characteristic feature of Western civilization, whether that feature is valued or rejected. For some of its denigrators, the tradition is too Jewish, too Oriental, an unseemly Semitic remnant within a West whose first duty is to be Aryan, or Christian. Others attach to it the weight of prohibitions, morality or prejudices from which the West should, rightly, free itself. Finally, for its adulators, the Judeo-Christian tradition is the means of asserting a historical, theological and ethical continuity between Juda-ism and Christianity, but often also a means of shrugging off Judaism in its specificity, in order to highlight a form of Judeo-Christianity that is more Christian than Jewish. I am not sure that these catego-ries are so interesting. In any event, something is hidden behind them which Jews may not be too keen to see: I mean, the fact that if Judaism occupies such a place in the West's consciousness or collec-tive unconscious, while being completely neglected elsewhere, this is thanks to Christianity and not only in spite of it. Since it defined itself in opposition to Judaism, but at the same time as the inheritor of Judaism, and since it has constantly renegotiated its relations with the parent religion, Christianity has objectively placed Jews at the heart of the debate, at the very heart of Western identity. That this has often involved rejection is of little matter. For Christianity has assured Judaism a cultural persistence and centrality that it would not otherwise have had. In Islam, things are already rather less clear.

EB: It is enough to go outside the frontiers of monotheistic culture, in Asia, to discover that there Judaism counts for nothing and for no one. That can be quite a relief for the Jewish traveller!

J–CA: Both the West and Jews tend to forget that certain issues which haunt us and tear us apart are of absolutely no consequence outside our little cultural universe.

EB: But, to return to the ambiguous relationship between Christianity and Judaism, it may be that it is at the root of anti-Judaism and later of anti-Semitism. The weight of a past debt, in a way.

J–CA: But I would stress that the debt is not only on one side. Christianity and Islam are not only offspring of Judaism; it is not always so easy to say which is the parent and which the child. If one is at all fair about the historical evolution of Judaism, one cannot but admit that it too has been a debtor. It has continually redefined, rethought and enriched itself, changing in response to the other two monotheisms that are at once close to it and different. Rabbinical Judaism would not be what it is if there had been no Christianity. Medieval Judaism, in both the Orient and the West, would not have become what it did without the Arab-Muslim philosophical, theological, linguistic and cultural challenge. Judaism is therefore a child of Christianity and Islam, perhaps as much as the other way round.

EB: These questions of descent are at the heart of a debate that people are now trying to calm. Dialogues, meetings and institutional links have created a new stability in relations.

J–CA: No doubt it was a good thing that the Pope went to Jerusalem. But the actions of the Pope do not much affect either Jews or de-Christianized Christians. A Western Christian must already have a special kind of informed and structured relationship with Christianity in order to ask questions about the Jewish roots of his tradition, or about the links that should be maintained with a still living Judaism. That is a welcome phenomenon, but it is limited to a minority. For most people, it all remains pretty vague.

EB: Still, you can't help noticing the interest that Christians, and not only Christians, have in the Jewish cultural heritage.

J-CA: That interest may not be such a new thing. The exegetical literature of medieval Christianity already concerned itself with 'the Hebrew truth', and in trying to discover it did not hesitate to turn to the judgement of the rabbis and their treatment of certain difficulties in the biblical texts. What is new today is that a current within Christianity can no longer form a clear view of itself without referring positively, and with a sense of guilt, to Judaism. This is a modern phenomenon, whose roots go back to the nineteenth century. Christian philo-Semitism is not a post-war invention.

EB: But the new awareness that came after the last world war has played a crucial role. The Jewish historian Jules Isaac, whose wife and daughter perished in the camps, worked towards a profound renewal of Christian–Jewish relations, founding in 1948 the Amitié judéo-chrétienne that still exists today and publishes the journal *Sens*. Co-author of the famous Mallet-Isaac history manuals, which helped to form generations of French schoolchildren, he urged Pope John XXIII to recast the Church's relations with Judaism. But it was only in the mid-1960s, with the Second Vatican Council and the *Nostra Aetate* declaration on non-Christian religions, that the Catholic Church officially broke with its 'teaching of scorn' and began to stress the underlying unity between Christianity and Judaism; it asked believers radically to transform their attitude to the Jews, stigmatized any manifestation of anti-Semitism and called for a climate of mutual understanding and respect.

J-CA: The friendship societies date from the post-war period. But what about the 1930s?

EB: Faced with the outpouring of hatred against the Jews, many Christians took their side. *La Vie catholique* (founded *inter alia* to combat the ideas of Action française), the intellectual journal *Esprit* and the Dominican weekly *Sept* were only some of the centres disseminating the principles of Christian philo-Semitism. Oscar de Férenzy, whose journal *La Juste Parole* appeared between 1936 and 1940, played a major role in this struggle.

J-CA: This revaluation of Judaism, as it were, and the recognition that it did not die with Christianity but may still be a living source of inspiration, cannot fail to gratify Jewish observers. Nevertheless, that is more a Christian than a Jewish affair. Christians cannot form a clear view of themselves without referring to Judaism, and they can refer to it in different ways. The dominant discourse today is rather encouraging, from a Jewish point of view, although it should be added that the Judaism which enjoys such enhanced standing among Christians is not one in which all Jews could so easily recognize themselves. For many Jews, Judaism has nothing to do with religion, and a secular Jew might not appreciate the way in which Christians smother it with a religious sauce, and a Christian one at that. Moreover, Judaism is not only what it shares with Christianity: a moral creed, a basis in the Ten Commandments, the Revelation, and so on. It is also the Law, which cannot be written off just like that. What is the validity of the Law? Was it merely the veiled annunciation of a world that was destined to do without it? What justification can there be for Jews today to continue observing all the provisions of the Law? Many of these questions are still outstanding.

EB: In this respect, the bitterness of the medieval disputes does not really conceal the reality of what was sometimes a more profound, more radical debate.

J–CA: There is no point in becoming nostalgic, and we should not attach inordinate value to verbal jousting that soon turned to the disadvantage of the Jews. But it is true that, from a certain point of view, the medieval period was a 'golden age' of intellectual dialogue between Judaism and Christianity. Despite the massacres, expulsions and persecutions, the cultural and ideological encounter seems to have then been greater and clearer than it was in late antiquity or than it became in modern times; Christian intellectuals displayed real interest (not always tainted with hostility or even apologetic purposes) in rabbinical learning. Of course, the Middle Ages produced an abundance of Christian polemical literature against Judaism. But, apart from the aim of converting the Jews – an aim, moreover, not always clearly attested – this literature sustained a determination to define Christianity in relation, if often also in opposition, to Judaism. At the same time, Jews began to produce a matching anti-Christian literature, in defence of Judaism against Christianity – one of the things you do not see in late antiquity, when Christian anti-Jewish polemics elicited nothing, or almost nothing, in response. At the moment, there is no fully convincing explanation of the reasons and the significance of this imbalance in late antiquity. The truth is that the first serious Jewish thinking about Christianity really developed only in the Middle Ages and the pre-modern era. It then emerged again, in a calmer, less polemical and sometimes brilliant form, among a number of Jewish thinkers of the late nineteenth and early twentieth centuries. Today, however, if we exclude a few marginal efforts that are not very convincing …

EB: In any case, it is now the relations with Islam that have become the least irenic.

J–CA: The problem for Islam is different: it stems from the reversal of roles, from the autonomy gained by the *dhimmi*, the protected second-class subject of old. On the ground, in Palestine and Israel, the *dhimmi* is now dominant and is reducing the Palestinian Muslims to a condition of 'dhimmitude'. And it must be added, after all, that certain forms of Islam have taken over all the clichés of Western anti-Semitism.

EB: Those clichés began to enter the Middle East in the nineteenth century, and since then the Israeli–Arab conflict has naturally played a role. But things are a lot more complicated. And perhaps we should avoid reducing the whole conflict to its religious dimension. In Israel itself the negative figure is not so much Islam as the Arab: or, rather, the two are closely entangled with each other. The average Israeli scarcely makes a distinction between the Arab enemy and the Muslim enemy, and this relationship to the Muslim (or Arab) Other remains ambivalent, even among Jews coming from North Africa. There is all the bitterness towards the Arabs from the time of their departure, which the present conflict can only exacerbate. But, at the same time, the Arab world of their origins tends to become an imagined lost paradise.

J–CA: In spite of everything, there remains a tendency to mythologize or idealize the Moroccan or Tunisian Arab they left behind. Often you will hear them say: 'Our Arabs weren't the same'; or 'Back in Tunisia the ones I liked most were not the Jews but the Arabs.' But there is also a profound enmity, a kind of determination to draw a line between themselves and the Palestinian or Israeli Arab. The two attitudes may go together in the same individual. There may also be a tendency to mythologize Islam as such, making it the closest thing there is to Judaism, as well as a violent and understandable rejection of hardline, fundamentalist Islam.

EB: The feelings that Jews from Arab countries feel or express are complicated by the variety of relations they used to have with their country of origin. It is well known, for instance, that the Iraqi Jews did not want to emigrate to Israel; recent work by historians suggests that it was Zionist agents who precipitated their departure by placing a bomb in a Baghdad synagogue that caused great damage and sowed panic among the local Jewish population. As to the North African Jews, they left because they had every reason to fear the future after the various states of the region became independent. It is quite a complicated story, therefore. Today, scarcely any Jews are left in the Muslim countries – except in Turkey, where there are said to be 15,000 to 20,000.

J-CA: Anyway, let us avoid idealizing things. Jews in Muslim countries did not generally experience the humiliations of Christian Europe. But that does not mean that, even in the Middle Ages, there were not extremist Islamic currents capable of decimating whole communities.

EB: Jews coming from Muslim countries kept a certain image of Islam, with its high points and low points, and they easily imagined that their lives there had been more pleasant. No doubt this was not entirely wrong, especially in the Ottoman Empire, whose structure was rather specific. In a mosaic of cultures and religions, where the central power was remote and the population was organized along confessional lines, both Christians and Jews had their place – even if it was not always as well defined as people sometimes think. When the equilibrium later broke down, through the rise of nation-states and the fragmentation of the Empire, things took a turn for the worse. It was these national demands, both within the Empire and then in the independent states resulting from its dismemberment, which poisoned inter-confessional relations in the late nineteenth and early twentieth centuries and, as we have seen in the tragic case of the former Yugo-slavia, right down to the present day.

J-CA: Something else we should bear in mind is that the age when the break-up was taking place also witnessed a growing pres-ence of the West, either through colonization (as in North Africa) or through a powerful economic thrust sometimes taking the form of a kind of economic colonization (as in the Ottoman Empire). As the intrusion of settlers turned communities against one another, Jews were caught in the middle and partly identified with the West – which created a new division between them and the local Muslim or Arab or Arab-Muslim population. They emigrated because they could not identify with the local nationalism, with the local Arab identity, having long had their eyes turned to the West.

EB: Everywhere, from India to North Africa, Jews took the side of the settlers, expecting from them an improved status and even access to citizenship. And when the settlers left and abandoned them, they followed in their steps. They could not keep going their own way in the new national states, in whose struggles they had not generally participated.

J-CA: So, not everything can be laid at the door of the Israeli–Arab conflict. The worsening of relations began before that.

EB: Today's Middle East was born out of the ashes of the Ottoman Empire and a disorder for which the European powers were largely responsible, having divided it up more with their own interests in mind than with those of the local populations. In the case of Israel, however, it seems to me that the conflict is not between Jews and Muslims but between Israelis and Arabs. It is a national and territorial conflict.

J-CA: Nevertheless, both sides instrumentalize the religious dimension. To a degree that varies with the needs of the situation, the national conflict is dressed up as a religious conflict.

EB: On the Israeli side, as we have seen, a good example of this confusion is a group like Gush Emunim, the Bloc of the Faithful, whose religious activists have taken over the Zionist ethos of work on the land – or, rather, occupation of the land. By combining these two sources of inspiration – irredentist Zionism and a combative religiosity – such groups are putting religion back at the centre of the national political arena. Nor are they alone in doing this: a coupling of religion and nationalism is also taking place among the Palestinians. It is not only political conviction, but also an intensely honed faith, profound despair and massive humiliation which lead people to sacrifice themselves in suicide attacks against the Israeli population.

8 | Secularization and Jewish morality

J-CA: But, without forgetting cases of political instrumentalization, let us come back to more endogenous considerations. Being-a-Jew goes beyond the religious dimension: it can even do without it altogether.

EB: Do you really think so?

J-CA: I am a little surprised that it is you who is raising some doubt! You know that that is where the difference lies between the rabbis and people like us, and that it even explains why we are generally optimistic, while they are rather pessimistic.

EB: Assimilation – yes, that is what haunts the rabbis.

J–CA: As well as quite a few community leaders.

EB: But maybe assimilation is not as much on the agenda as they think. Identities are re-forming, not necessarily being diluted. The excessive worries are perhaps due to a lack of historical vision.

J–CA: Some Orthodox have such a restrictive definition of Judaism that Jews like us no longer count as Jews.

EB: Maybe it's because we do not fulfil all 613 commandments laid down by the Law. But at least, with our work on the Jews, we are busying ourselves with the 614th.

J–CA: But there is no 614th commandment! You can invent one if you like, but it won't count.

EB: But look, we ourselves are going a little further. We mark the great points in life's cycle, celebrate the great festivals in our way, even if we do not practise in our daily lives. We behave exactly as other people do in other traditions: we take from religion only what helps us to organize the structure of our identity.

J–CA: But maybe the rabbis and upholders of Orthodoxy are not completely wrong. Once you give up the idea that the Jewish people is a people of priests, whose main function is to serve God and to apply his commandments, it does become very difficult to define a Judaism that can really hold up to the passing of time, or even to justify the simple fact of its continued existence. If the Jewish people is not first of all a people of priests, what is it? And why should it go on being what it is? That is the real question. The Orthodox have a simple answer: 'What was wrong was the betrayal, the renunciation.' That is all very well, but it is a little late in the day to be saying it. Such notions will not convince many people, and most Jews have well and truly given up that kind of definition of Jewish identity. It is not easy to propose something in its place, something that can unify and historically justify in the same degree. What historical justification can be given for the survival of a secularized Jewish people? Secular Jews struggle to find an answer, and that is doubtless why they reply in such diverse ways. Among both rabbis and secular Jews, therefore, there is a kind of disarray, a sense of sudden impoverishment as well as of a wide range of possible options and a great diversity of choices. That is what is sowing perplexity – not only the emptiness but also the superabundance.

EB: Still, I also see all these variants of being-a-Jew as a huge source of wealth. It is true that they have to be handled, and that that is a difficult task. Does a circular Judaism – which, in my view, is not Judaism – provide a way of handling these problems more easily? Is the best way of being a Jew to cut oneself off from the world and, in so doing, to undergo irreversible impoverishment? I am not an out-and-out supporter of universalism. The 'universal' is Christian. The universal is Christian, male and Western. But that universal deserves to be redefined and consciously assumed.

J–CA: The way you speak, the moderate differentialism that it expresses, has, if I may say so, curiously traditionalist echoes. God, as creator of the world, is certainly not forgotten in Orthodox Judaism, and, of course, he is always recognized as a universal power. But that God looks less interesting than a clearly more 'particularist' God, the one who reveals himself to the people of Israel and gives it a Law.

EB: But universality? The contemporary world wants Jews both to live as everyone else and to preserve a certain identity. Today, modernity permits us that kind of makeshift approach in which everyone 'does it their way' – and it's just too bad if a tension makes itself felt between religious Jewishness and secular Jewishness, between the Shabbat Jew and the Kippur Jew (who attends the synagogue only for that great autumn fast, often mainly to please his parents). It is that tension which makes Judaism a living reality, and its rifts also give rise to cultural production and encourage further thought that will make it possible to move ahead. No doubt I am dreaming. But it is a historian's dream: those are the tensions of the modern epoch, which have faced Jews ever since they left the ghetto. They have not been resolved, but Judaism has not disappeared for all that.

J–CA: All the dietary laws that Judaism imposes on the faithful are a good indication of these trends. In principle, they are a key element of social differentiation, since their strict application obviously limits contact between Jews and non-Jews. You don't go to eat with non-Jews, you don't drink with them. In fact, this system has a long history: the Bible already lists a number of quite precise dietary regulations, which then become wider and more complex in the post-biblical period and down to the Middle Ages. So, how do things stand today? Well, many a Jew is quite happy to be (more or less) kosher at home, but not kosher outside. It is a way of remaining Jewish while mixing with Gentiles. Let us note in passing that this kind of arrangement may not be as new as one might think. Already in the pre-emancipation period, there is evidence of meals in common – we do not really know what they were like. Compromise formulas seem to have been worked out at quite an early date.

EB: We know that, among certain elites in medieval Spain, laxity was pretty much the rule – even in sexual life! Dietary laws were doubtless not closely followed among such people, who ate at Muslim and later Christian tables. And what should we say of that secular Hebrew poetry celebrating the pleasures of the beloved and the flesh, good wine, fair women and beautiful boys? Mere conventions borrowed from Arabic models? Or evocations of life as it was being lived? At the end of the medieval period, this free lifestyle found other enthusiasts – for example, among the Portuguese Marranos who returned to Judaism in the late sixteenth and especially the seventeenth century.

J-CA: Nor should we forget that a constant feature of Jewish homilies, whether actually delivered or merely drafted, was a denunciation of the trespasses of the Jews of the time: our contemporaries are not measuring up; they are falling down in observance of the commandments; their faith is failing; the purity of their family relations is no longer preserved. Either denunciation of sins was simply integral to the literary genre of the sermon, or else our idealized view of the past has been rather wide of the mark. Laxity of morals and a merely approximative attitude to the Law would not seem to be practices that began only yesterday.

EB: The *carpe diem* morality expressed in the secular poetry is quite remarkable. Society events, court life, literary jousting, sumptuous feasts: they certainly enjoyed living well in those days. One and the same person – Judah Halevi, for instance – could at the same or successive moments of his life write epicurean verse celebrating the physical beauty of pretty boys, compose magnificent liturgical songs, defend Judaism against its detractors, write a work of science or philosophy, and finally, in old age, set off for the land of Israel. Is this the Jew who is usually thought of as wrapped up in himself, sheltered from all corrupting influences? The Judah Halevis, Abraham ibn Ezras and Solomon ibn Gabirols are sufficient evidence of the cultural interpenetration – and a little later, in the south of France, we find Jewish poets inspired by courtly poetry. Never has the Jewish world been as monolithic or shrivelled as certain contemporary representations would have us believe. It is as if a monolithic, shrivelled Judaism gave some people today a greater sense of security.

J-CA: Even the liturgy, on the face of it a more frozen side of Judaism, actually has a history rich in new developments. Its language is usually Hebrew, with a few passages in Aramaic, but at times it can also be Judeo-Arabic, Judeo-Spanish, Judeo-Persian or Yiddish. It has a number of key elements, which vary little from community to community and are capable of being integrated into different wholes. But one also sees medieval Spanish poets reject outright the ancient tradition of the liturgical poem inherited from the Holy Land, and propose completely novel rules of religious composition. During the morning service, men everywhere wear a white, fringed prayer shawl with black or blue stripes. All of them cover their heads during prayer, but the kippa or hat used takes the most varied forms. Similarly, in Muslim countries some usually took their shoes off before entering the synagogue. A diversity of rituals, texts and musical traditions is the rule. Change and external influences spare neither the forms of prayer nor those of worship.

EB: God himself is not safe – so the rumour has it.

J-CA: The debate is still going on about that. There is certainly a long tradition concerning the complete alterity of the godhead: his essence is usually, though not always, conceived as fundamentally other. Everyone agrees that he does not undergo incarnation, that he never takes bodily form. But, at the same time, he is someone near. It is not only the hidden God, or the terrible God, who reveals himself on Sinai. There is also an everyday God, who looks at what people do and judges it, who does or does not inscribe in the Book of the Living those who fast on Yom Kippur. There is also an immanent God – in a sense, a familiar God.

EB: It would even seem that he is there for non-believers. In the Eastern Balkan communities from which I come, people were often – sometimes since long ago – not very religious at all. Even for us, however, God was part of the landscape, in the same way as our neighbours. You didn't necessarily visit them, but there were things you didn't do because you never knew what they might say!

J-CA: You are right to stress that God is not only completely beyond what we are; he is also very close. And then, he has his inter-mediaries: the prophets. Elijah, for instance, that strange figure who is expected at the ritual Passover meal. In real life, he was certainly no joker: the Bible tells of him happily slitting the throats of idolatrous prophets. In popular tradition, however, he has become a very simple human character who brings tidings of good joy. He heralds the Messiah, of course, but he also tells individuals of some good fortune to come, offers a solution or a form of protection, gives a piece of advice.

EB: A curious proximity. Elijah: the messiah before his time?

J-CA: Certainly Elijah has a messianic dimension, but you might come across him on any street corner. He is a little like those Greek divinities who could take on the features of a beggar, a passer-by or a traveller. You find characters like that in Judaism, who in effect play the role of intercessors. The supernatural permeates the everyday life of traditional Jews. And then there are the saints – which is the right word for them.

EB: The Jewish cult of the saints always borrows some of its features from the local civilization. Esther, for example, becomes 'Holy Queen Esther' for the Marranos, a model who hid her religion to enter the gynaeceum of the Persian King Ahasuerus and later married him. It was her 'Marranism' *avant la lettre* which, in the second part of the story, enabled her to save her people from destruction.

J-CA: The same phenomenon exists within normative Judaism itself, where certain figures are the object of a real veneration. Their tombs have become destinations of pilgrimage – a practice especially common in North Africa. But one also finds it in Ashkenazi Judaism, as in Hassidism, with its charismatic *tsaddikim* who are at once community leaders, dynastic chiefs and miracle-workers. Who, in one Jewish shop or another, has not come across a photo of Rabbi Menachem Mendel Schneersohn, the now-deceased leader of the Lubavitch movement, or Baba Sale, the venerated Moroccan buried at Netivot, in Israel? They may not exactly be saints, but they are mediators between the divine and the human. Judaism has that too, even if it often claims the opposite. Such figures are not gods incarnate, but they are, like Jacob's ladder, the link between Heaven and Earth.

EB: What happens when God and his saints are missing, when religious practice has disappeared and commitment to the articles of faith has dwindled to a minimum, when Jews, having left their original milieu to face an outside world they value, nevertheless wish to retain their Jewishness as a strong component of their identity? What do they have left, especially if they are not, like you or I, 'Jews by profession'? What else – despite the reservations you expressed earlier – other than ethics? Jewish ethics, if it exists, is the religion of Jews who have lost all religion – in short, the religion of the irreligious. At least it has the merit of being universalizable: it can be addressed to others; it is neither abstract nor impracticable. Personally, I am in favour of a positive Judaism, and I live my Judaism in a positive manner. Like the philosopher Franz Rosenzweig, I feel myself to be a member of a people – but a people of the world. The Jew is the man of the world. This desire for alterity and this desire for justice are, in my view, characteristic of a Jewish way of relating to the world that still has strongly religious elements, without the punctilious observance of the commandments. I see it as a Judaism which, though secularized, remains Jewish. It is that in Judaism which guides me and still gives me an awareness of being Jewish, as well as the desire to remain Jewish. With that primacy given to life, proclaimed at every moment.

J–CA: Not in an undifferentiated way, though. I am thinking of a casuistic problem mentioned in the ancient rabbinical sources and reconsidered, in our own times, by a Jewish nationalist we have already come across: Ahad Ha'Am. Two men are crossing a desert and have with them only one goatskin of water. If they share its contents they will both die of thirst; if one drinks it all, the other will die but he will be saved. What is the most ethical solution to the problem? It is this: the man carrying the goatskin drinks the water and is saved. This may appear shocking, and contrary to the principle of a genuine altruism. Yet, if we imagine that both men are equally altruistic and share the same taste for sacrifice, the fear is that neither will agree to drink the goatskin of water. Life is the primary consideration, however. One of them must die, since then at least the other can be saved. And the choice must be made in all objectivity, without any pathos. The Bible, the objective source of authority, is clear on this point: 'Thou shalt love thy neighbour as thyself' (Leviticus 19:18). As thyself, not more than thyself. The one with the goatskin should drink: that is the only possible ethical decision, since ethics begins with one's duties to oneself. That is an idea which runs counter to spontaneous morality. Let us also note that, in this case, the solution to the dilemma is based on a scriptural text, and a precise interpretation – some will say an overinterpretation – of that text. Perhaps we should see this as typically Jewish. But I would stress that ethics is simply a human preoccupation. At least I hope it is.

EB: I am not at all religious, whereas at heart you are.

J–CA: Possibly. But that which was true one day may well cease to be true. My religion is highly residual: it has been reduced to the status of a question – a question, moreover, which does not torment me. That is a bad sign.

EB: For my part, when I am asked in what sense I am Jewish, I reply that I am Jewish because I observe certain rules, a certain kind of conduct which, though not strictly religious, stems from a past which is no longer my present but has left its mark on it. These norms of conduct are dictated to me by an experience of life, and perhaps also by a religion that I no longer know how to practise. You have known religion, you have or had more faith than I (no one could have less), so maybe your morality is made differently.

J-CA: What you call morality, I would have called a kind of relationship to the world that is shaped by one's Jewish condition and Jewish past. As I said, I find it very difficult to make ethics the distinctive feature of Judaism, because to reduce Judaism to ethics would involve diluting it into something that is no longer Judaism. And, strange though it may seem, to Judaize ethics is to imagine that certain moral demands might not be shared by others. All that worries me a little. I would rather tend to speak of a certain kind of Jewish attitude to universal ethical problems, an attitude determined or inflected by a Jewish experience of life and the constancy of a particular Jewish history. I can imagine that, in an individual Jew, a tendency to react intensely to injustice might be somehow reinforced by an awareness of the persecutions or injustices that he, his family or his people have undergone. But I wouldn't really go any further than that. The ethics of Mount Sinai? But what do people actually know about Sinai? I have the impression that this so-called ethical heritage of Mount Sinai is a kind of middle-of-the-road formula with no cutting edge, shared by all and shared by none. Judaism has, of course, produced a body of writing on ethics, and it is highly instructive to read it. But, I repeat, Judaism has also and mainly developed a way of thinking about the Law.

EB: Is not the ethics I have in mind a group unconscious, passed on to the least religious members of the group at the end of a long companionship in Judaism? That is more or less how I think of it. Judaism did not invent ethics, but ethics was also there in Judaism. And that ethics guided generations, in its religious form or in another.

J-CA: Let us say, then, that there is a Jewish application of ethics, a Jewish way of thinking about justice and putting it into practice.

EB: Not only justice. Attentiveness to others – to their weakness, their suffering, their poverty.

J–CA: Those are biblical themes, but also post-biblical. It is they which lay behind the creation of fundamental institutions in the Jewish community: a society to distribute clothing to the poor, another to marry poor girls without a dowry, another to visit the sick.

EB: You wouldn't deny that there is a distinctively Jewish way of handling ethical or social problems.

J–CA: Of course not. Take the *tzedakah*, for example, the act of 'charity' understood as a veritable tax, a returning to the needy of the share due to them. It is not only generosity, which comes like that – from the heart. One even sets limits to the charity: no more than a fifth of your income, no less than a tenth. The point is not to make yourself poor instead of the poor. Similarly, the giving should take place discreetly, so that 'the left hand does not know what the right hand gives'. I see that as a traditionally Jewish way of giving 'charity', which is to be found both in the texts and in practice.

9 | Being a woman and Jewish

EB: That does not mean that these ethical principles cannot be universalized: it goes without saying that I do not want to keep everything within a Jewish framework! Personally, though, I try to deal with my ethical conduct in that way, as if I really do have that legacy. Then there are also the regional peculiarities. Let us not forget that Mediterranean Jews may have a less individualist idea of society and human relations, which sometimes makes them closer to or more caring about other people. But those are just variants, and I think it is hard to define them in a strictly normative manner. Here is another question for you. Do you think that the status which traditional Judaism reserves for women is perfectly ethical?

J–CA: First of all – before we become sterner in what we have to say – let us be clear that the status of women should not be presented as if it was frozen once and for all. It evolved during the Middle Ages, under pressure from historical circumstances and the surrounding world. There was a move from acceptance or tolerance of polygamy to compulsory monogamy, among not only Ashkenazis but also Sephardis.

EB: Let us recall the famous rule forbidding polygamy in the Ashkenazi world, a rule attributed to Rabbi Gershom ben Judah, known as 'the Light of the Exile', who lived in the late tenth to early eleventh century AD. That and similar texts circulated with authority among Jews, and in fact the standards they laid down were already widely practised before their formal promulgation. But customs may have varied.

J-CA: The Sephardi and Oriental world was not uniform in this respect. Jews were generally monogamous, except in a number of outlying regions. In Morocco or Yemen, for instance, polygamy persisted until shortly before the emigration to France or Israel – residually, not as a normal institution – even if the rabbis advised against having more than one wife or family, on the grounds that they would be difficult to manage.

EB: Let us also remember the custom of the levirate, which was compulsory for a woman whose husband died without leaving descendants.

J-CA: But there were still two options: either the widow married the childless dead man's brother to give him a surrogate descendant, or she took part in a ritual involving removal of her brother-in-law's shoes, which freed her of the obligation to marry him. Historically, the rabbinical authorities tended to favour the latter solution, in order to avoid polygamy and forced marriages. The positive evolution of women's status is evident throughout the history of Jewish law. On the question of divorce, for example, although men still keep the initiative, a rabbinical court may exert pressure for an unworthy husband to grant the 'repudiation' that his wife demands.

EB: Think also of the unhappy case of a deserted wife whose husband refuses a divorce or disappears without trace. Unless it can be proved that he is dead, the rabbis forbid remarriage so as to avoid any risk of adulterous procreation.

J-CA: No doubt a lot remains to be done in Jewish law to strengthen the autonomy of women, and to make their status more like that of men.

EB: Still, many Orthodox women feel that they blossom as women in Judaism. It is difficult to draw a dividing line here between myth and reality. Perhaps these women are sometimes seeking to convince themselves, or even consenting to their own alienation (especially if they have returned to Orthodox Judaism late in life). In the long term, however, the status of women in the Jewish religion – as in all monotheisms – can hardly be described as equal.

J-CA: That is obviously true. But it is not easy to say whether that is an essential part of Judaism or only a hangover from traditional societies. In any event, it may have something to do with God's male-ness: God the Father – who is also the God of the Fathers, of Abra-ham, Isaac and Jacob – is clearly a male being, even if the kabbalistic tradition in particular also recognizes femininity in God. *Shekhina*, the divine immanence, the presence of God in the world, the part of God which resides on earth, is feminine. Femininity does have a place in the kabbalistic representation of the higher world. But the problems of hierarchy remain, even in the idea that the male and female in God are complementary and should be in harmony with each other. On the whole, what dominates is a strongly male image of the divinity. The tradition itself is carried by men: Abraham is father of the nation. There is also Sarah, of course, but it is not she but Abraham who dis-covers monotheism. And the transmission of knowledge, faith and values is also carried out by men.

EB: Yes, although there are some clearly defined exceptions. We know, for example, that in a situation of fear and withdrawal – when the home replaced the synagogue, which it was no longer possible to attend – it was the Marrano women who for generations were the re-positories and mistresses of the oral tradition that ensured the survival of a crypto-Jewish identity. When the written texts and male sociability lost the means of imposing themselves, it was women who re-created a tradition and passed on a whole body of ritual and learning.

J-CA: The same was true of the liturgy: the Marrano prayers were passed down by women. When men are forced to give up power, the model undergoes a real break. In the Marrano context, masculinity entered into decline and book-learning dropped out of the picture. Judaism ceased to be a religion of the written word and, in effect, became the religion of women.

EB: That did not last long. As soon as the crypto-Jews returned to mainstream Judaism in more clement lands, books once more gained the upper hand – and, with books, men again took charge of the ritual and therefore of the power of religious speech. It is always in periods of crisis that women have managed to create a place for themselves within Judaism; it was they, for example, who opened the way to a Jewish modernity in the period before emancipation. The *salonnières*, those cultivated Jewish women of the eighteenth century who had received from their demanding fathers a wide-ranging cultural educa-tion and an apprenticeship in languages and music, organized *salons* in their homes for the best non-Jewish society that brought together men and women, Jewish intellectuals and non-Jewish intellectuals, and thereby raised the image of Jews in the eyes of the intelligentsia. Women such as Dorothea Schlegel (daughter of the famous figure of the Jewish Enlightenment, Moses Mendelssohn), Fanny von Arnstein in Vienna, Henrietta Hertz in Berlin or Rahel Varnhagen (immortalized in Hannah Arendt's biography) were veritable trailblazers for the emancipation. At those crucial moments, while men were still hesitating, they took the plunge and acted as couriers of ideas.

J-CA: It was not only in periods of crisis or sociological transition that women played this kind of role. Even in the pre-modern era, one finds eminent (or dominant) female personalities come to the fore in a context of widowhood – for, in the end, it was when their husband died that women really came of age and achieved independence. There were businesswomen, female heads of families, and women in control of their own property and their own fate. The case of Gluckel of Hameln, in the late seventeenth to early eighteenth century, is emblematic in this respect: she was the first female memorialist in the Yiddish language.

EB: We should add that, for all the restrictions, women also cleared a path for themselves in the domain of the ritual – for example, through the *tehines*, those Yiddish liturgical compositions mostly written by women. Some were even able to read scriptural texts, and commentaries on them translated or compiled in Yiddish. In this way, women became more aware of the limits of the space given them by men, and were able to expand that space, however modestly.

J-CA: I agree that women had access to a certain kind of learning, including written learning, in the medium of the Jewish vernaculars, but most of the literature in question was produced by men for women. We therefore have to be a little more precise: it was male literature for a female public. Nor was it at the top of the hierarchy of knowledge, or of literature. Texts in Hebrew and Aramaic, the Scripture and the Talmud, remained an essentially male preserve. It is certainly praiseworthy to chart the history of the exceptions, citing this or that female single child whom her father brought up more or less as a boy. But that does not change the general picture.

EB: The vernacular often served as a refuge for excluded women. Thus, in the late eighteenth century, the Eastern Sephardi world threw up a new literature consisting of biblical commentary in Judeo-Spanish, which drew on tales, anecdotes and teachings from the

ancient rabbinical stock: the *Meam Loez*. This literature grew richer
in the course of the nineteenth and early twentieth centuries. One of
my own grandmothers was well known for her marvellous knowledge
of it: she could recite it by heart, and scholars were said to come and
consult her.

J-CA: She could recite it by heart, you say. Had she ever read the
texts in question, or was her knowledge of it purely oral? There have
always been knowledgeable women. But what were the nature and
the limitations of their knowledge? For a long time, scientific research
into Judaism and its history skipped anything to do with women.
Things have been progressing in these areas, especially on the other
side of the Atlantic, but is enough work being done on anthropology?
Is there enough research into domestic rituals or vernacular cultures?
The traditional scholarly emphasis on written texts in Hebrew or
Aramaic is still due to the domination of men. To be excluded from
the sacred language is no mere trifle. I always tell my students never
to forget that there is no gender parity in Judaism, and that what we
study are the words of men.

EB: Are you not going too far? After all, women did manage
to create a place, to clear a way for themselves, minor though it
remained. The appropriation of the texts in the vernacular was of
considerable significance for them; it was a strategy, a way of not
being totally excluded. Anyway, we should be wary of the myth that
all Jewish women were unable to read or write. Today we are less
ignorant than we used to be about the position of women in Jewish
culture: we know, for example, that they might be literate in Yiddish
while remaining illiterate in Hebrew.

J-CA: Most often, women found a way of affirming their cultural autonomy, even in relation to religious worship. There is even
an Orthodox female apology for all the special practices imposed on
women: abstinence from sexual relations and conjugal contact during
the menstrual period; the ritual bath marking the end of the period;
the concealment of the body and the hair because of their power to
arouse male sensuality, and so on. Both men and women have interpreted or experienced these rules in a variety of ways. But they could
also acquire a highly repressive tone, if what they mainly expressed
was male fear of everything in women that had to do with the mys-
tery of life and death. Unlike other religions, Judaism certainly did not
develop an excessive wariness of physical pleasure – on the contrary,

it attached great value to it, within certain limits. Yet Jewish men do have a traditional mistrust of women. Just think of the female demons associated with them (Lilith being the most famous case in point), even if women too could be their victims. Or think of the suspicion that women have a sexual appetite which is difficult to assuage. All the constraints imposed on women are also protective devices that men erect between themselves and women.

EB: They have been invented by men. It is a male reading of religion.

J–CA: That being said, there are ways (including Orthodox ways) of living with these prohibitions and restrictions which make it possible to subvert their primary significance, either in reality or in fantasy. Some Orthodox women, for instance, perceive all this as a way of affirming their autonomy: the fact that they must periodically keep a distance from their husband becomes a means of escaping male power, of ceasing to be a permanent object of desire in thrall to that desire. The way is thus opened to an almost 'feminist' reading of these prohibitions. Anyway, let us not reduce the Orthodoxy of Jewish women to wigs and woollen stockings.

EB: Jewish women, whether their heads are shaven or they are seen as sensual, have often been the stuff of fantasy for Christian men. This is a constant theme in literature. One has only to read Balzac's *Splendeurs et misères des courtisanes*, where the Jewess and the Oriental woman come together in a single character with irresistible seductive power, capable of ruining any man who surrenders to it. Nineteenth-century literature was very fond of this *femme fatale* – painting, too. Think of Delacroix, with his beautiful Jewish women from Morocco. The woman, the Jewish woman, the Oriental woman, with all her fascination, is the quintessence of the Other – the temptress or demon who catches the non-Jewish man in her toils. Think also of the stereotypes in the oldest pictorial traditions. What is a Jewish woman? Judith severing the head of Holofernes. Or Salome dancing and obtaining the head of John the Baptist. This attraction for the Jewish woman is still fully with us today, but it has taken a new form in which amazement is mingled with disbelief. Even the ultra-Orthodox woman excites the male imagination – this time as the woman who denies all sensuality and thus becomes still more strange and alluring. Even if she does not fit in with the norms, she exerts at least an intellectual attraction. But you are right: it is necessary to develop a more sophisticated picture. Religious, Orthodox women have not always been tied to the domestic world – and today they are so less than in the past. They work in various sectors of the economy, in professions ranging from psychology to computers. In this respect, modern Jewish Orthodoxy hardly differs from a certain kind of modern Islam. The tendencies are similar in the two.

J-CA: But that can also be the price for machismo. Once the Jewish man is someone who studies the Law, who spends all his time studying the Law, someone else has to keep the home going. And for a long time, while the man studied, it was also the woman who had to work – not only in modern society, but in traditional societies as well.

EB: Today, some Orthodox women express demands akin to those of women from other, non-religious circles, while giving them a different complexion more in keeping with their own experience. Our judgement of them should not treat them as a single bloc. Quasi-feminist voices are heard even within the groups in question. It is hard to believe, but …

J-CA: It's just that for those women it is still difficult to escape a traditional division of tasks. Femininity is posed as an absolute and certain tasks perceived as typically feminine: the education of young children, the observance of dietary rules at home, but also certain forms of philanthropy. Apart from the labour market, which is open to them but is part of the non-Jewish realm, there are a number of social activities within the Jewish community in which women can find fulfilment. But they are female activities. The model is holding up for the moment, at least in certain milieux, but it is collapsing among liberals and conservatives. There, what you find is a redefinition of gender roles, or even the breakdown of any division of roles. If women want it, they can have access to the same obligations, the same duties and the same rights as men, including in the field of religion and religious worship.

EB: This points to a real will for reform. In America today, you can find lesbian synagogues and gay synagogues. But this is all new, and far from being universally accepted! No religion seems to be without a repressive dimension: they are all rigid systems, even if some leeway may appear within them, and they are completely in tune with the society that harbours and uses them. Both Judaism and other religions move as society moves – no more and no less.

J-CA: Until the contemporary period, Jewish words were men's words. Talmud masters, medieval thinkers and jurists were all men. And men's words were most often misogynist – or philogynist, which is not much better. They valued the status of women, but only by locking it into an irreducible specificity. Women had children, ran the home and had a function in education – but a limited one.

EB: Religion played a role in this, by fixing and protecting a certain model. In fact, it merely ratified decisions made by men, conferring on them all the weight of a divine prescription. Thus, it is not surprising that Judaism condemns male homosexuality so severely. Recent trends across the Atlantic should not give us any illusion about what the situation has been like down the centuries: homosexuality repressed, condemned or assumed in secret, if at all. No doubt there have been many reasons for this, one being a determination to save the family and ensure reproduction at any cost.

J-CA: It is true that a dispersed, often migratory people may need a stronger family cell than other peoples. The family cell is Israel in miniature, the Sabbath table, the altar of the Sanctuary, the paterfamilias, the High Priest. People reproduced on a small scale what they could no longer have writ large, and the family was thus perceived by the rabbinical authorities as an assurance of continuity.

EB: But that is also how it was perceived by Christianity and Islam. Today, Judaism is adapting: the Reform movement in the United States gives its blessing to homosexual unions, even if these are not properly recognized as 'marriages'. You can be a rabbi, a woman and a lesbian. Or a gay rabbi.

J-CA: That, no doubt, is something typically American. But what seems to me a truly fundamental change is the access that women now have to knowledge. In the past, the education of Jewish girls was not very demanding: they basically learned to do what their mothers had done. Now all that is changing – or, anyway, women are demanding a change and eventually gaining it, especially in the Reform current. There has been a real turnaround: women study alongside men, in the same way and with the same texts, claiming the right to examine the knowledge they acquire. This has nothing in common with the Orthodox distillation of 'women's knowledge', which was already a feature of Jewish society before the emancipation. Today, the whole field of Jewish learning is available to Jewish women. And Jewish women are contributing to the production of this knowledge, or deeply transforming the way in which it has been traditionally interpreted.

EB: In Orthodox milieux, too, the picture is neither static nor homogenous. Abortion, though not considered equivalent to murder, is strongly condemned, but certain forms of contraception are sometimes tolerated. Outside male tutelage, some practising women set up working groups or scripture study circles. Again, it is mostly in America that the battle is being waged and that religious parity between the sexes is coming to be seen as a matter of course.

10 | To remain Jewish, to become Jewish again, or to reinvent Judaism?

J-CA: The traditional synagogue does not always show signs of great inventiveness. But Jews today demand from Judaism the creativity on which their futures largely depend. Of course, the contemporary epoch has not been without its strong, bold and inventive Orthodox rabbis; we should not think of Orthodoxy as a lifeless expanse – far from it. But how many Jews do such currents really affect? Are there so many Jews who think of themselves, and live their lives, as men and women of the Law? The legal emphasis in Judaism puts quite a few people off, and it is true that this kind of Judaism – at least in the West – shares with other religions the fact that it is on the defensive. This is especially the case in France, the land of secularism. Thus, if you are looking for creativity, inventiveness and conceptual richness, you are not likely to find it in official synagogues or their rabbis. But that is not all there is to Judaism: it involves a number of different currents, which do not express themselves in the same way, and which, in France, unfortunately express themselves rather little altogether. We should hardly be surprised that institutional Judaism, as a religion, displays the same weakness and rigidity as other Western religious traditions.

EB: In the United States, where diversity is the rule, the different sensitivities of contemporary Judaism can express themselves without complexes. In Israel, too, dissident voices are making themselves heard.

J-CA: France seems more consensual, or simply more silent and drab. But maybe that is only a surface impression.

EB: In any event, there is not just one Judaism. Some people do not want to understand this, and it is difficult to explain. Judaism today exists in several different forms. And the practices or positions vary considerably from one current to the next, from Reform liberalism at one end to ultra-Orthodoxy at the other.

J-CA: In the case of ultra-Orthodoxy, its rigorous insistence on the Law should not be seen as necessarily contrary to deep religiosity or genuine mysticism. One of the great Jewish legal experts, Joseph Karo, the author of a sixteenth-century code of Jewish law that is still an authority, was also one of the greatest mystics in the Jewish tradition, honoured for fifty years or so with visits from a celestial mentor. In these matters, everything depends on the interpretation. What meaning should be given to everyday practices? What is their weight in the economy of the sacred? Each human act on earth, even the humblest, has a cosmic impact and resonates in the upper spheres of the divine. Legalism and mysticism can very well go together, since it is possible to develop a mystical, theurgic interpretation and valorization of the practice of the commandments. To reduce even ultra-Orthodox Judaism to a dry legalism is obviously a mistake. No one will deny that it is articulated around a strongly legal way of thinking, but that is by no means all there is to it.

EB: Judaism has also stood out by virtue of its transgressors.

J-CA: Without a doubt. Periodically, a relationship of rejection or a penchant for relativism comes to light. There are antinomic traditions in Judaism which asserted themselves even in quite ancient times, albeit in a sometimes indirect manner.

EB: And they too are part of the richness of Judaism.

J-CA: Something essential risks escaping the attention of an outside observer: namely, the fact that minute observance of the Law does not necessarily involve mental anguish or an obsession with transgression. Most everyday Jewish gestures are performed naturally and with relative ease. They are a way of life, and in them the slightly sad legalistic dimension disappears. Many people who return to Judaism, or at least those among them who do not adopt extreme forms of Orthodoxy, are precisely looking for the comfort of a sacred existence lived in simplicity, the joy of commandments fulfilled with peace of mind.

EB: Currently, the tendency to return to stricter forms is coming largely from Israel, where some of the most secular layers of the population are falling back on religion. In the face of a conflict from which there seems to be no way out, a certain despair is beginning to make itself felt. The return to strict forms of religion affects many young people from groups that experienced a certain form of Judaism, com-

bined with everyday life in flexible domestic ways, which has begun
to crumble. The phenomenon is noticeable, for example, among children from Oriental milieux which, though not very observant, were
saturated with a traditional religiosity that imparted a Jewish content
to the simplest actions of everyday life. This model was broken by
emigration and integration, or as a result of the growing secularization
of Israeli society. The second or third generation therefore responds
to the vacuum with the means at its disposal. This return to religion
is a marked trend in Israel, and there can be no doubt that it has an
influence in the Diaspora. We shall have to see what the future brings.
I honestly believe that it is no more than one solution among others,
whereas some people imagine that it is the only legitimate path open
to Judaism.

J-CA: For my part, I find it difficult to identify with that trend,
even if I was asking similar questions myself twenty or so years ago.
What I see among many of those now 'finding their way back' does
not make me particularly optimistic. I sense that it involves a kind of
selective, ultimately very narrow re-Judaization, which is at the same
time terribly sure of itself and not devoid of hegemonic ambitions.
That is what worries me.

EB: I completely share your concern. But the extraordinary variety of the Orthodox palette can never be emphasized too much. In
France as in Israel, there are religious people whose lifestyle arouses in
me nothing but sympathy and respect. Similarly, many moderate (or
simply well-balanced) 'returnees' harbour no tendency to overcom-
pensate for past transgressions through an excess of rigour today; they
do not try to convince others with all their might in order to increase
their own conviction. Many religious people are even quite capable of
accepting that theirs is only one way of living Judaism today.

J-CA: That is certainly true. And, even if they hope that their
nearest and dearest will 'convert' to their model, they do not put any
pressure on them but merely testify through their own example to
what they see as the truth of their belief. It is not them I fear but
certain extremist currents, which the present situation makes more
visible and (in some eyes) more legitimate.

EB: And it is quite possible that that will not sort itself out. For
there is another reason for concern: the forthcoming disappearance
of the survivors of the Holocaust. If the Holocaust gradually loses its
function as a secular religion, or if this secular religion is no longer

enough, what will future generations be able to embrace? As we said before, the communion around the memory of genocide serves as a cement – and that cement is liable to break up. Will it last much longer? I don't know. I sometimes wonder whether, apart from religion, there is any other way out for those who want to remain Jews. What will provide them with an identity? How will people be Jewish in thirty years' time? I am not saying that the memory of the Holocaust will die out – far from it – but it is clear that time will take the edge off the religious feelings that surround it. What will then be left? And what will be left when the link is broken with the everyday experience of Jews from North Africa, with their tradition and their Jewish sociability? The link with Israel also weakens at times. No one knows what the country's future will be, or whether it can continue indefinitely serving as a prop for the identity of Diaspora Jews. This combination of factors really makes me wonder whether a certain Orthodoxy, a return to strict religious practices, will not be the only way open for those who still want to live as Jews. Do Jews have a future, then? And, if so, what might it be?

J–CA: That kind of concern with how Jews can survive as Jews is often foregrounded community leaders. For Jews to remain Jews is doubtless very good. But what worries me most is that I cannot always see where a creative, culturally productive Judaism will come from in the future. What kind of Jewish cultural production will emerge in the next ten, twenty, thirty or forty years? Israel is an important centre, where people create in Hebrew. But are we talking there of Jewish culture or Israeli culture? There is also the United States. But France? Or Europe?

EB: I can see another danger on the horizon – or another aspect of the same danger. You yourself referred a moment ago to the fact that a fringe of those returning to Jewish Orthodoxy would very much like to impose their own model outside. That is happening in Israel, where a fairly large religious minority exerts what some would regard as intolerable pressure on the secular majority. The big problem facing Israel today – apart from the Palestinians – is this division of society into two.

J–CA: In the Diaspora, at least, the pressure of the Orthodox is of course limited: both because there is nothing in national politics to increase their weight, and because religion in the West largely remains a private affair.

EB: There is still a tendency to separate good Jews from bad Jews – a tendency especially strong in, but not confined to, Orthodox milieux.

J-CA: You haven't mentioned the obsession with mixed marriages.

EB: That is a preoccupation for all minority groups. Endogamous marriage and the family in general are seen as a means, or even the only means, of preserving the group's cohesion and its distinctive ethno-cultural features. The principle of endogamy, both religious and ethnic, is not a new phenomenon and does not concern only Jews. It is an ancient and widespread preference, which has remained constant in many societies. Nevertheless, fear of exogamy has become a veritable obsession for rabbis, community leaders and quite a few ordinary Jews. As if it were the only danger threatening the future of the Jews! When you are in the United States you hear nothing else. The rate of mixed marriages is also high in France, but it is even higher on the other side of the Atlantic. But what safeguards Judaism there is the fact that some of its currents agree to live 'with' exogamy, instead of simply mobilizing 'against' it. After all, it is not the only danger lying in wait for a dispersed minority in an open society.

J-CA: The argument is that exogamy will directly lead to dilution of the community, to its inevitable effacement. But if people react differently, as in some currents of American Judaism, it need not mean that Jews who enter into such marriages will abandon Judaism; it could lead to a new form of Jewish identity, which allows people to marry outside the community while continuing to be members of it – and to pass that identity on to their offspring. Not all followers of Judaism today are making the same choice: either they regard exogamy as a major danger and wage (quite unsuccessful) war against its spread; or else, in the case of Reform Judaism, they merely note the trend, while acting in such a way that mixed marriages do not have the feared effect (either by making it easier for the non-Jewish spouse to convert, or by recognizing the Jewish identity of children even when their mother is not Jewish and agreeing to give them a Jewish education). These options are certainly shattering old models, but Jewish society had anyway been breaking with them for some time.

EB: Mixed marriages can be a factor of dilution or a symptom of dilution. But the real problem is extreme acculturation: the non-transmission of identity, of certain secular and not only religious values. Jews belong to a people. There is still a strange idea, common in the nineteenth century, that Judaism is mainly a religion, or even a denomination, and that only firm allegiance to its principles and practices is capable of ensuring its survival. I think that this is a mistaken view. Most Jews today who retain at least some solid chunks of their identity and heritage are members of a people (however you define that term) more than followers of a religion. And, even for an Orthodox, the Jew who takes only what he wants from all that is still a Jew: a bad Jew, but a Jew.

J–CA: Yes, but a Jew in need of redemption. And I don't want to be redeemed in spite of myself! But let us return to those de-Judaized Jews who 'find their way back'. They tell us, and tell themselves, that they are returning to 'authentic' Judaism. In fact, they are inventing a new Judaism which they see and claim as authentic. Unlike the returns that took place in the 1980s, what is happening today is not a 'cultural' return to the Judaism of one's parents or grandparents. The Orthodox models in greatest esteem today are mostly Ashkenazi models. This is rather paradoxical in the case of France, since the Jewish community there is chiefly Sephardi. The break therefore has several dimensions: a break with the Republic, a break with open, culturalist ways of returning to Judaism, and a break with the Judaism of one's parents, even when that was a traditional, practising Judaism. It seems to me that this amounts to a complete renunciation of the cultural layers that used to make Jewish identity so dense – and I find that worrying. This phenomenon of withdrawal, or reinvention of a tradition, is something quite new. Take the Lubavitchers, for example. What were they originally? A Hassidic movement from Eastern Europe which transplanted itself to the United States, with a headquarters in Brooklyn. It engaged in intense proselytizing among Jews all around the world, including in France, so that here it mainly involves an imported model alien to ordinary French-Jewish culture. It provides a clear illustration of the fabricated, reinvented aspect of the Orthodox return to Judaism that is prevalent today. I see it as a kind of ageing or rigidification. The historical irony is that Hassidism, an eighteenth-century mystical current which valued spontaneous religious devotion and insisted that the humblest (or least educated) Jew had access to complete fulfilment of his vocation, should have gradually drawn closer to its counter-model: the traditional Talmud-centred, elitist and legalist Jewish society of Eastern Europe. Hassidism sprang up to oppose that tradition and fought it for generations. But once common enemies appeared, in the shape of the Enlightenment, Reform Judaism and the emancipation, the road was open for a relative homogenization of traditional Judaism in Eastern Europe, whether Hassidic or not. Let us not forget either that the traditional Judaism of those regions was destroyed; only a tiny part of it had enough time, before the war, to find a new home in Palestine or the United States. What you find there today are new, deracinated (and significantly changing) forms of a religiosity and cultural tradition which had its *raison d'être* at a certain moment in European history. The currents or tendencies within Orthodoxy itself display renewed diversity and, naturally enough, are often in conflict with one another. But the question is whether, inside those currents, the forces of renewal are sufficiently powerful for that to continue and develop. The most curious aspect is that the traditional (Hassidic or non-Hassidic) Jewish model of Eastern Europe, though tragically uprooted and grown rigid with age, has transformed itself for the most secularized Jews into a kind of fantasy of lost authenticity. A real Jew, a genuine Jew, a Jew such as we should all have remained – even if we are careful not to become one again – is a Jew dressed in black, with a hat and locks. Hence a kind of shtetl romanticism, in which the small-town Hassidim of Jewish Eastern Europe continue to feed the imagination of the most de-Judaized Jews. But, of course, that is only one facet of Judaism.

EB: And maybe it is not as alive as some would have us think.

J-CA: The trickiest question is what will happen in the future. Will these Jews returning to Judaism be capable of passing it on? The 'returnees' may completely change their lives, but will the next generation follow them? They claim to embody continuity, and this is not entirely artificial; there is, of course, a degree of real cultural and theological continuity. But will they be able to ensure that it is still there tomorrow? Is it certain that the numerous children of the ultra-Orthodox and the repentant ultras will be capable of alone ensuring the survival of Judaism and the Jews? Can we legitimately say – to put it more generally – that only a 're-Judaization' of the Jews might shelter them from dilution? 'Re-Judaization': you find the idea of the 'truly Jewish Jew' as a leitmotif in contemporary Judaism, and not only among the ultra-Orthodox – as if it is not enough to be Jewish, as if you also have to double your Jewishness! The 'Jewish Jew' is the current fashion.

EB: You also see reactions in the opposite direction: not everyone sees modernity as the absolute evil; not everyone thinks that Jewish 'authenticity' must be built against it. But the taste for 'authenticity' is certainly widespread, as you say. We are a long way from the Jew of Sartre's *The Jewish Question*. In the nineteenth century, the birth of neo-Orthodoxy was a kind of reaction to modernity that was not purely and simply a rejection. You could be neo-Orthodox and strictly observant, and still integrate fully into modern society. Today, it is no longer 'the authentic' who dream of modernity, but the modern who dream of 'authenticity'. The currents favouring a return to intransigent Judaism often betray a wider malaise, a malaise which, in the case of France, grew out of an acute awareness that during the dark years the contract of trust with the state was broken, and which, in the case of Israel, reflects a crumbling of Zionist conviction.

J–CA: But the search for 'authenticity' can go a long way and involve the strangest deviations.

EB: Indeed it can. I think of a current that has recently been gaining ground in Israel, which presents itself as the inheritor of the teachings of the eighteenth-century figure Nahman of Bratslav – although this is strongly contested by the real followers of Bratslaver Hassidism. What you see are young Israelis who, having been through other 'experiences' in Thailand or elsewhere, find a way back to Orthodoxy in a kind of wandering sect. They discover 'authentic' Judaism not in study or common prayer, but in the forest or desert, close to springs and rivers. They do not work as a matter of principle – their secular parents are asked to pay for their sins – and instead sing and dance on street corners, selling to passers-by a literature that they have often not read themselves. It is pretty strange to see some of them, Sephardis, dressed in a black suit with a beard and locks, and on their head a large-brimmed *shtreimel* (the traditional fur- or velvet-lined headgear worn by Jews in Poland or Galicia); strange to see these young Sephardis searching for themselves in a life of wandering. These kinds of 'return' are severely criticized by institutionalized Orthodoxy, which sees them as deviant forms. But it is precisely such 'deviations' which arise when the relationship to all institutions, including the state, grows weaker. No state and no religious institution can any longer answer their desire for a total religion.

J–CA: How formidable is the illusion of theological, or cultural, authenticity! It would be interesting to find out the precise type of culture and the precise forms of training on which the return to Judaism is based. Nowadays, to return to Judaism does not mean to study the history of the Jews or Jewish thought; it is essentially a return to a certain practice, to the strictest possible observance plus an excessive revaluation of one stratum of Jewish culture and of Jewish religious culture. Excessive value is attached to Talmudic studies, for example – no doubt a feature of a certain kind of traditional Judaism, but actually corresponding to a strongly Ashkenazi model – or else to study of the Kabbalah, even among milieux on the periphery of Judaism. The idea is that the Talmud and possibly the kabbalistic tradition are the very heart of Judaism; that these classical sources represent something that has never changed but retained its original purity; and that they convey the ultimate truth of the message of Judaism. This appreciation naturally goes together with avoidance of the whole issue of the history of these texts – for example, with a refusal to see that there has been a Judaism without the Talmud, a Judaism without Joseph Karo, a Judaism without the Zohar (the kabbalistic reference-text which, for some, is equal in status to the Bible or the Talmud). For, although the Zohar is traditionally attributed to Simeon ben Yohai, a second-century Palestinian master, it was actually written much later, in thirteenth-century Spain. Many 'returnees' want to forget such details, and with them the historical depth and diachronic diversity of Judaism. They focus on a few texts and fail to see that Judaism is infinitely richer, infinitely more complex and contradictory. The quest for 'truth' is also a quest for coherence. But, if understood in that way, coherence is death.

EB: You must accept, though, that most Jews are cultural or psychological Jews and do not read the Talmud. Some may also keep up the traditions. To sacrifice to the ritual of the family couscous on Friday evening is also a way of being Jewish. Thank God, there are still thousands of ways of being a Jew. We are in an age of strongly asserted identities, no doubt partly as a result of the death of ideologies. The rigour or fanaticism of these newly religious young people makes me think of what we went through in the 1970s, with Marxism and other ideologies. Faced with the collapse of yesterday's certainties, they think they have found a lifeline across the centuries in the shape of religion. Parallel movements of withdrawal can be seen in the Islamic world, as well as in Christianity. But the churches are still pretty empty, whereas the synagogues are beginning to fill up. The ultra-religious crystallizations of identity must be taken into account, but it would be utopian to believe that all Jews will become Orthodox again.

J–CA: You mean it would be frightening to believe it.

EB: Let me stress again that it was the Reform liberals, not the Orthodox, who 'saved' American Judaism. Besides, the ultra-Orthodox fringe often does not mix with anyone else; it may sometimes be militant yet live a life of suspicious withdrawal, cut off from the rest of the Jewish world.

11 | Diaspora identities, Israeli identities

J–CA: In addition to the ideological commitment to certain truths or texts, another aspect that deserves to be studied is the way in which the return to orthopraxis functions. What does it mean in someone's life to return to a rigorous practice of Judaism? Does it correspond to any particular social-psychological profile? Is it a structuring phenomenon? Is not the focusing of so much energy and attention on everyday practices ultimately a way of avoiding certain questions? After all, the practical demands are something quite new for the 'returnees'. The seemingly complex and restrictive set of practices was a natural, unreflexive part of Jewish life for centuries, in both society and the family, experienced as neither novel nor restrictive. Today, however, the practice of Judaism – especially in a fragmented society like ours, which has relatively little room for certain lifestyles – implies a considerable effort of will and the learning of a number of everyday actions. It would be interesting to see with what that resonates, to what kind of demand it corresponds. The orthopraxis of our 'returnees' has been reinvented. And I know only too well – from my own experience – the obsessiveness to which it can lead or the kind of obsessional behaviour from which it emanates.

EB: And that's nothing in comparison with what awaits us after the construction of the Third Temple: the re-establishment of a pernickety sacrificial cult!

J–CA: Let us not jump ahead like that. A few small groups of extremists have periodically tried to lay the first stone of the edifice, on the famous 'Mosque Esplanade' – or Temple Mount, as it is known to Jews. There was a recent example in July 2001, which did not fail to arouse violent reactions among the Palestinians. Most religious people, however, calmly await the coming of the Messiah before making the least sketch for the reconstruction; some even wonder what could be done in a Third Temple after its completion. Animal sacrifices? That's not so sure. Think of the old Maimonidean interpretation of those rites as an ancient concession that God made to Israel when it saw other peoples honouring their divinities in that way – a kind of minimal sacrificial worship, cleansed, ethicized and normalized. And, in the end, perhaps it was meant to be no more than a moment in the history of Judaism. So, a Third Temple without sacrifices – why not? I don't know if I shall ever see it standing. Anyway, I have never visited the 'esplanade': when I was religious, I did not go there because of a formal rabbinical prohibition; and now that I am secular I still don't go there, because I basically see it as a Muslim site and, like others, I have no taste for political provocation. Judaism has shown that it is perfectly viable without the Temple. I would even say that Judaism has been what it is only since the Temple disappeared as a reality and became no more than a horizon. A Third Temple where sacrifices are performed: that would force me to rediscover Judaism as something completely exotic. It's no good my reading Leviticus, no good my knowing that close study of the sacrificial rites has always been part of Jewish learning. It is one thing to study a sacrificial cult and another thing to practise it. Judaism has replaced sacrifice with study: that has been its strength; that is its very foundation. Is it possible to move in the opposite direction: to reintroduce sacrifice and perhaps to end the pre-eminence that study has enjoyed for nearly two thousand years? That could prove fatal. I am not far from thinking that it is precisely a return to the origins which threatens to make Judaism lose its identity. For the identity of Judaism lies not in some mythified origins but in its history.

EB: Since we are into scaring ourselves, let us imagine an Israel inhabited by ultra-Orthodox. It would be impossible to live there. It would be a Jewish country …

J-CA: Jewish – perhaps …

EB: Anyway, it would no longer be Israel. I lived there for quite a long time, and my basic view is that Israel is first of all inhabited by Israelis, who, in most cases, are also Jewish. But imagine an Israel entirely inhabited by religious people. It would no longer be Israel: neither the Israel of those who dreamed it up, nor the Israel of those who built it, nor the Israel of those who presently live in that country. Israel is a country where many different groups of people live: totally anti-religious Jews, religious Jews, very religious Jews, Israeli Arabs,

Israeli Druze, Armenians, Christians from all backgrounds, Jews who have come from every other country and who sometimes, according to Orthodox norms, are not altogether Jewish. It is a country in constant movement.

J–CA: An Israel of Hassidim – what would that be like? One big community, on a planetary scale. Exactly what Israel should not become.

EB: It would be a Mea Shearim, the anti-Zionist ultra-Orthodox district of Jerusalem, expanded to the proportions of a state. Is Mea Shearim Israel?

J–CA: Can I return to less gloomy considerations and ask whether the rabbinical authorities themselves are always absolutely convinced that Judaism is passed down through them alone?

EB: We should not imagine that all these authorities, despite their rigour, are unaware that there are several variants of Judaism today. The Reform movement knew how to position itself so as not to lose what was about to be lost to Judaism for ever, and the extreme rigour of some Orthodox authorities may perhaps be bound up with a fear of being overtaken.

J–CA: A certain kind of religious Judaism would have us believe that study of the texts and observance of the commandments have alone guaranteed the survival of the Jewish people. Maybe, maybe not. Things happened in a different way – otherwise women would not be Jewish, or less so. They do not have circumcision to make official their entry into the community. They did not have the bar mitzvah ritual to mark their coming of age. They have never practised more than a reduced number of commandments. They have generally been excluded from study. Nevertheless, as far as I know, Jewish women are fully Jewish.

EB: As we said before, the practice of Judaism has been historically coloured by local specificities.

J–CA: And it is precisely that local colour, not an abstract list of commandments, which has made people Jews.

EB: Take the case of France. In the first half of the twentieth century, the 'Israelites' saw Jews arrive en masse from Eastern Europe – practising or just 'very Jewish' Jews, socialist Jews, and nationalist Jews. As far as these newcomers were concerned, you were a Jew in the street, at home, everywhere. This did not prevent the growth of a strong attachment to France, but the Jacobinism of the 'Israelites' was dented as these Jews brought a revival of Jewishness to France. The war initiated major breaches and undermined the almost organic links that had developed with France, either placing religious faith in danger or galvanizing it. Later, in the 1950s and 1960s, the Jews who came from North Africa had a traditional (not Orthodox but traditional) background, and they too sparked off a religious revival in France. Paris today has some two hundred kosher butchers, a host of kosher grocery stores, and supermarkets with kosher shelves. France is an interesting case because Judaism there has drawn sustenance from a number of waves of immigration. Today, of course, the younger generation is generally less observant, but we can also see comprehensive or selective returns to Judaism. The United States has also developed an extraordinary diversity, with different forms specific to the country. Reform Jews, reconstructionists (who regard Judaism as a religious civilization in movement rather than a revealed teaching and law), the conservative or Masorti movement and all manner of Orthodox share out the terrain. In Germany, the arrival of large numbers of Russian Jews and the settlement of Israelis from old stock will doubtless lead to a still more complex reconfiguration of Jewishness. No uniformity, then, and quite a lot of change. Today's Jews have grown out of these tendencies, either chosen by themselves or imposed by history.

J-CA: It is doubtless true that there was a general (and unavoidable) decline in the practice of Judaism around the world in the nineteenth and twentieth centuries. But we should not think that until recently Jews were all good Jews, or that in the East European ghettos everyone studied the Torah and spoke Yiddish. There is a veritable myth of excellence lost, as well as a temptation to deplore the supposed fact of its loss. This kind of modern complaint about the decay of Judaism in modern times is a veritable constant of Judaism. In fact, it is a thoroughly medieval idea to imagine that our forebears were better than ourselves. You must know the Talmudic formula: if we are men, our ancestors were angels; and if they were men, we are donkeys. This retrospective vision of a lost golden age was tirelessly taken up by both ancient and medieval Judaism, and even seems to be a feature of contemporary Judaism.

EB: It is the myth of a blessed age when Jews lived in a world that was theirs, and when a great and genuine Jewish creativity could develop because the Jew was only Jewish.

J-CA: To be Jewish is to be Jewish plus something else. Our dear fellow-Jews who are tempted to withdraw into themselves all speak, as far as I know, French, English, Russian, German or Dutch. However great the resistance to cultural mixing, there is no escaping the fact that it is always present in some degree.

EB: In Israel such mixing has even asserted itself as a model, at least among the secular population. To go abroad once or twice a year, to watch and listen to foreign broadcasts: all that is valued as a life-saver. I recently learned from a good source that cable television is supposed to have helped change the behaviour of the average Israeli. It would seem that the old kibbutznik type, not very polite or refined, shoddily dressed and stuffing himself on American fast food, is in the course of disappearing; that young Israelis are more and more sensitive to good manners; and that the health food craze, imported from the United States, is sweeping the country. Such are the benefits of contact with others. It works for Jews and it works for Israelis (who are not only Jews).

J-CA: Jews, Israelis – the distinction is not clear in everyone's mind.

EB: It makes me think of what someone said to me when I returned from a research assignment in Israel, an assignment unfortunately prolonged by the outbreak of the Gulf War in 1991. After an absence of two weeks, instead of the few days initially envisaged, I heard a secretary in my department say to me with the most sincere admiration: 'Ah! How courageous they are in your country!' I did not understand at once. But then I realized that for her 'Jew' and 'Israeli' were one and the same.

J-CA: I, with my perverse mind, would have said to myself: 'Huh, it's strange that she finds "us" courageous precisely at the moment when "we" are remaining passive!' You remember, it was the first time in its history that Israel did not respond to attacks on its territory; this could have given the impression that it was shrinking from a conflict. But you are right: the distinction is not always clear for ordinary people. Not everyone is aware that there are also Israeli Muslims, Christian Arabs, Christian Armenians and so on. Israeli nationality or citizenship is easily confused with belonging to the Jewish people.

EB: In the same way, you can be a Diaspora Jew, have Israel as a major identity reference, and never wish to go and live there. The possibilities are endless: Zionist Diaspora Jew, non-Jewish Israeli, post-Zionist Israeli Jew ... Nor should we forget that, in its stronger moments, Zionism built itself up in opposition to its image of the

Diaspora Jew – a puny figure corresponding quite well to anti-Semitic stereotypes. That Jew was repudiated to strengthen the foundations of Zionism, and to boost the image of the risk-taking pioneers who went off to build a new nation and with it themselves.

J–CA: Quite a lot of Diaspora Jews today continue to internalize that hierarchy. They do not dare to criticize Israel too much, because they still have a little of the old inferiority complex of the Jew who has done nothing heroic and risks nothing in his comfortable existence in the West.

EB: The Jew from the 'Galut', from the Exile, was a type of Jew who was supposed to disappear. But Israel is in the process of coming to terms with its past, with its Other, with the Diaspora, so that perhaps Israeli and Diaspora Jews are starting to be less alien to each other. Assuming that this tendency continues, I wonder whether it will not lead to a re-Judaization of Israeliness, without necessarily implying a massive return to religion. Similarly, identification with the experience of the genocide, deliberately kept up over the last few decades among generations born inside the country, may also contribute to a strengthening of the Jewishness of Israelis. At a number of levels, however, the condition of Diaspora Jews is still quite remote from that of their fellow-Jews in Israel.

J–CA: You sometimes see that in the tiniest details. Jews in France, non-practising as we are, are tempted to conform to certain minimal practices capable of holding things steady and reminding us of our identity. In Israel, we would probably feel less need for that kind of thing: we would have only to follow the calendar, not working on Saturdays instead of Sundays and replacing our customary public holidays with the great Jewish festivals. We would think less about it and allow ourselves the luxury of being even more secular! People are more naturally Jewish in Israel, so they think less about the question than in the Diaspora and are therefore, at least in one sense, actually less Jewish. To take another example: here in France, full respect for the Jewish dietary laws would create a social barrier and rule out a lot of social interaction. In Israel, you can always engage at home in forbidden combinations of meat and dairy produce, but once you go out to a restaurant it becomes difficult not to eat kosher. The big difference is between a minority status and a majority status.

EB: In Israel, you can be a perfectly secular Jew yet remain Jewish. In the Diaspora, to be a Jew, you have to want it and to make at least a minimal display of it – by celebrating the major stages in life's cycle or the year's main festivals in a particular way, even if you do not attach any religious importance to them. A visible link is necessary to maintain a minimal sense of belonging. In Israel, secular Jews stay at home at the Jewish New Year because everything is shut, whereas in France you would have to ask for a special day off from work. That would link you to a definite practice, even if you did not observe it yourself.

J–CA: And it would immediately signal your difference. It is that difference which necessarily disappears in Israel, to be replaced by a number of others: Ashkenazi/Oriental, religious/secular, majority-Jewish/minority-Arab. Then another question emerges. Are you still Jewish, outside the context of the Jewish/non-Jewish difference?

EB: I think everyone answers that in their own way, and it's good that they do.

J–CA: Anyway, to be Jewish is still to be divided against yourself: to discover in your own kind, in your fellow-Jew, someone perhaps very different from what you are yourself. The religious Jew perceives the non-religious, agnostic or atheistic Jew as a strange and alien, perhaps even illegitimate creature, who is nevertheless mysteriously close. And vice versa. The Jewish people is thus divided against itself: its diversity compels it to see itself always as other and not as unified. But the individual Jew is also divided against himself or herself, bearing a multiplicity of not always compatible references and having to live with the incompatibility.

EB: What should we say about Israeliness, then? It seems to me an essentially incomplete identity, because it was born out of exile and based on a break with exile. The problem is that exile is constitutive of all Jewish (including Israeli) identity. The Zionists wanted to remove it from the picture and thought they could create a complete Israeli identity out of nothing. But that identity does not exist. It is not a failure – perhaps even that is success. In any event, the project was always going to be double-sided. They hoped that Israel would become a melting pot, that the mingling would lead to the crystallization of an essentially Israeli identity. At the same time, demographically and culturally, they sustained the project with wave after wave of immigrants from the infinite diversity of the Diaspora. There is no uniquely Israeli identity. And now, with two successive Intifadahs, Israelis find themselves face to face not only with their own past and that of their people, but also with the Palestinian Other, the enemy so close to themselves, who has himself probably forged equally complex relations with 'the land of Israel'.

J-CA: You cannot deny the existence of an Israeli identity, though. When does it manifest itself? When a Diaspora Jew and an Israeli meet each other. The difference is there to be seen in their relationship to the country, to the place. Now, after all, there is also a shared cultural heritage – linguistic, culinary, historical and existential. To quote Saul Tchernikowsky, the Hebrew poet who died in 1943, 'man is only the reflection of his country's landscape'.

EB: It is true that the Israelis, like any other people, have developed a close, nationalist relationship with their land – even if that land often escapes them. Today, when the horizon looks bleak and nothing seems able to halt the spiral of violence, people are anxious and ask themselves: 'Where should we go? What should we do? It is our land here: we grew up in it.' A colleague said to me recently: 'There are odours in spring, flowers in spring, that I cannot do without. Even if I can earn a better living under other skies, I need to smell those flowers in the spring. And, come summer, there is a wind in Tel Aviv that you don't find anywhere else.' That expresses a real sense of roots.

J-CA: In that sense Zionism has worked. And no Jew from the Diaspora could feel that kind of bond with Israel. There are two kinds of nostalgia: that of the Israeli who is far from home; and the more mythical, more imagined nostalgia of the Diaspora Jew who dreams of Israel.

EB: The person who spoke to me of that wind and the smell of those flowers lives for part of the year in Germany. Of course, Germany occupies an ambivalent, problematic place in the Israeli imagination. It's a strange combination. But that complexity also makes up the identity of an Israeli.

J-CA: Israeli identity is perhaps precisely that: a strong awareness of the problem it represents for anyone laying claim to it. For people in France, French identity is not usually a problem. But Israelis are all the more Israeli when they are led to ask themselves what it means to be Israeli.

EB: Israel is the homeland of Israelis and the imagined homeland of Diaspora Jews, or at least part of them. Here too there is a wide range of attitudes. And since Israel is an imagined homeland, the relationship that people have to it is even more complex. An Israeli feels himself to be Israeli, in touch with the land in which he lives, with

the problems of the day, problems of the environment or personal
security. But, because he is fortified by his identity, he now and then
allows himself to criticize his country. Without beating about the
bush, indeed sometimes with an extraordinary crudeness, he will say
what he thinks about his leaders' policies or the history of Zionism. In
the Diaspora, the relationship with Israel is all the more passionate for
being imagined, and Jews are quick to feel guilty towards the distant
homeland. Any criticism of Israel is felt as a real wound, as if no one
should touch something that is not experienced on a daily basis, that
has no concrete existence in your life. This explains why the relationship is so peculiar.

J–CA: But it is not structured in the same way for everyone.

EB: No. The relationship to Israel is also defined by one's attitude
to the country where one lives. But there is no point in speaking here
of dual allegiances. The imagined homeland is a 'homeland' between
inverted commas, a well-nigh inaccessible place.

J–CA: Although it really does exist, it is paradoxically an inner
homeland.

EB: Maybe some people in Jewish institutions can give an
impression of soaring flight. But ordinary Jews generally live their
relationship with Israel in accordance with the contract that binds
them to the modern state of which they are citizens. The inner homeland belongs to their private life. Of course, this private conviction
may also express itself outside: not only have Jews overcome the stage
of feeling ashamed of their Jewishness, but many proclaim it loud and
clear, and an attachment to Israel is often an integral part of it. The
institutional Jews often find themselves torn between the need to
maintain good relations with the Jewish public and the need not to
upset the authorities too much. And so they zigzag as best they can.
Jews today are perhaps more or less doomed to live like that. Dual
allegiance? Probably not. Polymorphous identity? No doubt about it.

J–CA: This multiplicity of allegiances and superimposition of
sometimes contradictory identities has become an ordinary part of
the modern or 'post-modern' condition. It is not only Jews who live
like that.

EB: I think that nowadays we should speak above all of the paradoxical Jew. The Jew is a paradox – that must be accepted. Non-Jews
think of the paradox as a contradiction, but it is not really one. It is the
present lot of numerous minorities. In Judaism, some elements inher-

ited from the past or generated by a complex present serve to reinforce this factual condition. People should not be afraid of being paradoxical.

J-CA: But that is what Zionism wanted to end, in its way. It had the idea of creating a unified Jew, in full correspondence with the world around him. But it has not really achieved this: either for Diaspora Jews, of course, or even for Israelis. The Jew is a paradox, but that does not have to tear people up inside. The paradox can be lived joyfully.

EB: Nor does it imply any lack of affection for the country in which one lives.

J-CA: On the other hand, it would be a mistake to see this merely as a product of modernity. There is nothing essentially modern about the mental structures induced by dispersion and exile: modernity simply makes them more systematic and more visible, mainly because they are no longer characteristic of Jews alone. The mobility, the capacity to see oneself, the relationship to others, the multiplicity of referents: these are an ancient legacy of the Jews which is now be-coming universal. Before the modern age, Jews bore some of these characteristics within themselves. Today, they are only more widely perceptible, doubtless because many more doors are open to Jews, but also because the whole of Western society is affected by them.

EB: The music of Leonard Bernstein or the films of Steven Spiel-berg may have something Jewish, but they are immediately received and appreciated by a non-Jewish audience. That was perhaps not so readily the case before emancipation, when the universality of Jewish cultural works, with a few exceptions, was not immediately seen by others.

J-CA: Does that mean that modern Jewish cultural productions are less Jewish? Or has the non-Jewish public also changed? Perhaps this points to a kind of encounter between the traditional Jewish con-dition and the modern Western condition. I am from here, I am from somewhere else, there is no place, there is no time: all junctions are possible, as networks form and break up in perpetual movement.

EB: Nevertheless, Jews develop a special relationship with modernity by virtue of their very history. They are not afraid to invest in novelty, because no ties are required to master it – on the contrary, a lack of ties makes the task easier. Every innovative sector, every modern activity not yet dominated by a tradition, is more easily acces-sible to them than to others.

J–CA: But modernity has not brought only progress for Jews. Racial theories, anti-Semitism and the death camps are a monstrous product of modernity, obstinately sending back to Jews a negative image of themselves, even at a physical level.

EB: For a whole period, Jews did indeed try to rid themselves of the physical defects that others attributed to them. Appropriation of the stereotype went so far that some did not even hesitate to have an operation, thereby helping to create a veritable caste of Jewish cosmetic surgeons in early-twentieth-century Central Europe.

J–CA: Fortunately, we are no longer in that situation; it marked an extreme limit. Surgical intervention is one of the ultimate consequences of a will to become other than the person you are in the imagination of those who hate you. There is a phrase for that: Jewish self-hatred. It was typical of those regions and of that moment in the history of European Jewry.

EB: A change of name and religion still left it open whether one was a Jew. So people started to change their faces, in a radical internalization of their rejection by others. The last stage of this process was self-annihilation, suicide. It was the option chosen by the anti-Semitic and anti-feminist Otto Weininger, a Viennese Jew who converted to Protestantism and died in 1903. Having studied a number of similar trajectories, the German-Jewish cultural historian and philosopher Theodor Lessing developed the concept of Jewish 'self-hatred' in the early 1930s. In fact, it is a concept that can be applied to many other oppressed minorities: homosexuals or blacks, for example.

J–CA: Self-hatred is one possible reaction on the part of a minority group exposed to widespread hostility. By taking over the Other's discourse, you justify it and legitimate it in your own eyes: 'I am just like others say I am. They hate me, and I hate myself.' The minority simply takes on board the discourse of the majority, and turns it against itself. And if you feel completely incapable of regeneration, incapable of reshaping yourself and shaking off the image that others pin on you, all you have left is suicide.

EB: But we should not confuse the pathological phenomenon of self-hatred with distant and ironical yet fundamentally benign Jewish ways of relating to oneself.

J–CA: The issue is different there. The self-mockery so characteristic of a certain Jewish humour has nothing to do with self-hatred. The Jew who makes fun of Jews really is making fun of them: he sees what is not right in how they behave. At the same time, though, he has real compassion for the Jews he mocks.

EB: He sympathizes with their neuroses, their difficulties in life, their love for their mother.

J-CA: Yes, that is the self-divided Jew in humorous mode: nothing painful, nothing dramatic.

EB: On the contrary, it is even positive. There is nothing positive in self-hatred. For what is hate? Is it the other side of the coin of love, or is it non-love? What weighs most heavily is the non-love, the lack of love, which prevents me from loving myself. Not by chance was it in Central Europe that the concept, and the reality, of Jewish self-hatred was first developed. There, the conditions were such that upwardly mobile Jews came up against insuperable limits and outright anti-Semitism.

J-CA: There is no self-hatred if there is no rejection by society in general.

EB: In France, a Jew might be rejected but also become justice minister (like Adolphe Crémieux) or a professor at the elite Collège de France (like the Hebrew scholar Salomon Munk or the Indianist Sylvain Lévi). Popular anti-Semitism existed, but it did not necessarily stop Jews from rising up the ladder.

J-CA: Self-hatred arises only when all horizons are blocked, when ambient hostility is combined with an incapacity to overcome it in any way.

EB: But since we are compiling a list of grave and less grave mental disturbances to which history has made Jews more prone, in certain situations, why should we not mention some of the supposedly typical phobias? Neurosis is not a Jewish disorder. But is it an accident that Freud, a Viennese Jew, was the one who ensured its 'fortune'? This does not mean that psychoanalysis is a Jewish science. But is it surprising that certain characteristic obsessions can be found in the Jewish world? In fact, they are present in all minority groups which are, or have been, exposed to persecution. Certain 'character neuroses' that affect people all around the world do seem to be more common among Jews: a tendency to anxiety, for example, or some attitudes of a paranoid type, or fear of illness.

J-CA: This means that enemies are found everywhere except where they really exist. Such imaginary enemies make it possible not to think about others.

EB: Let us be wary of clichés. Not all Jews develop the same neuroses at the same time! There are numerous variations, depending on the historical context, social conditions and pressures, and local cultures. The films of Woody Allen, for instance, have helped to popularize an image of the Jew that is by no means universal; Allen himself is the inheritor of a whole American-Jewish literary tradition that focuses on a certain type of *luftmensh*, a single man in the big city, a tormented, alienated intellectual torn between different cultural worlds and moral values. What is Woody Allen's Jew if not a reincarnation of the Ashkenazi cultural myth of the *shlemil*, that unlucky type who tries to tame a hostile world? He is therefore not a 'typical' Jew – at most a 'typical' Ashkenazi-Jewish New York intellectual.

J-CA: It is all there, though: sexual problems, huge psychoanalyst's fees, a fascination with non-Jewish women, some major problems with the mother, and a neurosis that is in the end quite creative.

EB: Are the much-talked-about relations between mother and son really so peculiar to Jews? Does one not find that mutual excess of love in all societies where the family is of utmost importance?

J-CA: It's certainly true that the Italian mother can be as all-consuming as the Jewish mother. And, in a dispersed minority group, the weight of the family is naturally greater.

EB: Still, we do see a tendency in many Jewish mothers to over-protect their children, to worry too much about what they eat, and to wean them later than their non-Jewish counterparts would. With so much on the debit side, it would be hard not to develop a few neuroses.

J-CA: Remarkably enough, this set of disturbing handicaps is usually associated in people's minds with exceptional intelligence. Jewish intelligence …

EB: Assuming it exists, it is not so difficult to explain. So long as Jews were a minority in societies that presented them with a powerful challenge, they wanted to and had to do better than others. And when you do better than others, you attract hatred and envy and awaken feelings of unease. Who does not have in their head the names of those (more or less controversial) 'Jewish geniuses' of the last two centuries: Marx, Freud and Einstein? I do not know whether Marx, who converted to Protestantism at the age of six, can be considered a model of Jewish intelligence; his relationship to Judaism was ambivalent, not to say downright negative. But that did not prevent him from having good relations with his wealthy uncle Lion Philips – the originator of the famous brand name – or from being friendly with Heinrich Graetz, the great historian of the Jews. Nor, incidentally, did it stop Bakunin from treating him as a Jew! All three of the great names I mentioned have left their mark on people's minds. But we should not exaggerate: the fact that Jews tend to be hypochondriac, or to develop certain neuroses, does not mean that they are destined to become geniuses. They do have a few to show for themselves, but not as many as that.

J–CA: There are also others who, however neurotic, do not strike one as in any way genius-like! The challenge of minority status favoured the development of certain talents and perhaps a stronger tendency to react to stimuli. But Jewish intelligence as such is a fantasy, sometimes concealing a rather dubious way of looking at the world. The Jew is supposed to be of more than normal intelligence – which suggests something supernatural, suspicious, even a little demonic.

EB: Let us also remember that, once the first generations of immigrants had battled their way through, Jews showed a natural inclination to become like everyone else again.

J–CA: The world is full of quite ordinary Jews whom non-Jews simply do not notice. And when I say ordinary, I do not mean that they are often not engaging individuals.

EB: The outbursts of Jewish creativity are quite explicable if we bear in mind that, in the United States and elsewhere, the leading lights were children of immigrants who no longer had even a vague desire to return and were keen to get on in life.

J–CA: Since American society, which was explicitly built on immigration, placed the highest value on self-fulfilment, enterprise and inventiveness, it was inevitable that Jews would respond to such stimuli. Let us, above all, avoid attributing Jewish intelligence to some special ontological characteristic. But, to return to Woody Allen, here is a likeable man who tends to make Jews in general appear likeable. As you have already pointed out, however, his films show us no more than a small fringe of the contemporary Jewish world; they should not make us overlook its infinite diversity. The shtetl Jew or the New York Jew is a thousand miles from the gallant characters in Albert Cohen's novels. The forms of Jewish self-irony vary from one cultural area to another: the Eastern Judeo-Spanish, for instance, make fun of themselves in their own special way, with a sense of ridicule and a taste for mockery quite different from the bitter-sweet self-mockery common among Ashkenazis.

EB: In any event, the tendency to self-mocking detachment may well be a constructive feature.

J-CA: Who knows if it is not this capacity to see oneself with eyes that are not one's own which makes people intelligent?

EB: So, you are coming back to intelligence. Didn't we move on from that? But it may be worth mentioning that the attachment to study evident among at least some Jews may tend to promote intelligence. You find something rather similar in the Asian communities which succeed in America: the idea that study is a dependable value, a sure means of getting on in life.

J-CA: The old tradition of valuing knowledge must also have played a role. Wealthy Jewish merchants used to try to find a poor husband for their daughter, but he had to be a doctor of law and spend all his time studying. The son, for his part, having been freed from money worries, could hope to pursue an intellectual or scientific career.

EB: Do not forget the overprotective tendencies of so many Jewish parents, which mean that their children have not been allowed to assert themselves in physical fights or confrontations with the all-too-violent world around them. Instead, the utmost value has attached to intellectual achievement, as the only way to rise in society, to become free – and to charm people! This emphasis on books, though not shared by all components of the Jewish world, has for many been the secret of success: culture and science are sound investments, and can easily be taken with you if the need arises – like music and certain musical instruments.

J-CA: The centrality of the book is certainly one of the distinctive features of the Jewish cultural tradition. In the modern age, however, it has mainly taken the form of direct participation in the building of Western culture.

EB: Indeed, if you look for the birthplace or privileged expression of Jewish modernity, you will find it also in literature. In the nineteenth-century aftermath of the Jewish Enlightenment in Eastern Europe, a secular Jewish literature emerged which corresponded to the great Western canons, autobiography being the first genre to establish itself. These new authors, themselves from religious backgrounds, yearning to emancipate themselves and to integrate into the surrounding society, expressed their discomfort at being caught between two worlds. Their attempts to leave the one gave them a sense of betrayal, while their attempts fully to join the other gave them a sense of rejection. Autobiography is an individualist form of writing: it marks a passage from community to individual. *Aviezer*, the work by Mordekhai Aharon Guenzburg that appeared in 1864, would serve as a model for other autobiographies by Jewish writers.

J–CA: The first Hebrew novels began to appear around the same time, written in a biblical language that was considered purer, or more literary, than Aramaic-influenced rabbinical Hebrew. Abraham Mapou, Kalman Schulman and Mendele Moykher Sforim – a pseudonym meaning 'Mendele the Itinerant Bookseller' – were some of the first names to signal the renewal of a Jewish literature in Hebrew as well as Yiddish. The new Yiddish literature involved both an acclimatization to Western models and a defensive response to the invasion of modernity.

EB: You find the same phenomenon among the Eastern Jews, who were producing a literature in Judeo-Spanish at the same time that they were being Frenchified at the schools of the Alliance israélite universelle. It was precisely the tensions between tradition and modernity which drove their creativity forward. Nor should we forget the later literature of the emigration; American Yiddish literature, in particular, distinguished itself in the novel, poetry and theatre. Isaac Bashevis Singer is perhaps the best known of these writers, but there are many others. In Palestine, later Israel, a whole autochthonous body of Hebrew literature took shape. Who, in France, has not heard of the works of Amos Oz, Abraham B. Yehoshua and David Shahar, or even the police novels of Batya Gour? In the United States, Cynthia Ozick and Philip Roth are just two of a plethora of Jewish writers in the English language producing literature that gives full scope to the self-doubt, irony and humour (now caustic, now gentle) of the Yiddish world. Rebellion, heartbreak, internal exile, the family, the quest for a political and personal morality: these are among its recurrent themes.

J–CA: France has not lagged behind either. In the 1920s and 1930s, Richard Bloch, Armand Lunel, Irène Nemirowsky and a few others produced a considerable body of literature with Jewish themes, and the arrival of the Jews from North Africa later gave it a spectacular fresh momentum. Many people have heard of Albert Memmi, but the late 1970s brought Katia Rubinstein's *Mémoire illettré d'une fillette d'Afrique du Nord*, followed by Marco Koskas, Paula Jacques, Nine Moati and, more recently, Éliette Abécassis and others. The first works by these authors have usually been autobiographical. Writers of Ashkenazi origin have also been appearing on the scene.

EB: Arnold Mandel, Berthe Burko-Falcman, Georges Perec, Myriam Anissimov, Henry Raczymov and so many others. The full weight of the Holocaust is felt in this literature, even if it is not necessarily the main theme. At the same time, Clarissa Nicoïdski – herself of Judeo-Spanish origin – has evoked her childhood, the war years and the lost Ladino language. None of these writers defines himself or herself only in terms of a Jewish identity, and some have been quite capable of moving outside the Jewish world. In other cases, such as Robert Bober or Patrick Modiano, the Jewish identity is on the margins, or stuff of the imagination.

J-CA: Of course, the writers we have been discussing did not mark the entry of Jews into the world of literature; there was already a rich tradition, both religious and secular, in the pre-modern era, when the fact that literature was religious did not mean that it was not literature. The pleasure of the written word is not a recent discovery in the Jewish world. It is quite possible to make a literary analysis of the traditional mystical, legal or even philosophical texts, and to find at least as much of interest in the forms of expression in classical and medieval Jewish culture (where the commentary was the leading genre) as in the content and the ideas which that culture conveyed. On the other hand, it is perfectly true that the typical literature of the nineteenth and twentieth centuries that we have mentioned did mark the entry of literature with Jewish themes into modernity. The emergence of the novel and especially autobiography is a clear symptom of this. That was also the way in which a literary modernity originally constituted itself in the West.

EB: It is clear that Rousseau's *Confessions* served as a model for the first Jewish autobiographical writers of the Enlightenment. It should be stressed, however, that the real novelty was the emergence of Jewish literature as part of world literature, so that most non-Jewish readers have come to see it mainly as literature *tout court* (and only secondarily as Jewish literature). Albert Cohen is read by everyone, as is Primo Levi. In 1966 the German poet Nelly Sachs shared the Nobel Prize for literature with the great Hebrew writer Shmuel Yosef Agnon, and in 1978 it was the turn of Isaac Bashevis Singer to be honoured. Elias Canetti received the prize in 1981, and, although his is not a 'Jewish oeuvre', the first volume of his autobiography – *The Tongue Set Free* – evokes the Judeo-Spanish world of his childhood.

J-CA: For Jews, then, literary modernity was the moment when Jewish literature freed itself of religious models and became recognized as literature in the outside world.

EB: But in what way is this secular literature still Jewish? One writer might express nostalgia for the (mythified) Jewish small town of Eastern Europe, while another might raise Jewish moral demands or cast a vaguely Jewish gaze over the world.

J-CA: Not all literature that speaks of Jews, nor even all literature written by Jews, is necessarily Jewish literature. Both qualities seem necessary – and perhaps more besides. Yet sometimes less is enough. Jewish literature is definitely like Jewish identity: hard to pin down!

EB: A number of writers do, however, claim to be looking at the world in a distinctively Jewish way: for example, Bernard Malamud, Leon Uris and Chaim Potok in the United States. But others, sometimes the same people – Malamud again, Norman Mailer or Saul Bellow – have helped to fashion the cultural hero of modern America. You find this ambiguity everywhere. What, for instance, is a 'Jewish' film? A film made by Jews, for Jews or about Jews? Or what is a 'Jewish' intellectual? Raymond Aron was a French intellectual. But he responded to de Gaulle's declarations concerning a supposedly 'self-assured and dominant' Jewish people, and in 1968 he published *De Gaulle, Israël et les Juifs*. When was he a French intellectual, when a Jewish intellectual, and when just an intellectual?

J-CA: What is true of intellectuals, novelists or artists is true of any rank-and-file Jew. He is never 100 per cent a Jew, twenty-four hours of the day. He has activities, commitments and affiliations which mean that he is always something more besides.

EB: And then, Jewish writers touch all kinds of readers, because every Jewish theme is filtered and universalized through literature. They move from the particular to the universal. The elements of their imagination are drawn from a history and common fund shared with their group; they enrich their vision with a certain moral sense and both a personal and a collective legacy of responses to a particular experience. But they address themselves to everyone. When I read Albert Cohen, I find in his characters all the folklore of my childhood. But that is not what interests me in his work. What interests me is what he draws out of those characters, what makes their experience fundamentally human. In this way, Cohen is capable of affecting others besides myself, because this human experience becomes the experience of us all.

J-CA: May I express one reservation here? Cohen speaks of the world you knew, and your reading of his work does not treat it as folklore. A non-Jew or even an Ashkenazi, however, who has not had that experience and starts out knowing nothing about the Judeo-Spanish world, might well be dazzled by the folklore and lose sight of the literary and universal dimension of Cohen's work.

EB: As far as I am aware, no one has ever said that Albert Cohen was a great writer because he spoke of the Jews of Corfu! The *Livre de ma mère* is the book of his which affected me the most. But, beyond the figure of the actual mother, with her typically Judeo-Spanish traits, what you mainly discover in reading it is the lack of understanding between a mother and a son.

J-CA: Despite this self-affirmation through literature and art, Jews who do not necessarily recognize themselves in the characters of a novel or film sometimes feel not so much that they are objects of hostility as that they are not being understood for what they are. They suffer, or think they suffer, from a kind of general lack of understanding – or, in some cases, denial – of what Judaism means in everyday life, as well as of its historical development and cultural wealth. And, when the opinion that people have of these is positive, it often seems to refer to a rather abstract Jew who does not exist in reality.

EB: In the end, though, all minorities in France are victims of a lack of knowledge. Arabs, Turks, Armenians: who knows what about them?

J-CA: Sometimes people are no more ignorant about the wealth of Judaism than Jews are themselves. But it is not just ignorance: there are a whole host of images.

EB: Not necessarily negative ones.

J-CA: Sometimes they can even be positive, it's true, but they still seem to stand in the way of a recognition of Jews in their otherness.

EB: Anyway, you have to know what you want; the wavering images have something to do with Jews themselves. Let me tell you about an incident I recently witnessed. Just before Passover, I went to buy some things in a kosher shop – the kind of place where, at that time of the year, you meet all kinds of Jews, by no means only Orthodox. I noticed a middle-aged man, well dressed and with a distinctly 'accultured' appearance, who was looking through the magazine displays with obvious signs of unease. In desperation he finally turned to one of the shop assistants, a North African Jew wearing a black skullcap, and said: 'I'm looking for a kind of little roll … You know, that cement people eat … ' The assistant smiled broadly and replied: 'But what is the cement you are looking for?' Feeling a little embarrassed for him, I took a packet of the substance in question from beside the check-out and discreetly placed it in his hands. It was *haroset*, a ground mix of apple, dried fruits, wine and cinnamon, which is traditionally prepared at home but also sold in grocers' shops in little rolls of white paper. On the Passover evening table, it symbolizes the mortar used by Hebrew slaves in the building of the Pharaoh's towns. So that was the cement. As for the poor shopper, it may be that he was embarking on a return to Judaism. But that did not stop the other playing the part of the uncomprehending assistant. How could such disparities fail to maintain a certain lack of definition in people's minds?

J-CA: And the minimalist, but not completely wrong definitions of Jewish identity that you often hear today are not likely to settle matters: for example, that you are a Jew if that is what you say you are, regardless of your ancestry, beliefs and culture; or if most of the people around you say that that is what you are; or if you keep asking yourself what it means to be a Jew … Such definitions express the contemporary fragmentation, as well as the frequent difficulty of un-ambiguously stating the positive content of the identity to which you refer. How can one not be surprised that non-Jews therefore tend to focus on stronger, simpler images – of strict religious observance, for example, and of a break with the cultural values of the surrounding world? Of course, behind those images, behind that reality, the same complexity remains. But who actually knows that? There are plenty of *baalei teshuva*, or 'repentant ones', in the ranks of the ultra-Orthodox. They look as if they are fully 'on the inside', even when they have only just arrived from 'the outside'. How can one explain to people, or even get them to recognize, that the return-to-Orthodoxy tend-ency may be only the continuation, in a different form, of a return that was fashionable in the 1970s and 1980s, when a lot of Jewish ex-leftists and sixty-eighters, as well as the generation immediately after them, rediscovered from a secular point of view all the richness of the Jewish legacy? You remember the turbulence of the 1980s. You were actively involved in it.

EB: The Judaism in question was so 'cultural' and so non-religious that, when I once helped to organize some meetings on Mediter-ranean and Oriental Jewish culture at the Pompidou Centre, together with Jacques Hassoun, Annie Goldman and others, the date we chose happened to be that of the Jewish New Year! None of those organizing the event had thought of that. The problem had never occurred to anyone. We certainly came in for some rebukes from the rabbinate: it was all very well to be working for the greater glory of Jewish culture, but it was a bit much to be doing it on a particularly solemn religious holiday when no one was supposed to work! We wanted others to recognize us for what we were, not in some ancestral religion but in a cultural identity at once ancient, composite and reconstructed.

J-CA: That was the period of the great surge in Jewish studies in France, which produced most of today's researchers and lecturers.

EB: For some it meant a real change in their academic career during those years. In fact, most of us came from other disciplines.

J-CA: Secular or even academic study of Judaism and the history of the Jews became one of the main ways in which the return to Judaism took place in the 1970s and 1980s. At the same time, there were the efforts inspired by Neher or Lévinas to regain a Jewish sense of meaning. What is Jewish consciousness? What can Judaism offer in reply to the great questions of the epoch? The two approaches were often combined, and the same people could be found working on both the cultural and the philosophical level. Today things are quite different: the forms in which people are returning to religion mark a break with that previous movement – or, at least, they continue it only by subverting it, or aim to move beyond it. But the fact remains that, as far as Judaism, including secular Judaism, is concerned, lively forces are still active in France.

EB: France does indeed provide a base for a reflexive Judaism that is moving with the times, for Jews who are active in society and active in their way of being Jewish. I don't only see grounds for pessimism. There are many centres of great vitality. We have spoken of the United States; we are now speaking of France.

J-CA: France has the peculiarity of being the only country in the Diaspora where a majority of the Jewish community is Sephardi. Already Westernized in their country of origin, these Sephardis also maintain here many of their distinctively Oriental elements. There is Israel, of course, where the tensions are pregnant with menace. But there is a strong potential in various places in the world.

EB: We should also consider Central and Eastern Europe, where things are less clear but still on the move. There is a real awakening in Hungary, for example. In Germany, where 100,000 Jews now live, even non-Jews weighed down by guilt and a sense of irreparable loss are looking again at the time when Jews were a real and integral part of the German-speaking world. Britain's community of 300,000 is the second largest in Western Europe, enriched during the last few decades of the nineteenth century by the arrival of Jews from Eastern Europe, and it has developed a stabler Judaism unscathed by war. Everywhere, the question of Jewish identity is being posed, and solved in a variety of ways. Europe and its Jews are together looking for references in a space currently undergoing reconstruction.

12 | From communal affirmation to the temptation to withdraw

J-CA: I more or less agree. Nineteenth-century Judaism invented new forms of Jewish identity, some of which have continued to develop and prosper down to the present day. Twentieth-century Judaism was marked by the experience of devastation and deracination. The Muslim countries have been emptied of their Jews. Eastern Europe has been emptied of its Jews, through either extermination or emigration. But I fear that the century now beginning will produce new roots mainly through support for a model of religious closure.

EB: Does that mean that religion is what will remain to Jews when they have lost everything else?

J-CA: When they have lost everything that makes up the substance of Jewish life, perhaps they will be left with no more than that as an anchor.

EB: Let us not forget the memory of persecution.

J-CA: Another legacy of the century now over. The memory of past suffering welds the group together and legitimates its claims.

EB: All contemporary assertions of identity are based on a memory of persecution or oppression. You are what you are, you affirm it, you proclaim it – and you do this all the more when you have been or are a victim. This does not apply only to Jews. Who has not been the victim of one group or another? Think of the American Indians, or the Beurs [second-generation North Africans in France], or homosexuals. But this emphasis on victimization strengthens group identity even more than individual identity: it leads, whatever anyone says, to a revival of ethnicism – even in France. There is no point in getting hot under the collar about multiculturalism, because the fact is that it is already advancing in society. It is also a fact that withdrawal is one of its symptoms, but withdrawal bearing a double sign. Forget the Jews and think of France's young Muslims, those who used to be called 'Beurs'. Studies have shown that many of them are attached to the model of Jewish integration, but use it only as a reference. They want to integrate, not to surrender their identity or to run the risk of assimilation; integration for them does not necessarily mean a total loss of group identity. That is also how things worked out in the end for Jews, but with the greater discretion required in the nineteenth century. Today, a young woman can be a practising Muslim even if she dresses in Western clothes; or she can be modern even if covered up.

J-CA: There are many possible combinations to try out.

EB: Not even the state has much leverage over these trends. Conflicts in other countries may become transformed, inside France, into elements that define people's identity, as we saw in the case of those young Muslims who set fire to synagogues at the start of the second Intifadah, in autumn 2000. Was it right to describe those attacks as anti-Semitic? The young people in question identified with the Palestinian cause, with the Palestinian stone-throwers, with a suffering that was not directly theirs. And this proximity, real or imagined, was stronger than all the fine lessons in republican morality. We should not get too panicky: I remember that, while all this was going on, I went shopping in the eighteenth arrondissement in Paris and received greetings for the Jewish New Year from Muslim Arab shopkeepers.

J-CA: But let us come back to the bitterness.

EB: The history of relations between the Jews and France, the first country to emancipate them and to give them citizenship, is mostly in the nature of a love story. But now all that is being forgotten as a recently acquired bitterness is constantly renewed. After the last war, French Jews again wagered on integration and pressed on with efforts to rebuild their lives. But the nineteenth-century model had had its day: the dark days of the war had taken their toll, even though France was one of the Nazi-occupied countries where the Jewish population, in proportion to its size, had suffered the fewest losses. Out of 320,000 Jews, nearly 75,000 perished during the conflict. Memories of this betrayal by the Republic, however, have never ceased to fuel the bitterness of which you speak, and the fact that we are now living in an age of assertive identity has obviously played a role in this. De Gaulle's inept (to say the least) remarks during the Six-Day War did nothing to help matters. Then there was the terrible attack on the synagogue at rue Copernic in Paris, in 1980. All these events and resentments have combined to foster a gradual withdrawal on the part of French Jews.

J-CA: We should not overlook the communitarianism, or quasi-communitarianism, of the French state itself.

EB: I think that both the religious institutions and the public authorities have an interest in strengthening this trend, whether in relation to Islam or to Judaism. Communitarianism is a simple means for the state to control minority groups; the creation of the Consistories in 1808 was designed to achieve precisely that. But what does communitarianism really mean today? When a Jew says that he is Jewish, and expresses a desire to act as such in the name of or for the sake of his group, is that communitarianism? In 1870, Adolphe Crémieux obtained French nationality for the Jews of North Africa, having previously fought, in 1846, to eliminate the *more judaico* oath required of Jews involved in court proceedings. Can that be described as communitarianism? Nevertheless, for the state authorities it is simpler to negotiate with structured communities and their presumably representative spokespersons than it is to deal with completely fragmented groups.

J-CA: As far as community notables are concerned, this gives them power (or an illusion of power) that they could not obtain anywhere else. How many Jews vote in the Consistory elections? Who elects the chief rabbi of France? Which Jews even know how it happens? Yet representatives of the Jewish institutions feel themselves to be invested with authority, at least when they are consulted by the state. How many Jews recognize themselves in the declarations of Chief Rabbi Sitruk? Are some of them not rather irritated or worried by his ceremonial expression of good wishes to the President of the Republic, at the beginning of each year?

EB: That is not going to stop the state from continuing with things as they are; it wants to have someone to speak to. It tried to come to the same arrangement with Islam in France, but the plan for a Muslim 'consistory' floundered for a long time because Islam is also a complex reality with lively inner conflicts, in an age of generally tough identities. We are no longer in the nineteenth century, when Jews dreamed of nothing other than integration.

J-CA: The Jews do not only have consistories – which in

principle are now merely religious associations. They also have the CRIF,[2] which sees it as its duty to receive the powerful of this world from time to time.

EB: The CRIF – which, at the time of its foundation, was called the Conseil représentatif des israélites de France – is a secular political structure. For a long time the chief rabbi of France was not at all recognized as a political representative of the Jewish community, and it has to be said that today he tends to set himself up more and more as an interlocutor of the state. Traditionally, in the Jewish world, the role of intermediary has devolved to secular figures – so what we see here is a blurring of functions that often makes different institutions compete with one another. Communitarianism? That may be the aim of the public authorities, as well as an aspiration on the part of those who run Jewish institutions. But it is a dream of control completely out of their reach. Who would control such a polymorphous community?

J-CA: Communitarianism is also a kind of hobby horse agitating the minds of our republican Orthodox. So where is the communitarianism they fear so much? There is no community or institution that really sets itself up as an intermediary between the individual and the state. Groups appear, organize and try to operate as lobbies: it hardly gets any further than that. Most Jews can recognize themselves as Jewish and feel part of a community, without belonging or paying a subscription to anything, without thinking of themselves as represented either by the chief rabbi of France, or by the CRIF or by any secular notables. They have a sense of belonging to a community, but it is not their only sense of belonging. They might also be signed-up supporters of an aid agency or an environmental group, or have a membership card in a political party of the Right, Left or Centre, or have a passionate interest in Bordeaux wine or stamp-collecting. There is no danger of communitarianism so long as the state refrains from giving further credit or authority to certain institutions.

EB: Withdrawal into the community is nevertheless a reality, and I am not thinking only of the most religious. I come across more and more Jews who seem to live in a kind of aquarium: they listen to Jewish radio stations, read Jewish newspapers, live with other Jews,

2 The Conseil représentatif des institutions juives de France, the Representative Council of the Jewish Institutions of France.

go out to see Jewish films. The self-enclosed detachment of certain Orthodox is understandable, given their lifestyle and the dietary laws they follow. That is not what is most disturbing, or most surprising. I am talking now about the rest. Since October 2000, when the cycle of violence began again in the Middle East, a certain kind of discourse has become more and more widespread. 'We have been betrayed, the media are against us, French policy is directed against Israel, anti-Semitism is rising again from the ashes.' This defensive retreat is what I find the most worrying. We should not generalize, should not see things in black and white. It may be no more than one of those passing crises which the Jews of France have known before. Their passionate love for the Republic has naturally had its ups and downs, like all passions. It is not that kind of self-absorption which worries me, but rather the cultural sterility that it threatens to induce in the medium term.

J-CA: I agree that it leaves little room for Jews who would dearly like to be both inside and outside. If the choice is between barricading yourself inside your four walls and being totally outside, it is understandable that some still prefer to take refuge outside.

EB: A schizophrenic development is something else to be feared. You are a citizen, you go out to work, you are not visible as a Jew – but as soon as you step inside your home or your community, you live entirely as a Jew and only as a Jew. In that kind of schizophrenia, what space is left to be receptive to non-Jews, or to Jews who live differently, who wish to move around and to keep ideas circulating with them?

J-CA: A certain kind of integrationist Judaism has long had as its watchword: 'Be a Jew at home and a man outside.' Personally, I am not against a (perhaps slightly provocative) reversal of the formula: 'Be a Jew outside and a man at home.' The important thing is never to stop thinking of yourself as a human being within a horizon of universality. Why should you not bring the outside world inside, while also, within certain limits, showing your Jewish identity outside? There is no compulsion to choose one camp or the other, and a lot to be lost by doing it.

13 | Israel seen from within and from the Diaspora

EB: Unfortunately the question of Israel, which occupies many people's minds, drives more than one to fall into univocality. Yet in this area there are so many different views, so many different attitudes. Is enough care being taken to listen to them?

J-CA: We should not let ourselves be trapped by the public, or official, discourse of certain community institutions. There is no point in denying that it exists, but we should take it for what it is. There are other discourses as well, which are less often expressed, because people are either unable or unwilling to express them. Fear weighs down on them with all its force: fear for Israel, fear for its existence and for the lives of friends or relatives there.

EB: Nevertheless, during the second Intifadah, quite a few 'Jewish' petitions were circulated and published which did not necessarily accord with the official discourse of the Jewish institutions. In fact, they often vigorously opposed it. This was one indication of the range of opinions. But, as you rightly said, what one hears most are not opinions but fear – that great fear for the existence of Israel! Still, for a historian, there is no real reason to think of that fear as absurd. Israel might disappear. It would not be the first time in history that the Jews lost their political autonomy, their territorial base. I am not uttering these words to give myself a frisson. I am simply thinking that the real threat to Israel is not war but the inability to make peace. Peace, not further escalation, is the best way of removing the fear. How we get it is another matter. But it certainly won't be through being anti-Palestinian, through closing our ears to the suffering, expectations and demands of the Palestinians. Even at the present moment, that is not how the fear for Israel's survival can be dispelled.

J-CA: Yes, the danger for Israel comes not only from its objective external enemies but also from its internal tensions and the difficulties it faces in handling the crisis. The danger is not necessarily where you think it is. But it does exist. The late Israeli scholar Yeshayahu Leibo-witz is one of the few thinkers who has not been listened to enough. In his view, it is the occupation not the return of the Arab territories which corrupts Israel's identity and threatens its future existence.

EB: At least in Israel you can hear dissident voices; the capacity to take a distance is more widespread there. Not everyone has it, of course, but historians, sociologists and political scientists have for quite some time been producing analyses that deserve to be given greater attention, and which are not really being heard in the Diaspora. This whole post-Zionist generation – people like Baruch Kimmerling, Ilan Pappe, Uri Ram, Sammy Smooha or Amnon Raz-

Krakotzkin – are helping to deconstruct the official discourse. The Benny Morrises and Tom Segevs have long been writing about the 1948 crisis and the expulsion of the Palestinians, reviewing from scratch the whole history of the war of independence. It is now known, for example, that the Palestinians did not leave fully of their own accord or simply under the influence of Arab propaganda. The work of Tom Segev is regularly translated and published in France: the Jewish media speak of it, and he has not been subjected to inordinate criticism in the organized community, no doubt because his is a voice coming from inside Israel and no one has felt entitled to say: 'Look at this anti-Semitic Israeli.' But have people listened closely to what he has to say? When a Frenchman, even a French Jew, says something disturbing, a ton of bricks come crashing down. What accusations are not hurled at him? Yet there is no anti-Semitism in that. Unfortunately, there are many other discourses that assist our understanding which large parts of the Jewish community in France still do not want to hear. In the United States, at least, the political options are more varied and new voices are not stifled. The Jews of France are lagging somewhat behind. Not all the Diaspora communities develop exactly the same attitude to Israel, even if Israel remains an essential component of their identity.

J-CA: One idea we need to abandon, in my view, is that the creation of the State of Israel marked the fulfilment of messianic prophecies. Perhaps it was not even the beginning of the beginning. What madness it is to debase messianism into politics! What a crime against messianism! And what a suicidal way of conducting politics! Let us strip that country of dreams which it has no mission to fulfil. Israel wanted to be a Jewish country, or a country for the Jews. Today, its aim should be to become a place of secure settlement for those who live there; it cannot be a country based on occupation; it is not the vocation either of Zionism or of Israel to occupy territories inhabited by non-Jews. Too many Jews in the Diaspora never manage to take on board these few elementary truths. But they have been said loud and clear in Israel itself.

EB: Perhaps the focus should not be so much on the hatred between the two peoples. The conflict cannot be reduced to an explosion of more or less irrational passions: there are reasons for the war, and for the hatred. It seems to me that recently some of the Jewish media have put a little too much stress on an implacable

Palestinian hatred for Israelis. Hate has long been cultivated on both sides, not only one, and now people are suffering the consequences. But that is not the only element in play. Demonization of the Other as the one to blame for everything will not leave any chance of achieving peace. One side at least much take the necessary step and leave hate behind. Will some think this is just naïve? The difference, today, is that unlike the Israelis (or at least some Israelis) the Palestinians apparently refuse to revise the myth of the land which both they and their enemies have developed – and which, in many respects, they have actually borrowed from their enemies.

J–CA: But how could they revise it when they do not have a land or a state, and when all they have known until now are subjugation and dispossession? It is understandable that the myth is showing some signs of weakness in Israel, but how can the same thing be expected of the Palestinians? On the other hand, it is true that the themes are similar: attachment to the land, loss of the land, return to the land, diaspora, ancient roots, legitimacy, historical rights and victimization.

EB: You are overlooking Jerusalem.

J–CA: Jerusalem was not at first such a big issue for Zionism, even though the country's first Hebrew university was founded there.

EB: Indeed, the first Jewish pioneer settlements in Palestine did not take root in Jeruslaem. Apart from the mistrust that these agricultural workers felt for city life in general, Jerusalem stood for the ancient Jewish community of Palestine with all its peculiar quirks, a religious population always praying and studying the Torah to save the Jewish people, a Jewish exile population par excellence. The pioneers preferred to settle in areas without religious associations and for a long time remained distrustful of Jerusalem.

J–CA: Still today, even if they insist that the State of Israel must have a united Jerusalem as its capital, many Israelis see it as a reminder that the 'land of Israel' has always been and still is also someone else's land, and Jerusalem also someone else's city. It is the city of Orthodox and ultra-Orthodox, some of them even anti-Zionist, and it is the city of the Arabs, the city of Islam. It exerts a kind of twofold spell or fascination, and for that reason always ends up becoming an issue – not only between Jews and Arabs, but also among Jews themselves. To choose to live in Jerusalem is not a neutral act. You could live in Tel Aviv instead, precisely so as not to be put through Jerusalem, the city of the Other.

EB: In fact, some academics who teach in Jerusalem do choose to live in Tel Aviv, as a neutral city.

J-CA: Or a Jewish city par excellence. It started out, in 1909, as a new city built by Jews where only Jews lived, and it came to symbolize the whole Zionist enterprise. It is a coastal city alongside Jaffa – alongside it, not in its place. Tel Aviv evokes the re-establishment of a Jewish presence on the soil of Palestine, but also a reconstruction that parts company with all models and turns its back on any awkward presence.

EB: I should also mention that the first settlement of Jewish pioneers from abroad was Rishon LeZiyyon, now less than ten miles from Tel Aviv and a long way from Jerusalem. The New Jew naturally dreaded getting too close to a city heavy with thousands of years of history.

J-CA: Let us look at the ambiguities. Jerusalem, city of the Jebusites, is said to have been conquered by King David, and his successor, King Solomon, to have built the First Temple there as the site of temporal power and God's residence on earth. A mythical place, on which Jewish expectations of redemption centred for centuries, Jerusalem is also the symbol of independence, the capital and anything else you care to mention. It is therefore a powerful messianic-Zionist symbol, but also the exact opposite: the city of exile. The ultra-Orthodox district of Mea Shearim, in Jerusalem, contains the whole exile transplanted to the land of Israel.

EB: If you look at a map of the first pioneer settlements, you will see that they faced away from Jerusalem. For Israel, however, there is also the question of the state – not only a question of geography or territory. Quickly grasping the dimension of the Arab problem, a thinker like Ahad Ha'Am, in the late nineteenth or early twentieth century, had a quite different goal in mind: namely, that Palestine should become a centre of Jewish culture, not a Jewish state.

J-CA: And, by radiating out, that centre of culture would enable the Diaspora to protect itself against the dangers of assimilation and the temptations of the open society. The ambition of Ahad Ha'Am was to create an area of secular Judaism, a Palestinian Jewish culture strong enough to feed, enrich and regenerate the Jews who remained in exile. And that, we should note, is not exactly what we are witnessing today.

EB: Diaspora Jews, especially from France, latch on to everything in Israel that can reinforce their identity. But they will not find that in a short story by Aharon Appelfeld or a novel by Yaakov Shabtai. What will actually reinforce the Diaspora Jews in their Jewishness will, on the contrary, be the religious currents active in Israel; and they will find reassurance about their own future from a particular political figure there, or a particular ruling party. Instinctively they will support the government of the day – whether Netanyahu, Barak or Sharon – because it represents and fights for Israel, and because many Diaspora Jews still see Israel as a last refuge in case of adversity. We should not forget this aspect. Strong governments are more highly regarded for being strong. Israel, at least in people's imagination, brings security and protection to the Jews of the Diaspora. All this leaves no scope for a post-Zionist discourse, which is rejected out of hand.

J–CA: It calls too many things into question. In the end, the diversity and depth of Israeli culture do not really reach the Diaspora – if they did, they might well destabilize it. What the Diaspora seeks in Israel are not its living elements of secular culture but its least Zionist side: a religious identification, the myth of Jerusalem.

EB: Yes, secular culture is certainly lively there, with major literary, artistic and intellectual movements. But this goes unnoticed in the Diaspora, which fixes only on what it sees as the twin sources of its survival: the state and religion. As the state and religion are also moving, however, it is difficult to keep up with them except in fits and starts, according to the rhythm of government change.

J–CA: You speak of twin sources, but I might just as easily speak of twin crutches that make the Diaspora overlook its own creative forces. The Diaspora is more than just a fragile Jewish universe that can survive only by identifying with a state; it houses a rich and productive Judaism. There is a slight tendency to ignore or undervalue it. Things are happening on both sides, but they are not appreciated for what they are. Not all eyes are directed at Israel, and even there some eyes are turned outwards.

EB: Personally, I have never had a Diaspora attitude to Israel. I am myself a former Israeli and I also have Israeli citizenship. I am a *yoredet*, an emigrée: literally 'one who has descended', thereby reversing the 'ascent' to Israel advocated by Zionism. And I feel as much Israeli as French. What counts for me in that country is what is actually happening there. And when I talk to some of my Jewish friends about the simplicity of this relationship, I sometimes get the impression of having descended from another planet. I allow myself to criticize Israel, sometimes quite vigorously, but I tremble at each new incident. I know there is scarcely anything effective I can do to help restore peace, although it is the only thing that preoccupies me. When you are Israeli, peace is not an abstraction; you know the costs of war. When you are Israeli, you cannot ignore the fact that there are the Palestinians. The Diaspora Jew can dream, can act as if there were no Palestinians – but not an Israeli who has lived every day in contact with them. Often I tell myself that many Israelis, from North Africa or the Middle East, share certain values with Muslims. Israel belongs to the world of the Eastern Mediterranean, more than people care to think, even if it is also a country turned towards the West. In many aspects of life – ways of eating or shopping, favourite styles of music, and so on – Israelis are Eastern Mediterranean. Everyone knows that there is not just one Israeli cuisine, that each ethnic group has kept the culinary traditions of its place of origin. Yet the few dishes that are today considered 'typically Israeli' – falafel or houmous, for example – are in fact typically Middle Eastern. There is also an Israeli body language, as well as a climate that favours life on terraces and out of doors. In a country whose population is an improbable mixture of European and Oriental, the Mediterranean imposes many of its customs. It is a society which has evidently become 'Levanticized'.

J-CA: For the better and for the worse!

EB: Things can change again. The arrival of a million immigrants from Russia, who have nothing Eastern Mediterranean about them, has turned relations upside down.

J-CA: Until the recent Russian wave, Israeli society had a Sephardi majority. Now that is again not the case.

EB: Politically, however, Israel has always been Ashkenazi, with a ruling elite turned towards the West. There are still not many Sephardis in the senior ranks of the civil service or the academic world – a disparity which reflects the dangerous imbalance on the political level.

14 | Jewish intellectual freedom and the weight of conformism

J-CA: In any event, to return to our main concern here, Israeli culture remains largely impenetrable to the Diaspora Jew. The problem is already one of language, as few Jews in the Diaspora speak

Hebrew well enough to enter the culture on an equal footing. From this point of view, Israel does not correspond to the vision of a centre of culture radiating out to the Diaspora; what it radiates is rather fascination and imagination. But, while the cultural distance between Diaspora Jews and Israelis has proved to be quite considerable, the Diaspora can still pride itself on what at least seems to be a degree of intellectual vitality. The official academic recognition of Jewish and Hebrew studies, the ever growing number of books published in this field testifies to the growing legitimacy that this culture has been acquiring outside the Jewish world. The books to which I refer are being produced by 'ordinary' publishers, not those which specialize in Judaism. Lecturers and researchers in this field find it reasonably easy to fit into the general structures of academic institutions or the CNRS (the French scientific research centre). But it remains very difficult to gauge the impact of this stronger cultural position on the Jewish community itself.

EB: The recent boom in Jewish studies is bound up with the return to Judaism that many intellectuals have effected in the last few decades. Before, academic research on Judaism and the Jews was the preserve of a few rare specialists with only a small readership. Again this raises a number of questions. Do Jews really read such books? What do they mostly read? Do they read at all? What do they expect from their intellectuals? Words of comfort? Judging by the sales figures, we may well wonder whether the Jews, the 'People of the Book', actually buy books with a Jewish theme. We should note that many of them seem to have been more affected by the publication in French of great texts from the Jewish tradition than by the appearance of critical or historical studies. No publishing house is unaware of this. The aim of any responsible author is doubtless not so much to write for hypothetical Jewish readers as to open new horizons for a broader non-Jewish public. As you see, I continue to think that it is possible to make advances through knowledge, and that sometimes – not always – rejection of the Other stems from ignorance of what he or she really is.

J-CA: There is another phenomenon to which you have already alluded. A large minority of the Jewish population expects to be re-assured, to have its value recognized in its own eyes and those of the outside world. But that is certainly not the role of the Jewish intellectual who focuses his attention on the Jews or Judaism; he is not there to reinforce identities or to weld communities together, but rather to stimulate reflection, to challenge ready-made images, to show that things are always more intricate than one thinks. And that kind of work is not always well received at first.

EB: Nor does it always have the intended effect. People arrive with preconceived ideas and go away still carrying them. They come to our courses for five or six years and ask the same question for the umpteenth time. Even if our writings do not address some of the obsessions of Jewish readers, they are often read through their prism, not for what they really are. In such cases, a book quite simply has no reception.

J-CA: On the other hand, if a book of yours happens to be promoted beyond a Jewish readership, if it is successful or earns respect in the wider intellectual community, there can sometimes be a knock-on effect within the Jewish community.

EB: It seems to be a feature of all minorities to seek the approval of the rest of the world, before moving on, often still cautiously, to adopt a new cultural product. Some people shut themselves up in one-dimensional thinking, with its clear-cut and doggedly cultivated axes of identification. And, as soon as you write something that points in a different direction, you are exposed to a flood of negative epithets: your text is 'anti-Semitic', your book is 'anti-Semitic', 'anti-Israeli', 'anti-Zionist', 'self-hating' and so on. It would be wrong to think that all Jews react like that. But I am not an ideologue, only a modest producer of ideas, and I am not here to give my backing to assorted clichés. On the contrary, even if it is not to the liking of all Jews, I must try to push things forward a little. Sometimes I manage to do that in my lectures. Sometimes, not often enough, a student says to me about a historical event: 'For years I've had this or that way of thinking about it. Now I've discovered to my surprise that you can think about it quite differently.' If I can at least tell others how I see the Jews and their history, basing myself on research that is as far as possible without preconceptions, then I think I will have done my job. I have also noticed that more and more non-Jewish students are writing theses under our supervision. They show up with a few ideas gleaned from here and there, but not completely fixed, and are capable of showing a lot of good will. The quality of their work is ample evidence that they are still capable of new discoveries. And that is the kind of thing that encourages us, rather than a struggle lost in advance against water-tight banalities. Jewish studies are like any other studies: they are not reserved for Jews alone.

J–CA: I detect another danger against which it is not easy to protect yourself. When the unconventional discourse that you try to present finds an echo outside the Jewish world, it can often be neutralized from within by people who cannot and will not see what is new or unsettling about it. There is a certain lack of clarity in the status of a Jewish academic. We work on Judaism: we are not spokespersons for the organized Jewish community. We must never be where we are expected to be. We are smugglers across frontiers. Our calling is to make everyone feel a little awkward. If we don't achieve that, what good are we? This freedom comes at a price, in that some will read us badly or not at all. But that is only normal. The search for 'roots' feeds on answers not on questions, and what we can offer is not what it hopes to find. There is an intellectual public out there which is made up of Jews as well as non-Jews. And, clearly, the main readership for a book about Judaism will not necessarily be Jewish itself.

EB: My own experience makes me think that, for a lot of middle-class people in particular, the fact that they have lived through certain things gives them the conviction of knowledge. That is the core of the problem.

J–CA: We live, perhaps wrongly, on the myth that Jews have traditionally valued knowledge and learning. We gave way to it ourselves a moment ago when we talked about 'Jewish intelligence'. But a more commonly heard idea is this: 'We know all that already; we know it better than you do because we have experienced it ourselves.'

EB: But you don't hear it in connection with biblical, talmudic or kabbalistic texts. There attitudes tend to be humbler, because the texts are sacred and are supposed to bear the ultimate truth.

J–CA: Humility is compulsory in that context, as is acceptance of scholarly mediation. The first obstacle is linguistic, since people are not born with a knowledge of Hebrew or Aramaic and do not pick it up just by living. The fact remains, though, that most people put a premium on being, essence and nostalgia, and easily turn their back on learning, research and the painful acquisition of knowledge. 'It's enough that I'm Jewish.' That kind of maxim tends to make our function appear less legitimate.

EB: Are we not also perhaps victims of a devaluation of secular discourse?

J-CA: That goes without saying.

EB: So the problem is also the following. Who has authority to speak about Judaism? A godless female Jewish, or non-Jewish, historian of the Jews? A youngish, smooth-faced, non-religious man who thinks of Judaism as he would about any other religious tradition?

J-CA: It is clear that, for large sections of the Jewish community, what you are gives credence to what you say. And many do not recognize ordinary intellectuals or scholars as fully legitimate.

EB: At the same time, intellectual discourse about the Jews has become increasingly female over the past twenty years or so, with more and more women historians who are Jewish or have a Jewish background. I do not know what is the reason for this: perhaps the greater openness in the period since 1968, or the relative devaluation of this kind of work. In any event, does the discourse in question really correspond to the expressed needs? What do most people expect? A way of speaking that is either entirely secular – the kind you find among writers of novels, for example – or else fundamentally religious. I cannot see much room for a third type of discourse, except in the case of personal testimony. First-hand testimony does correspond to some of the crystallizations of the present period; such words are audible. We are living in an age of overproduction of such accounts, as words that were never spoken (especially about the Holocaust) make themselves heard. I see nothing wrong in this – on the contrary. But it means that personal testimony, which is by definition irrefutable, has acquired a kind of holy status. Nor should we forget that we are living in a time when anyone can be asked to say what they think about anything. Everyone has an opinion about everything, and every opinion is legitimate. If the voice in question arises out of personal experience, then nothing can be opposed to it – only another experience. What objection can be made to a memory, or to a person's suffering? Among the evident plurality of discourses, the only one lacking is a discourse about discourses that operates with critical distance.

J-CA: Let me say that the average Jewish reader has almost the same attitude to the sacred or canonical texts of Judaism. A critically detached historical approach to them is usually repudiated, or simply considered uninteresting. The text itself is supposed to say all it has to say. From it alone we are supposed to derive its entire meaning. It has the same value as personal testimony. The two phenomena go hand in hand: prostration before personal testimony and prostration before the sacred text. A detached approach that deconstructs and reconstructs thereby loses its legitimacy and authority.

EB: The weight of conformism, alas, does not affect only Jews. All too easily, in matters concerning the Jews, one discourse tries to impose itself by crushing all others. Take, for example, the furore unleashed by the appearance of Norman Finkelstein's recent book *The Holocaust Industry*. Are we going to start banning the publication of books because they are polemical? Doesn't that land us in an embarrassing kind of Stalinism? After all, to accept the principle of democracy means to accept real freedom of expression. I myself read the book soon after it appeared in English. It is certainly far from perfect: I myself immediately pointed out its highly polemical tone, and a lot of what you read in it is pretty questionable. There is a kind of leftist inspiration behind it, as well as old resentments possibly associated with the author's own life. OK, you can even completely disagree with Finkelstein. But what are that French lawyer and his association doing when they threaten the author and publisher with prosecution for incitement to racial hatred? It is really too much – or too ridiculous. If you step out of line, you can expect to be put on trial. Let us criticize, denounce, publish articles, continue the debate – but above all let us try to expand it. Is the thirst for courtroom justice not hypocritical? Maybe Finkelstein does not say what you want him to say about the less than noble uses to which the memory of genocide is put, about what some have called the 'Shoah business'. But does that mean you try to shut him up? To think of putting him on trial is to deny any scope for the exchange of ideas, to ask judges to solve a clash of ideas which, in a society that calls itself democratic, should be settled only with words.

J-CA: Such behaviour both induces and feeds on an extreme simplification of the debate. Did Finkelstein say some shocking and revolting things? He certainly did. But he said other things that are definitely less so – things with which we can even agree. Instead of selecting these out and giving them serious thought, his detractors preferred to go in for amalgams such as: Finkelstein = anti-Zionist = anti-Semitic = historical revisionist. And soon they were thinking of legal action, without even realizing that this gave his book free publicity that they should logically have denied it. All this makes me feel uncomfortable, because I have no wish to live and think in that kind of regime, and because Finkelstein's book anyway does not dispute the reality of the Holocaust. Has it been used by the revisionists? But who isn't used by the revisionists? The Israeli post-Zionists certainly are. You see them quoted all the time on websites run by revisionists, Roger Garaudy supporters and others.

EB: There are similarities with the Renaud Camus affair, which was not so important and hardly deserves to be called an affair. The result was that a rather obscure author was given inordinate publicity. It would have been better not to talk about him, not to react, so that the whole thing fizzled out into silence and darkness. But everyone got much too steamed up about it – even the minister of culture and communication. From one day to the next, the name of Renaud Camus became known to a lot of people. I don't deny that we have a duty to fight against anti-Semitism, but in that case it all went a little too far. His few words about the growing Jewishness of a France Culture programme deserved to be shrugged off and forgotten.

J-CA: I think there was also a little Parisianism in the whole business. Did it advance anything by one iota? I don't think so.

EB: In one degree or another, all of us are in the psychological state of the intellectual warrior, who jumps on anything said or written, any little sign, and denounces it with sound and fury. The anti-Semitism of Renaud Camus? OK, he said some things that were more than dubious.

J-CA: Let us be clear. It is right to fight against real dangers, but was there really a danger in that case? In my view, that is not where the danger lies. Other things deserve more attention and more combativeness. Perhaps the constraint on all of us to be 'right-thinking' is a good example of a real danger. Besides, too much moralism in intellectual debate is not good either for morality or for intellectual debate. None other than Paul Ricoeur, himself a friend of Emmanuel Lévinas, came in for unjust criticism after the publication of his last book *La Mémoire, l'Histoire, l'Oubli*.

EB: It is the need to shout one's moralism from the housetops which is so astonishing. I find it disturbing, because our society is neither moral nor just, its politicians are not all clean-handed, its intellectuals are sometimes ambivalent, and its economic priorities are not always very honourable. And yet, for reasons that are by no means clear, this society lines up behind an ultra-moralistic position, a collective expiation either through denunciations of anti-Semitism or through a cult of the Holocaust.

J-CA: This fuels a thoroughly simplistic view of the world, in which there are only goodies and baddies, only people on the right side and people on the wrong side. We know that history has not been like that, but people demand it nevertheless. They demand transparency and simplicity.

EB: The truth!

J-CA: But there is not one truth. In history there have been executioners and victims, as well as masses of people who have been neither the one nor the other, but who in certain circumstances might have become either executioners or victims. You find more than one complex itinerary, where someone on the Right with quite nationalist leanings, who might have been expected to support Pétain and make a pact with the devil, eventually joined the Resistance and helped to save numbers of Jews. Or vice versa. Manichaeism is dangerous and can end up backfiring on the Jews themselves, who are neither simple nor transparent. You sometimes have to resign yourself to a lack of transparency, to accept that people and societies have a long and complex history. You may have to accept duality. For duality is not always the same as duplicity.

EB: Who can boast of being simple? It is this thirst for clear-cut truths and absolute morality which shocks me, in a world otherwise prepared for many a compromise. Is all this activism really in the service of ideal justice and truth? Or does it not involve a mere instrumentalization of the Shoah and anti-Semitism, a mobilization of these themes for other purposes? The hubbub is so Parisian. I am not aware that Finkelstein's book provoked such a storm in the United States, where discordant voices are more common, even if a number of harsh reviews appeared in the press. Over there, intellectuals and academics are capable of a calmer approach. One of my colleagues in New York, for example, a well-known academic specialist on Judaism, recently told us that he had declined huge sums for the setting up of a Holocaust study centre at his university, because he did not want to make the Shoah a central focus of his teaching programme. When students ask him to supervise theses on the question, he prefers to encourage them to look for a different subject. The way in which it has been blown up is truly worrying, and Americans – who are most affected by this – are also the most aware of what is happening. People do not hesitate to criticize the Simon Wiesenthal Museum of Tolerance in Los Angeles, or to describe it as a 'Holocaust Disneyland'. Nor do they hesitate to question the policies of the Holocaust Museum in Washington. Does that bring threats of legal action? Yet the United States is certainly a country given to litigation. In France we have the Gayssot Law against racism and denial of the Holocaust, and this has its good and its bad side.

J-CA: You remember the Yahoo affair and those Nazi memorabilia that could be bought on the Net?

EB: It's exactly the same; nothing escapes the hunt. But I don't think that is the best way of combating anti-Semitism.

J-CA: It may be the worst.

EB: Before the violent outburst against Finkelstein's book, there was the kind of cult in some circles surrounding Goldhagen's *Hitler's Willing Executioners*. Everything in German culture was supposed to have led irresistibly to the Holocaust. The Germans close to being ontologically anti-Semitic: what a godsend! I am simplifying, but some analyses were not far from that kind of Manichaeism. If you don't say this or that, if you don't fall into line, you risk ending up in court.

J-CA: There can be no intellectual debate in a society which says: 'Watch out, everything you say may be used in evidence against you.'

EB: Only debate in which there is a real clash of views has a chance of dispelling ready-made ideas. Some people do have a taste for boldly striking out on new paths. No one should issue us with instructions on how to use the only instrument that can guarantee a little freedom: the instrument of thought. Words must have the right to circulate. Of course, that does not include words which deny the reality of the Holocaust. But let us not impose a leaden silence, let us not drown out the discourse of others, and let us not look for enemies where there are none. Previously there used to be Jew and anti-Semite; now there are supposed to be Jew, anti-Semite and anti-Semitic Jew. If, as some say, it is a Jewish characteristic to develop a critical sense and not to think what everyone else is thinking, then we must not lose it. If we lose that too, we Jews will have lost everything. Fight anti-Semitism? Of course, but in different ways – not with that indiscriminate pursuit of minor matters. The real task is a task of construction: to write and pass on the history of the Jews who lived before and continued to live after the extermination; not to centre everything on death and the cult of death.

15 | Fascination with suffering or the challenge of life: a critical choice

J-CA: In fact, why should Jews continue to be shut up in the absolute otherness that comes with the status of absolute victims? Jews are men and women. And I can't see how they would consent for long to confine themselves or be confined in that status. Like you, I think it is more important to educate the public about the history of the Jews, the history and cultural richness of Judaism. Jews are people in movement, not born martyrs. Let us remind people that Jewish societies are and have been living, creative societies, where certain things have been and still are experienced in joy.

EB: There is no point in playing with expressions like 'memory work' or 'memory duty'. What counts is to convey what Judaism was, to understand what Judaism is, and to think about what Judaism might become – not to detach the future from the past.

J-CA: And to restore to the past all its historical depth …

EB: … while remaining in the present. This involves some very modest tasks: the writing of books about the Jews that will also be read by non-Jews; the inclusion of the history of the Jews and Jewish thought in competitive entrance examinations; and the teaching of this history (which is not all a vale of tears) in our classrooms. Young people need to be shown that being a Jew is a way of living.

J-CA: And not only a fate of death.

EB: A way of living which has its peculiarities but can also contain a wider message. I think that the very experience of exile, which lies at the basis of a certain Jewish identity, is capable of speaking to everyone.

J-CA: You remember, we started off talking about the dimension of exile, as the first pillar of any definition of Jewish identity. Now we have come back to it, and to the possibility of its universalization. For, quite simply, exile may be at the heart of the human condition itself. To each their own exile … Mine was a kind of voluntary, internal exile, a chosen exile, where the memory of persecution did not play any role. Curiously, my road to Judaism passed through the discovery of Israeli literature and modern Hebrew, during a study trip to the Hebrew University in Jerusalem more than twenty years ago. The strong attachment to Israel that I have developed over the years has never really made me think of leaving France as a serious or likely option. Israel has been no more than a detour, a way of discovering

Jewish reality. It helped me to cultivate a thirst for knowledge, which I eventually tried to assuage in a more classical, 'diasporic' manner, by making medieval Jewish culture in the Diaspora my special field of research. The paths of exile can sometimes be very tortuous. Nowadays, when I arrive in Israel I don't really feel at home, but nor do I feel all that far from home. In a way, perhaps, the country is so close to me that I don't feel the need to go and live there.

EB: For myself, I am a random Jew. I have no homeland, no attachment to a particular territory. But I do have a physical link with Israel. Nearly all my family is there. Some of my relatives arrived there as long ago as the 1940s, and I myself was a member of a Zionist youth organization. I left at the age of fifteen. I am an Israeli, I have no complexes, and I have no accent in Hebrew. It is true that I feel more at ease there, but I am intellectually more attached to the West. Intellectually attached to the West, emotionally to Israel and ancestrally to the East, I nevertheless remain without a homeland or even a real mother tongue (because of an excessive multilingualism). At bottom, perhaps I am more Jewish than Israeli. My language of culture has been French, although for a time in my childhood it was English – something I have repressed for various reasons. I am a convinced Americanophile. But in Israel I see all the bad aspects of America magnified and indiscriminately taken over. Then I feel distant, both from Israel and from America. Culturally, I feel more in tune with France. In Israel the anxiety stifles me, but at the same time you feel alive. Everything is inordinately important there, everything has an exceptional place, everything is the object of debate, everything deserves long conversations, heated discussions and arguments. I am still an Israeli, then, but with a strong element of the Diaspora Jewishness. You, on the other hand, are perhaps too French.

J-CA: 'Too French' may be saying too much. I agree that what mainly defines me is my Frenchness, that that is what I am made of. I do not have doubts about my French identity, even if I have made an effort to put some disorder into it. But I certainly am a 'Frenchman born and bred' – that is the bedrock. Maybe the role of my mother and her native soil …

EB: You are a Diaspora Jew when you are in Israel. I am one everywhere.

J-CA: One thing does draw me closer to an Israeli, though, and that is the fact that I am at least 50 per cent a Gentile. Because of this,

I live my Jewish identity in a fairly simple – dare I say calm? – manner. It is not a source of embarrassment for me or something I feel a need to proclaim at the top of my voice; it is simply something that became quite natural to me. Strangely enough, this Gentile side today enables me to live my Jewish identity in a way that the Zionists could only have dreamed of! With complete equanimity. It was sometimes a problem for me in my youth, but today I am a Jew – full stop. And French – full stop. Neither an 'Israelite' nor anything else. This natural, untroubled experience of Jewish identity is perhaps the one thing I have in common with the Israeli or Zionist ideal – even though I live here in France!

EB: Still, we live in an ever more secular, ever more homogenized society; we see disappearing before our eyes the customs that used to give all the flavour and texture to a religion that was not only the Law but also the little everyday tasks, the little pleasures of a Sabbath that was not very Orthodox yet shared with the family, the pleasures of the various dishes, rituals and even little superstitions. Are not many non-religious Jews deprived, consciously or unconsciously, of this everyday Judaism?

J-CA: What you are describing is the dimension of pleasure in Judaism, which seems to me as essential to it as anything else. To enjoy life, to give thanks to the Life-Giver, is a fundamental obligation. 'Man shall be held to account for all his eye has seen and he has not consumed', says one text from the Talmud. Unfortunately Jews today are sometimes deprived of that pleasure.

EB: Conscious of this lack, we set up associations for trips down memory lane, we listen to the songs of our ancestors sung by operatic voices quite unlike the broken, not always melodious voices of our grandmothers, and we organize big get-togethers to savour the dishes that we have never known before. In this way, people create a universe in the belief that they are re-creating it.

J-CA: The aim is to convince oneself that everything dead can be revived.

EB: And why not? Such associations have always existed; they group together several generations, as fathers and mothers come with their sons and daughters, grandparents with their grandchildren, to taste, listen and see, sometimes also to buy a book or two. In the past, associations of this kind wove the fabric of solidarity in the community, whereas nowadays their aim is to gather people together and to serve as a cultural transmission belt. The transmission is often very modest, for they can only transmit the things that an association can transmit. None of that can replace the words of a father, mother or grandparents. But these associations do become places of life. They give too much of a role to 'memory' and too little to history, I agree, but there is nothing new about such a tension within Judaism. They still serve as substitutes, breathe life into the community, socialize its members, and try to revive as best they can the family festivals that used to be such an important part of Judaism.

J-CA: This is new, and undoubtedly difficult, for the ordinary run of Jews: what used to be lived naturally has become an object of effort. Here, in my view, lies a large part of the problem of the self-definition of Diaspora Jews.

EB: Do the Jews have a future? They have survived the worst, and they will save themselves in their way and change. But the quality of their future will largely depend on their capacity to resist the spell of suffering, to stop seeing the real or imagined hostility of others as the main cement of their own identity. Judaism has a duty to take up the challenge of life.

J-CA: Do the Jews have a future? It's a strange question – the kind you might address to a prophet (which, I admit, is a Jewish profession), not to a historian (which is already less Jewish). Anxieties are contained within it. But the very lack of completeness suggests that they will be overcome. In any event, I do not see any Jewish future which is not intimately bound up with the future of humanity.

EB: The Jewish experience – like the Gypsy, Black, Armenian, African-immigrant or homosexual experience – is a human experience. The future of the Jews does not concern the Jews alone, and Jews are not the only people who can speak about the Jews. Sometimes, when I teach about the Holocaust, I am asked: 'You're a Sephardi, so what do you know about it? You never saw Auschwitz.' And I reply: 'So, am I supposed to speak only about what I have known in my lifetime – between 1950 and the present day?' No experience of life can remain completely impervious to the experience of others.

J-CA: Let us not forget that Judaism offers the possibility, for every non-Jew who wishes it and proves worthy of it, to become a Jew himself. Obviously I am not calling on anyone to take that step. But its mere existence as an option seems to me highly instructive. Even if Judaism does not involve the active seeking of converts, it does keep Jewish identity open for everyone. I translate this as meaning that everyone, Jew or non-Jew, can have access to an understanding of Jewish identity, no doubt with a certain effort on their part.

EB: But you have to make an effort for anything. Men to understand women, or women to understand men. And the reader to understand this book.

A Bibliographical Guide

This bibliography evidently does not aim to be exhaustive: it presents a few classic texts, critical studies and synthetic overviews among the countless works available today concerning the questions on which we touch in our dialogue. The reader may find in it some of the information that he or she does not already have, as well as other ways of considering the richness and complexity of Jewish life.

Attias, Jean-Christophe and Esther Benbassa, *Israel, the Impossible Land*, trans. Susan Emanuel (Stanford, CA: Stanford University Press, 2003). A study of the relationship of Jews to the land of Israel and of how this has varied over time, enabling us to understand how it still has not been possible to share this land now claimed and held sacred twice over.

Baer, Yitzhak F., *Galut*, trans. Robert Warshow (Lanham, MD: University Press of America, *c*.1988). A history of the representations of exile in the Jewish world, from the end of antiquity to the beginning of the contemporary era, by a Zionist Jewish historian, born in Germany in 1888, who was one of the founding fathers of the 'Jerusalem School'. Originally published in German, in Berlin, in 1936.

Bauer, Yehuda, *Rethinking the Holocaust* (New Haven, CT and London: Yale University Press, 2001). One of the great historians of the Judeocide asks whether it can be compared with other genocides, how the Jews reacted to the drive to exterminate them, and what is the link between this tragedy and the establishment of the State of Israel. In the author's view, the Holocaust should not be surrounded by mysticism. It was an action conducted by human beings against other human beings. It should therefore be seen as an event that does not go beyond the bounds of the explicable.

Benbassa, Esther, *The Jews of France. A History from Antiquity to the Present* (Princeton, NJ: Princeton University Press, 1999; softcover edn, 2001). A history of the Jews from antiquity to the end of the twentieth century.

Benbassa, Esther and Aron Rodrigue, *Sephardi Jewry. A History of the Judeo-Spanish Community, 14th–20th Centuries* (Berkeley, CA and London: University of California Press, 2000). A long-range study of the history of the Iberian Jews in Spain and in their principal places of exile.

Ben-Rafaël, Eliezer, *Qu'est-ce qu'être Juif ?, suivi de 50 Sages répondent à Ben Gourion* (1958) (Paris: Balland, 2001). In 1958, David Ben Gourion, first prime minister of the State of Israel, questioned fifty Jewish intellectuals coming from every different horizon. The author publishes their answers to the question: 'What is it to be a Jew?', and tries to to develop his own answer in an essay on 'Jewish identities'.

Berkowitz, Michael, *Zionist Culture and West European Jewry before the First World War* (Cambridge: Cambridge University Press, 1993), and *Western Jewry and the Zionist Project, 1914–1933* (Cambridge: Cambridge University Press, 1997). Two classic studies of the ambivalent impact of Zionism and Zionist culture in emancipated Jewish circles of Western Europe and the United States up to the eve of the Second World War.

Biale, David (ed.), *Cultures of the Jews: A New History* (New York: Schocken Books, 2002). A compilation on the diversity, richness and historical development of Jewish cultures – a development inseparable from their interaction with the cultures of the host societies.

Cohen, Jeremy, *Living Letters of the Law: Ideas of the Jew in Medieval Christianity* (Berkeley, CA and London: University of California Press, 1999). How Latin Christianity formed and re-formed its representation of the Jew. From the Jew as witness to the truth of Christianity (St Augustine) to Judaism as heresy (in the thirteenth century). History and doctrines of Christian anti-Judaism.

DeKoven Ezrahi, Sidra, *Booking Passage. Exile and Homecoming in the Modern Jewish Imagination* (Berkeley, CA: University of California Press, 2000). On the poetry of exile and return to the native country in contemporary Jewish and Hebrew literature, in a period marked by the American conquest of space, the Zionist adventure and the destruction of European Jewry.

Esprit, 'Le poids de la mémoire. Comment transmettre le souvenir? Le pardon dans l'histoire', July 1993.

— 'Les historiens et le travail de mémoire', August–September 2000.

Fackenheim, Emil L., *What is Judaism?: An Interpretation for the Present Age* (Syracuse, NY: Syracuse University Press, 1999). The impact of the genocide of the Jews on contemporary Judaism. The author rejects the idea of a possible theology of the genocide, while urging the Jewish people to commit themselves to their own survival and that of the State of Israel.

Feiner, Shmuel, *Haskalah and History: The Emergence of a Modern Jewish Historical Consciousness*, trans. Chaya Naor and Sondra Silverton (Oxford and Portland, OR: Littman Library of Jewish Civilization, 2002). A fundamental study of the nineteenth-century Jewish Enlightenment and its role in the development of a modern Jewish historiography.

Finkielkraut, Alain, *The Imaginary Jew*, trans. Kevin O'Neill and David Suchoff with an introduction by David Suchoff (Lincoln: University of Nebraska Press, *c.*1994). How Alain Finkielkraut (b.1949) moved 'from ostentation to fidelity', how he got over narcissistic reference to a glorious and tragic Jewish past, enabling him to tear 'the seamless web of a calm and studious existence'. A searching look at Jewish identity, emblematic of the state of mind of an Ashkenazi intellectual elite that was born in France after the genocide and reached maturity in and after 1968.

Friedmann, Georges, *The End of the Jewish People?*, trans. Eric Mosbacher (Garden City, NY: Doubleday, 1967). Reflections on Israeli society as it appeared to an observer in the mid-1960s, and on the dangers that seemed to him to threaten the survival of the Jewish people as such: Diaspora assimilation on the one hand, Israelization in the new state on the other.

Funkenstein, Amos, *Perceptions of Jewish History* (Berkeley, CA: University of California Press, 1993). On the changing historical consciousness of Jews from the Bible through to Zionism and the genocide.

Goldberg, Theo D. and Michael Krausz (eds), *Jewish Identity* (Philadelphia, PA: Temple University Press, 1993). A collection of philosophical essays on the nature of Jewishness and what may be understood by cultural identity.

Grosser, Alfred, *Le Crime et la Mémoire* (Paris: Flammarion, 1991; 1st edn 1989). A book which argues that the memory of yesterday's crimes should lead us to fight against the crimes being committed today, and that the uniqueness of a crime against humanity cannot be decreed, even when it is a question of Auschwitz.

Kertzer, David I., *The Popes Against the Jews: The Vatican's Role in the Rise of Modern Anti-Semitism* (New York: Knopf, 2001). Having had access to previously closed Vatican archives, the author argues that Pius XII's highly controversial attitude during the Second World War was only the most visible and most recent outcome of the Church's anti-Jewish policy, which contributed throughout the nineteenth and early twentieth centuries to the emergence of a modern anti-Semitism that would make the Holocaust possible.

Kugel, James, *On Being a Jew* (Baltimore, MD: Johns Hopkins University Press, 1998). This imaginary dialogue on contemporary Jewish identity, though a long way from our own positions, is full of deep insight. It takes account especially of the particular realities of North American Judaism.

Lévinas, Emmanuel, *Difficult Freedom. Essays on Judaism*, trans. Sean Hand (Baltimore, MD: Johns Hopkins University Press, 1990). A collection of articles on Judaism and Jewish identity. An advocate of direct personal encounter and readiness to serve, appealing for holiness but also justice, Emmanuel Lévinas (1906–95) has compelled philosophy, the daughter of Greece, to enrich itself with the early insights of a Hebrew tradition often obscured in the West. Lévinas largely initiated, and left his mark on, the emergence of new Jewish thinking in France.

Lewis, Bernard, *The Jews of Islam* (Princeton, NJ: Princeton University Press, *c.*1984). A history of relations between Islam and the Jews, from the seventh to the twentieth century, by one of the greatest contemporary Jewish orientalists.

Mendes-Flohr, Paul, *German Jews. A Dual Identity* (New Haven, CT: Yale University Press, 1999). As they integrated, German Jews fervently embraced the religion of education and self-improvement, seeing *Bildung* as capable of creating a neutral society, a social and cultural space in which special kinds of belonging no longer played a role. This ethos was rapidly taken over for the construction of a collective German identity, leaving Jews alone with their disappointed ideal. Through the examples of Hermann Cohen, Heinrich Heine and Franz Rosenzweig, the author shows the complexity of the identity of German Jews who did not abandon their Jewishness while seeking to build bridges between German culture and their own.

Meyer, Michael A., *Response to Modernity. A History of the Reform Movement in Judaism* (New York: Oxford University Press, 1988). Traces the history of the Jewish Reform movement, born in Germany and inseparable from the efforts of German Jews to achieve integration and emancipation.

Mintz, Alan, *Popular Culture and the Shaping of Holocaust Memory in America* (Seattle and London: University of Washington Press, 2001). How contemporary film production has shaped the popular American perception of the Holocaust. An in-depth consideration of representations of the genocide, the ways in which it has been appropriated and interpreted, and the possibilities and limits of memory work.

Neher, André, *Moses and the Vocation of the Jewish People*, trans. Irene Marinoff (New York: Harper Torchbooks, *c.*1959). An attempt to explore the foundations of Jewish identity. André Neher (1914–88) contributed to the renewal of Jewish and Hebrew studies in France after the war, and was a strong Jewish voice also listened to in non-Jewish circles. He went to live in Israel in 1967, following the Six-Day War.

Novick, Peter, *The Holocaust and Collective Memory: The American Experience* (London: Bloomsbury, 2000). On the ubiquitous presence of Holocaust memory in the United States, a country which had no direct responsibility in the extermination of the Jews and did not directly suffer from it. The author analyses the shift from relative obliviousness to the tragedy during the Cold War to the hypermnesia that began with the Eichmann trial in 1961 and the Six-Day War. He emphasizes the Zionist policy of the Jewish organizations that use the memory to justify unswerving support for Israel and to impose a religion of the Holocaust as a pillar of contemporary Jewish identity in societies where anti-Semitism is tending to disappear.

Pines, Shlomo, *Studies in the History of Jewish Thought*, ed. Warren Zev Harvey and Moshe Idel (Jerusalem: Magnes Press, Hebrew University, *c.* 1997). A collection of scholarly studies in which medieval and pre-modern Jewish thought appears as a major locus of exchange with non-Jewish religious and philosophical traditions. The very continuity of Jewish culture is treated as a problem requiring explanation, not as a self-evident fact.

Robin, Régine, *La Mémoire saturée* (Paris: Stock, 2003). General reflections on contemporary abuses of memory and the forgetting that they inevitably produce.

Rosenbaum, Alan S. (ed.), *Is the Holocaust Unique? Perspectives on Comparative Genocide* (Boulder, CO: Westview Press, 1996). Can the genocide of the Jews be compared with that of the Armenians, Gypsies or North American Indians? This work brings together different views on the question, without reaching any real consensus.

Rothschild, Fritz A., *Jewish Perspectives on Christianity* (New York: Continuum, 1996). How five great contemporary Jewish intellectuals – Leo Baeck, Martin Buber, Franz Rosenzweig, Will Herberg and Abraham J. Hersche – thought about Christianity and its relations with Judaism. An analysis and a selection of texts.

Scholem, Gershom G., *The Messianic Idea in Judaism and Other Essays on Jewish Spirituality*, foreword by Arthur Hertzberg (New York: Schocken Books, 1995). An excellent initiation to the major issues raised by the history of mysticism and messianism in the Jewish world, from the origins to the contemporary period. Gershom Scholem (1897–1982) helped to place the Kabbalah at the centre of Jewish studies, breaking with the academic tradition initiated by the 'Science of Judaism'. The reader should be aware, however, that Scholem's approach has itself sometimes been severely reappraised by a later generation of researchers (of whom Moshe Idel is the best known and the most often translated).

Segev, Tom, *The Seventh Million: The Israelis and the Holocaust*, trans. Haim Watzman (New York: Hill and Wang, 1993). From the rise of Nazism to the arrival of the first German refugees and the extermination of European Jewry, the author examines the reaction of the Jewish community in Palestine, which lacked compassion for its persecuted fellow-Jews, even when it encountered survivors. Segev also traces the vagaries of the ideologization of the genocide, and its instrumentalization to serve the cause of the State of Israel and to shape a collective Israeli identity.

Silberstein, Laurence J., *The Postzionism Debates: Knowledge and Power in Israeli Culture* (New York: Routledge, 1999). An up-to-date account of the historical debate of the last twenty years, and of its cultural significance and social-political implications.

— (ed.) *Mapping Jewish Identities* (New York and London: New York University Press, 2000). A book which distances itself from essentialist representations of Jewishness and provides the conceptual tools for a sophisticated understanding of the multiple and shifting ways of being a Jew.

Soloveitchik, Joseph Dov, *Halakhic Man*, trans. Lawrence Kaplan (Philadelphia, PA: Jewish Publication Society of America, 1983). Defence and illustration of the validity and value of a rigorous practice of Judaism, by the intellectual leader of Jewish Orthodoxy in the United States.

Stanislawski, Michael, *Zionism and the Fin de Siècle. Cosmopolitanism and Nationalism from Nordau to Jabotinsky* (Berkeley, CA and London: University of California Press, 2001). Discusses the trajectories of three key figures: the writer and critic Max Nordau, who worked alongside Herzl; Ephraim Moses Lilien, the first great Zionist iconograph; and Vladimir Jabotinsky, the founder of revisionist Zionism. This study locates the emergence of the Zionist option in the wider context of a fin de siècle marked by social Darwinism and the positivism of Russian radicalism, as well as by Symbolism, Decadentism and Art Nouveau.

Sternhell, Zeev, *The Founding Myths of Israel: Nationalism, Socialism, and the Making of the Jewish State*, trans. David Maisel (Princeton, NJ: Princeton University Press, c. 1998). The Zionist revolution that got under way a century ago was principally a national, cultural and political revolution, much more than an attempt to create a different society. This explains Israel's alignment with the values of the bourgeoisie and state capitalism which are part of the legacy of its founding fathers.

Swirski, Shlomo, *The Oriental Majority*, trans. B. Swirski (London: Zed Books, 1989). A critical study of the ethnic division of labour in Israel that was unfavourable to Sephardis, and of the development towns where they were concentrated without any great prospects of social ascent. The book also lets activists speak from these circles which took up the struggle to make the voice of their people heard.

Todorov, Tzvetan, *Mémoire du mal, tentation du bien* (Paris: Robert Laffont, 2000). One does not escape evil by taking oneself to be an embodiment of good, or by giving lessons on morality to one's fellow-citizens and other countries. The author considers the defeat of twentieth-century totalitarianisms by a democracy not immune from the 'temptation of good', which cultivated 'moral correctness' at home while dropping atom bombs abroad. It was also a century of lucid men and women who lit up these shadows. An invitation to use memory properly.

Trautmann-Waller, Céline, *Philologie allemande et tradition juive. Le parcours intellectuel de Leopold Zunz* (Paris: Cerf, 1998). A work on the origins of the 'Science of Judaism', which tried to establish Judaism as an object of scientific study. This movement, born out of debates among German Jews on modernity, throws light on Jewish identity during the period of emancipation and integration in Europe.

Union des étudiants juifs de France-SOS Racisme, *Les Antifeujs. Le Livre blanc des violences antisémites en France depuis septembre 2000* (Paris: Calmann-Lévy, 2002). A work on the recent upsurge of anti-Jewish actions in France. Has the merit of presenting facts and figures.

Vidal-Naquet, Pierre, *The Jews: History, Memory, and the Present*, trans. and ed. David Ames Curtis, with a foreword by Paul Berman and a new preface by the author (New York: Columbia University Press, 1996). Collection of prefaces, studies and analyses of issues in ancient and modern history, by a French Jewish academic and intellectual actively involved in the ideological debates of his time who tirelessly probes the great questions facing contemporary Jewish consciousness. A meditation on the uses of memory and history.

Vital, David, *The Future of the Jews* (Cambridge, MA: Harvard University Press, 1990). One of the greatest historians of Zionism anxiously evokes the contemporary erosion of the Jewish world, which is blowing apart the idea of a 'Jewish community' and isolating Israel (now separated from the American Diaspora especially).

Wasserstein, Bernard, *Vanishing Diaspora: The Jews in Europe Since 1945* (Cambridge, MA: Harvard University Press, 1996). In an ever more secular world, the danger of disappearance weighing on the Jewish communities of Europe (including Russia) is perfectly in tune with all the aspects of modernity.

Webber, Jonathan (ed.), *Jewish Identities in the New Europe* (London and Washington: Littman Library of Jewish Civilization, 1994). How do the Jews of Europe, both East and West, see themselves? As a religious minority, an ethnic group, or simply members of the wider European cultures in which they live?

Yerushalmi, Yosef Hayim, *From Spanish Court to Italian Ghetto: A Study in Seventeenth Century Marranism and Jewish Apologetics* (Seattle: University of Washington Press, 1981). A general survey of Marranism and the return to Judaism among Marranos at the dawn of modernity.

— *Zakhor: Jewish History and Jewish Memory* (Seattle: University of Washington Press, c. 1996). A history of the ways in which Jews have related to history, from antiquity to the contemporary period. The author illustrates the novelty as well as the vulnerabilty (in the Jewish world) of the status of a historian of the Jews.

Index

Zed titles on Israel/Palestine

Esther Benbassa and Jean-Christophe Attias, *The Jews and Their Future: A Conversation on Judaism and Jewish Identities*

1 84277 390 9 | 1 84277 391 7

Marwan Bishara, *Palestine/Israel: Peace or Apartheid — Occupation, Terrorism and the Future*

UPDATED EDITION

1 84277 272 4 | 1 84277 273 2

Uri Davis, *Apartheid Israel: Possibilities for the Struggle Within*

1 84277 338 0 | 1 84277 339 9

Nicholas Guyatt, *The Absence of Peace: Understanding the Israeli-Palestinian Conflict*

1 85649 579 5 | 1 85649 580 9

Hussein Abu Hussein and Fiona McKay, *Access Denied: Palestinian Land Rights in Israel*

1 84277 122 1 | 1 84277 123 X

Peretz Kidron (compiler and editor), *Refusenik!: Israel's Soldiers of Conscience*

1 84277 450 6 | 1 84277 451 4

Ephraim Nimni (editor), *The Challenge of Post-Zionism: Alternatives to Israeli Fundamentalist Politics*

1 85649 893 X | 1 85649 894 8

Rosemary Sayigh, *Too Many Enemies; The Palestinian Experience in Lebanon*

1 85649 055 6 | 1 85649 056 4

For full details of this list and Zed's other subject and general catalogues, please write to: the Marketing Department, Zed Books, 7 Cynthia Street, London N1 9JF, UK; or e-mail: sales@zedbooks.demon.co.uk

Visit our website at: <http://www.zedbooks.co.uk>

About the authors

Esther Benbassa is professor of Modern Jewish History at the École Pratique des Hautes Études, Sorbonne, and director of the Alberto Benveniste Center for Sephardic Studies and Culture (EPHE). Several of her books have been translated into English: *Haim Nahum: A Sephardic Chief Rabbi in Politics* (1995), *The Jews of France: A History from Antiquity to the Present* (1999), and with Aron Rodrigue, *A Sephardi Life in Southeastern Europe* (1998) and *Sephardi Jewry: A History of the Judeo-Spanish Community, 14th–20th Centuries* (2000). She is also the author of *Une diaspora sépharade en transition (Istanbul, XIXe–XXe siècles)* (1993). She edited or co-edited *Cultures juives méditerranéennes* (1985), *Mémoires juives d'Espagne et du Portugal* (1996), *Transmission et passages en monde juif* (1997) and *L'Europe et les Juifs* (2002).

Jean-Christophe Attias is professor of the History of Rabbinic Culture at the École Pratique des Hautes Études, Sorbonne, and a member of the Centre d'Études des Religions du Livre (Centre National de la Recherche Scientifique / EPHE). He is the author of *Le Commentaire biblique: Mordekhai Komtino ou l'herméneutique du dialogue* (1991) and of *Isaac Abravanel: la mémoire et l'espérance* (1992). He edited or co-edited *De la Conversion* (1998), *Enseigner le judaïsme à l'Université* (1998), *Messianismes: Variations autour d'une figure juive* (2000) and *De la Bible à la littérature* (2003).

Jean-Christophe Attias and Esther Benbassa have also co-authored in English *Israel: the Impossible Land* (2003), and in French *Dictionnaire de civilisation juive* (1997), *Le Juif et l'Autre* (2002), and edited *La Haine de soi: Difficiles identités* (2000).